The Pirates

SCALE IN MILES

0   500   1000   1500   2000

The Seafarers THE PIRATES

TIME LIFE BOOKS ®

Other Publications:

THE ENCYCLOPEDIA OF COLLECTIBLES
THE GREAT CITIES
WORLD WAR II
HOME REPAIR AND IMPROVEMENT
THE WORLD'S WILD PLACES
THE TIME-LIFE LIBRARY OF BOATING
HUMAN BEHAVIOR
THE ART OF SEWING
THE OLD WEST
THE EMERGENCE OF MAN
THE AMERICAN WILDERNESS
THE TIME-LIFE ENCYCLOPEDIA OF GARDENING
LIFE LIBRARY OF PHOTOGRAPHY
THIS FABULOUS CENTURY
FOODS OF THE WORLD
TIME-LIFE LIBRARY OF AMERICA
TIME-LIFE LIBRARY OF ART
GREAT AGES OF MAN
LIFE SCIENCE LIBRARY
THE LIFE HISTORY OF THE UNITED STATES
TIME READING PROGRAM
LIFE NATURE LIBRARY
LIFE WORLD LIBRARY
FAMILY LIBRARY:
  HOW THINGS WORK IN YOUR HOME
  THE TIME-LIFE BOOK OF THE FAMILY CAR
  THE TIME-LIFE FAMILY LEGAL GUIDE
  THE TIME-LIFE BOOK OF FAMILY FINANCE

The Cover: The most flamboyant of all
18th Century pirates, foul Blackbeard struts
ashore in this 1734 engraving sporting
pistol-packed bandoliers and a coiffure
of smoldering locks designed to convince
all beholders that he was a fiend from
hell. In the background, lackeys are loading
bales and barrels of provisions onto
the pirate's waiting vessel.

The Title Page: Weighing 150 pounds, this
painted metal chest is believed to have
belonged to pirate Thomas Tew, a Rhode
Islander who was one of the first and
greatest captains to plunder Indian Mogul
riches in the Eastern Seas.

The Seafarers

THE PIRATES

by Douglas Botting
AND THE EDITORS OF TIME-LIFE BOOKS

TIME-LIFE BOOKS, ALEXANDRIA, VIRGINIA

Time-Life Books Inc.
is a wholly owned subsidiary of
TIME INCORPORATED

FOUNDER: Henry R. Luce 1898-1967

Editor-in-Chief: Hedley Donovan
Chairman of the Board: Andrew Heiskell
President: James R. Shepley
Vice Chairman: Roy E. Larsen
Corporate Editors: Ralph Graves,
Henry Anatole Grunwald

TIME-LIFE BOOKS INC.

MANAGING EDITOR: Jerry Korn
Executive Editor: David Maness
Assistant Managing Editors: Dale M. Brown,
Martin Mann, John Paul Porter
Art Director: Tom Suzuki
Chief of Research: David L. Harrison
Director of Photography: Robert G. Mason
Planning Director: Thomas Flaherty (acting)
Senior Text Editor: Diana Hirsh
Assistant Art Director: Arnold C. Holeywell
Assistant Chief of Research: Carolyn L. Sackett

CHAIRMAN: Joan D. Manley
President: John D. McSweeney
Executive Vice Presidents: Carl G. Jaeger
(U.S. and Canada), David J. Walsh (International)
Vice President and Secretary: Paul R. Stewart
Treasurer and General Manager: John Steven Maxwell
Business Manager: Peter G. Barnes
Sales Director: John L. Canova
Public Relations Director: Nicholas Benton
Personnel Director: Beatrice T. Dobie
Production Director: Herbert Sorkin
Consumer Affairs Director: Carol Flaumenhaft

The Seafarers
Editorial Staff for The Pirates:
Editor: George G. Daniels
Picture Editor: John Conrad Weiser
Text Editor: Anne Horan
Designer: Herbert H. Quarmby
Staff Writers: Susan Bryan, Gus Hedberg,
Henry Woodhead
Chief Researcher: Martha T. Goolrick
Researchers: William Banks, Carol Bok, Jane Coughran,
W. Mark Hamilton, Barbara Levitt,
Katie Hooper McGregor, Peggy L. Sawyer, Nancy Toff
Art Assistant: Santi José Acosta
Editorial Assistant: Feroline Burrage

Editorial Production
Production Editor: Douglas B. Graham
Operations Manager: Gennaro C. Esposito
Assistant Production Editor: Feliciano Madrid
Quality Control: Robert L. Young (director),
James J. Cox (assistant), Michael G. Wight (associate)
Art Coordinator: Anne B. Landry
Copy Staff: Susan B. Galloway (chief),
Elise D. Ritter, Ricki Tarlow, Eleanor Van Bellingham,
Florence Keith, Celia Beattie
Picture Department: Dolores A. Littles, Cathy Doxat-Pratt

Correspondents: Elisabeth Kraemer (Bonn); Margot
Hapgood, Dorothy Bacon (London); Susan Jonas, Lucy
T. Voulgaris (New York); Maria Vincenza Aloisi,
Josephine du Brusle (Paris); Ann Natanson (Rome).
Valuable assistance was also provided by: Enid Farmer
(Lexington, Mass.); Colleen Mitchell (London); Carolyn
T. Chubet, Miriam Hsia (New York).

The editors are indebted to Barbara Hicks, Curt
Prendergast, Mary Y. Steinbauer and David Thomson
for their help in the preparation of this book.

The Author:
Douglas Botting published his first book—
about a summer spent roaming around Arabia—while still an undergraduate at Ox-
ford. As writer and photographer, he has
traveled to Siberia, the Sahara and Matto
Grosso, and once made a 2,000-mile trip up
the Amazon River in a fishing boat captained by a Brazilian smuggler who called
himself a pirate. Botting has written Wilderness Europe in The World's Wild Places
series and Rio de Janeiro in The Great Cities
series for Time-Life Books. Among his other books are Pirates of the Spanish Main
and Humboldt and the Cosmos.

The Consultants:
John Horace Parry, Gardiner Professor of
Oceanic History and Affairs at Harvard
University, was educated at Cambridge
University, where he took his Ph.D. During
World War II, he served in the Royal Navy
and rose to the rank of commander. He is
the author of 10 books, including Trade
and Dominion, The Discovery of the Sea,
The Spanish Seaborne Empire and Europe
and a Wider World.

Richard Knight, as a youth in London, was
nurtured on the Gosse collection of pirate
books in the National Maritime Museum,
and subsequently became an avid collector
and noted student of all things piratical.
The author of a number of articles on pirates, he lives in Kent, England, where he
works at his second love: restoring to mint
condition vintage racing autos.

William Avery Baker, a naval architect and
engineer, has designed and supervised
construction of a number of reproductions
of 17th and 18th Century sailing craft, including the "Mayflower II," which sailed
from England to Plymouth, Mass., in 1957.
He is curator of the Hart Nautical Museum
at the Massachusetts Institute of Technol-
ogy, where he took his degree.

Second printing.
Published simultaneously in Canada.
School and library distribution by Silver Burdett Company,
Morristown, New Jersey.

Library of Congress Cataloging in Publication Data
Botting, Douglas.
   The Pirates.
   (The Seafarers; v. 1)
   Bibliography: p.
   Includes index.
   1. Pirates. I. Time-Life Books. II. Title.
III. Series.
G535.B62   910'.453   78-91928
ISBN 0-8094-2652-8
ISBN 0-8094-2651-X lib. bdg.

Contents

A gallery of rogues who made war on the world

"I am a free prince," boasted pirate Charles Bellamy to the captain of a Boston merchantman captured off South Carolina in 1717, "and I have as much authority to make war on the whole World as he who has a hundred sail of ships at sea and an army of 100,000 men in the field." However grandiose Bellamy's assertion may sound today, it was not without foundation in his own day. For Bellamy lived at the zenith of the Great Age—some said Golden Age—of piracy, when thousands upon thousands of brigands made what amounted to war all along the sea-lanes of the world.

Although the era lasted scarcely 30 years, in that time the pirates plundered shipping to the point where normal commerce—and even the economy of some countries—was threatened. Spanish, French, British, Dutch, Indian, Arabian, it made no difference what flag a vessel sailed under. The pirates turned their hands against all men, and every vessel was fair prey. So immense was their booty and so powerful their impact that the most fearsome of the pirates and their exploits became legends in their own lifetimes— the fiendish Blackbeard forcing a Portuguese captive to eat his own ears, nose and lips; Captain Kidd stringing up an entire crew by their arms in the tropical sun to make them confess the location of their gold; Henry Every ravishing, then falling in love with and marrying the daughter of the great Mogul of India.

But if some of these tales were largely apocryphal, the truth about the pirates was incredible enough. Who these men were, why they suddenly burst on the world and how they met their doom has fascinated historians for years. Perhaps the best account of the pirates and their crimes was an encyclopedic tome published in 1724 and entitled *A General History of the Robberies and Murders of the most notorious Pyrates*. Its author, everyone is now pretty certain, was the novelist Daniel Defoe, writing under a pseudonym. The woodcuts on this and the following pages were made to illustrate a 1725 English edition of Defoe's chronicle—and to satisfy the 18th Century curiosity to see what the rogues looked like.

How accurate these depictions are can only be conjectured. The name of the artist is lost to history, and Defoe does not go into the matter. But it seems likely that they were done from descriptions provided by Defoe from his extensive studies of the pirates and their ways.

Defoe did not approve of the pirates he wrote about. Quite the contrary. Describing a devastating raid on a Newfoundland fishing fleet, he wrote, "They are like mad Men that cast Fire-Brands, Arrows, and Death, and say, are we not in Sport?" And when one of the raiders was captured and hanged, Defoe reflected, "Thus we see what disastrous Fate ever attends the Wicked, and how rarely they escape the Punishment due to their Crimes."

Yet Defoe strove to understand the pirates, and at times exhibited admiration for these bold seafarers. They were often brave men and wise warriors, he wrote in his preface, and Rome was founded by men no better. "If the Progress of our Pyrates had been equal to their Beginning, had they all united, and settled in some of those Islands," he concluded, "they might, by this Time, have been honoured with the Name of a Commonwealth, and no Power in those Parts of the World could have been able to dispute it with them."

Henry Every

*One of the most famous of pirates, Every seized such spectacular
treasure in the Red Sea in 1695 that word of his coup
made him a hero to every unemployed seaman and underpaid
wretch in England and the colonies. In the eyes of the
poor, wrote Daniel Defoe, Every "raised himself to the Dignity of a
King, and was likely to be the Founder of a new Monarchy."*

Edward England

*After the British Navy drove him from the Caribbean in 1718,
England made himself a scourge of the African waters. "He had
a great deal of good Nature," wrote Defoe, "and was always
averse to the ill Usage Prisoners received." This unusual
kindness proved his undoing: he was deposed for freeing a
captured merchant captain and died a beggar on Madagascar.*

Stede Bonnet

A retired Army major, Bonnet was portly and clean shaven and wore a gentleman's powdered wig. He was such a dandy that the satanic, unkempt Blackbeard burst out in guffaws when the two met off South Carolina in 1718. A bungler and a dude, Bonnet was ousted from his ship by Blackbeard —"laid aside," as Defoe put it, "not withstanding the Sloop was his own."

Charles Vane

*Though he had boldly defied two British men-of-war at Nassau
in 1718, Vane was voted out of his captaincy for cowardice by
his crew when he later wisely retreated before a more heavily
armed French warship. He was soon caught and hanged, and as
Defoe reported, he "died in Agonies equal to his Villainies
but showed not the least Remorse for the Crimes of his past Life."*

John Rackam

Known as Calico Jack for the bright cotton clothing he often
wore, Rackam was the man voted into Vane's captaincy.
He went on to plunder the West Indies until his capture in 1720.
But Rackam's place in history rests on his great romance with
the lady pirate Anne Bonny. Afloat or ashore, according
to Defoe, Rackam "had nothing but Anne Bonny in his head."

12

Bartholomew Roberts

*A superlative seaman who became the greatest pirate of his day,
Roberts launched his career in 1720 for all the wrong reasons,
according to Defoe. "He could not plead Want of Employment, nor
Incapacity of getting his Bread in an honest Way, but frankly own'd,
it was to get rid of the disagreeable Superiority of some Masters he
was acquainted with —and the Love of Novelty and Change."*

Howell Davis

*Among the most guileful of all pirates until his death in 1720,
Davis often posed as a merchant or even a pirate hunter,
the better to size up his prey. His cutthroat crews, who easily could
have mutinied and overthrown their captains, conceived "so
high an Opinion of his Conduct, as well as Courage," recounted
Defoe, "that they thought nothing impossible to him."*

Chapter 1

A Golden Age for daring sea rovers

t 5 o'clock on the afternoon of April Fool's Day, **1719**, the English slave ship *Bird Galley*, carrying cargo from Holland to the West African coast, entered the mouth of the Sierra Leone River on a strong flood tide and dropped anchor for the night. She was not alone. A long way up the river her crew could see another ship at anchor and, unknown to them, there were two more hidden behind a bend.

As evening came, all was quiet on the river. At 8 p.m. the commander of the *Bird Galley*, Captain William Snelgrave, went below and sat down to supper in his cabin. But he had barely eaten more than a few mouthfuls when the officer of the watch reported to him that he heard the rowing of a boat. As a precautionary measure, Captain Snelgrave went up on deck immediately and ordered Simon Jones, the first mate, to go into the steerage and send **20** men straightaway up onto the quarter-deck with firearms and cutlasses.

Dusk falls quickly in the tropics, and it was already too dark to see what kind of boat was approaching. Standing there in the heat of the African night, Snelgrave could gather nothing but the rattle of oars in their rowlocks and the soft splash and drip of water from the unseen blades. As the sounds grew louder he ordered his second mate to hail the visitors. Across the black river an English voice called back: they were off a Barbados ship and they came from America. A second or two later a volley of small-arms fire exploded in the darkness and the captain knew at once what kind of men were coming toward his ship.

Snelgrave shouted out to the first mate to open fire. But nothing happened. Shortly afterward, one of his officers informed him that the crew refused to bear arms. The captain was astonished. He was not the brutal kind of 18th Century sea captain who might expect his orders to be disobeyed when so much was at stake; he believed in treating his crews humanely. Though he was a slaver, he was an honest and reasonable man and was much admired by the men who served under him. He went down into the steerage. He asked the men brusquely why they had refused to fight. Their response was even more astonishing than their refusal: they could not find the chest in which the weapons were stored. This, as Snelgrave later learned, was true—for reasons of his own, his first mate, Simon Jones, had hidden it.

By now, the strange boat had come alongside. There was nowhere for the men of the *Bird Galley* to hide, nowhere they could go to evade the approaching terror. They listened in fear to the muffled voices, the dull thud of feet on the deck overhead. Dark shapes against the starlit sky, the invaders swarmed up onto the quarter-deck, then drew their pistols and fired down into the steerage, hitting one of the sailors in the buttocks and

Merchant vessels crowd the docks of Bristol, England, in this tidy 18th Century view that belies the port's true nature. Bristol was home for Britain's slave fleet, whose hardened sailors were prime pirate recruits—among them the infamous Blackbeard and Bartholomew Roberts.

wounding him so severely that he later died. Then they tossed a number of grenades down. Stunned by the noise and flash of the explosions, the acrid smoke and confusion, the *Bird Galley*'s men cried out for quarter.

Snelgrave had never come face to face with pirates before. He was to see all too much of them in the next weeks. By great good fortune, he lived to tell the hair-raising tale and returned to London to publish a volume entitled *A New Account of Some Parts of Guinea, And the Slave Trade*. It is a fascinating document. For Snelgrave was a cool, acute and not altogether unsympathetic observer. And his account of his experiences among the pirates offers rare insight into these strange practitioners of one of the oldest yet least understood of seafaring professions.

The first man Snelgrave laid eyes upon was the pirate quartermaster, leader of the boarding party. Who was the captain of the *Bird Galley*? roared the marauder. "I had been so till now," replied Snelgrave. In a fury, the quartermaster demanded to know how Snelgrave had dared order his crew to open fire; he had heard him give the order several times, the pirate said. Snelgrave told him that he believed it was his duty to defend the ship—to which the quartermaster made no reply, but pulled out his pistol, clapped it to the hapless Captain's chest and pulled the trigger. Snelgrave just had time to knock the gun aside before it went off, and the bullet creased his side, leaving him bloody but still alive. When the pirate quartermaster saw that the captain was still standing, he took his pistol by the muzzle and brought it down on Snelgrave's head, knocking him to his knees.

Snelgrave was dazed only momentarily. Finding some secret spring of strength and courage, he raced up out of the steerage on to the quarter-deck. But there was no escape. On the quarter-deck he was confronted with an even more vicious villain, the pirate boatswain. The boatswain lifted up his broadsword and aimed a huge blow at Snelgrave's head. The captain ducked, and the sword bit a hole an inch deep in the quarter-deck rail and shattered with the force of the impact. Wild with rage, the pirate boatswain began to belabor the poor captain with the butt end of a discharged pistol. By now some of the crew of the *Bird Galley* had ventured on deck, and they pleaded with the boatswain. "For God's sake don't kill our captain. We never were with a better man." But all they achieved by this intervention was to divert the boatswain's rage from the captain and to themselves.

Only a few minutes had passed since the pirates had boarded the *Bird Galley*, but the ship was theirs. The quartermaster came back up on deck. In a calmer mood now, he took Snelgrave by the arm and told him no harm would come to him provided the pirates received no complaints about him from the *Bird Galley*'s ordinary seamen. The pirates then fired a victory salvo with their small arms.

The scene that followed might have struck Snelgrave as comical in other circumstances. Hearing gunfire, the pirates on the mother ship— the one anchored up the river—had cut their cable and come down on the ebb tide. When they saw the *Bird Galley* alight with candles and lanterns they jumped to the conclusion that their boarding party had been wiped out in a vain attempt to take the merchant vessel. In misguided revenge, they opened a furious fire on the *Bird Galley*. Confusion reigned as the pirate ship blazed away in the dark at the pirate prize. At last, Snelgrave, watching with bemused disbelief, suggested to the pirate quartermaster that he should hail his shipmates and tell them that the prize had been successfully captured. Much to his amazement, the quartermaster turned on him angrily and demanded to know whether he was "afraid of going to the Devil by a great shot." On his part, the pirate announced, he hoped to be "sent to hell one of these days by a cannon ball." However, he followed Snelgrave's advice and shouted to his comrades that he had taken a great ship with plenty of liquor and loot on board. The firing stopped immediately.

Shortly afterward the pirate commander, Captain Thomas Cocklyn, a short, squat Englishman, came on board. He issued an order for all the live fowl on the *Bird Galley*—geese, turkeys, chickens and ducks—to be killed and cooked, and they were put into an immense cauldron with no more preparation than drawing the guts and singeing the feathers; along with the fowl went some Westphalian hams and a pregnant sow, which the pirate cook simply disemboweled and threw into the brew with the bristles still on.

While the pirates feasted, poor Snelgrave contemplated the disastrous turn of events. It had been his misfortune to fall into the clutches of a flotilla of pirate ships commanded by three notorious captains—Cocklyn, Howell Davis and Oliver La Buze, the Buzzard.

The morning after his capture, 10 of Snelgrave's crew joined the pirates, among them first mate Simon Jones, who told him that he was turning pirate because his marriage had broken down at home and he no longer loved his wife. He confessed that this was why he had hidden the arms chest before the pirates boarded the *Bird Galley*. He had suspected from the start that the boat rowing toward them was filled with pirates and had made up his mind to sabotage any attempt to defend the vessel.

After Snelgrave's wound was dressed, the captain was summoned before Cocklyn, who told him: "I am sorry you have met with bad usage after quarter given, but 'tis the fortune of war sometimes. I expect you will answer truly to all such questions as I shall ask you, otherwise you shall be cut to pieces. But if you tell the truth, and your men make no complaints against you, you shall be kindly used."

The most important question Cocklyn asked Snelgrave was about the sailing qualities of the *Bird Galley*, which the pirates had decided to take over as their new raiding vessel. Cocklyn was apparently satisfied with the answers. From then on, Snelgrave was allowed to move about as he pleased, and he observed the pirates' antic world with a mixture of horror and fascination.

Chaos was never far from these mercurial men. The crews of the three pirate vessels took turns plundering the *Bird Galley*. Snelgrave stood helplessly by and watched as Cocklyn's and Davis' men "hoisted upon Deck a great many half hogsheads of Claret and French Brandy; knock'd their Heads out, and dipp'd Canns and Bowls into them to drink out of: And in their Wantonness threw full Buckets upon one another. And in the evening washed the Decks with what remained in the Casks. As to bottled Liquor, they would not give themselves the trouble of drawing the Cork out, but nick'd the Bottles, as they called it, that is, struck their

necks off with a Cutlace; by which means one in three was generally broke. As to Eatables, such as Cheese, Butter, Sugar, and many other things, they were as soon gone."

At one point, staggering into Snelgrave's cabin, some pirates tripped over one of several bundles of goods, including some fine garments that he had been allowed to keep for private trading. Complaining that they could have broken their necks falling over these bundles, they threw all but one overboard. And yet, while one lot of pirates was throwing Snelgrave's possessions into the sea, another lot was bringing him liquor to drink and slices of boiled ham served up on a ship's biscuit, telling him they felt sorry for him. Soon afterward the pirate quartermaster kicked Snelgrave's gold watch about the deck, chortling that it made a "pretty football," and a drunk stole his hat and wig.

There was a great deal about pirate behavior that Snelgrave found incomprehensible. For one thing, he was astounded that the pirate captains had so few privileges that were not shared by their men. One day the three captains came to Snelgrave and demanded his embroidered coats because they were "going on shore amongst the Negroe-Ladies" and wanted to look their dandiest. Cocklyn, the shortest of the three, was given the longest coat, scarlet in color, embroidered with silver, and reaching almost to his ankles. When he groused about this, the other two captains told him that African ladies knew nothing of European fashions and would probably think he was the most important man of the three because of the generous cut of his coat.

When the three captains rowed ashore for a long night's dalliance, the crews they left behind were not amused. In the democratic society of the pirates, the captains had been expected to secure permission from the quartermaster before seizing Snelgrave's garments, and they had failed to do so. "The Pirate Captains having taken these Cloaths without leave from the Quarter-master, it gave great Offence to all the Crew, who alleg'd if they suffered such things the Captains would for the future assume a Power, to take whatever they liked for themselves. So, upon their returning on board next morning, the Coats were taken from them, and put into the common Chest, to be sold at the Mast." One of the pirates, a man named Williams, who was the quartermaster of La Buze's ship, blamed Snelgrave for having put the pirate captains up to it in the first place and threatened to kill him. But Snelgrave was told that Williams always talked like that; he was advised to call the man "Captain." This had a magical effect, and Williams, instead of killing Snelgrave, gave him a keg of wine and was his friend and protector from then on.

At last, after what seemed a lifetime, the pirate captains and a number of crewmen held a council and decided to free Snelgrave. He was a good fellow, they judged. "And now, the Tide being turned," recalled Snelgrave, "they were as kind to me, as they had been at first severe." As a gesture of respect, the pirates gave Snelgrave one of their prizes, the *Bristol Snow*, in exchange for the *Bird Galley*, together with what was left of the *Bird Galley*'s cargo, plus several thousand pounds worth of goods taken from earlier prizes. The pirates even helped Snelgrave's crew transfer the goods.

Later, the pirate captains held a farewell gala aboard Davis' ship—

which almost proved disastrous. In the middle of dinner a fire broke out when someone accidentally set a candle too near a cask of rum and blew it up. A number of pirates fled to the boats or huddled together at the far end of the bowsprit because there were 30,000 pounds of gunpowder on board; others were too drunk to care. But 16 men fought the fire for nearly two hours until it was finally extinguished. A few of the pirates were so grateful for Snelgrave's help with the fire that one man proposed the good captain "be obliged to go down the coast of Guinea with us, for I am told we cannot have a better pilot." But Captain Davis of the third pirate vessel caned the man off the quarter-deck. And so on May 10, 1719, more than a month after his capture, Captain William Snelgrave's sojourn among the pirates ended. With what remained of his crew, he boarded the vessel the pirates had given him and sailed safely back to England to recount his experience.

Captain Snelgrave's misadventure came at the height of the greatest outburst of piracy in all the annals of seafaring. Historians with a keen sense of irony have called it piracy's Golden Age—as in fact it was, for some pirates. It lasted barely 30 years, scarcely a wink of time's eye, starting at the close of the 17th Century and ending in the first quarter of the 18th. In those tumultuous years, a number of political and economic circumstances conspired to send uncounted thousands upon thousands of desperate men swooping down upon the sea-lanes of the world. Mostly they were English and American mariners, with a scattering of French and other nationalities. Whatever their home ports, in their lust for treasure and adventure—or merely to vent some inner rage—they ravaged the coasts of North and South America and Africa to the point where no merchant vessel without escort could count herself safe. The Caribbean became a virtual pirate lake, and the Bahama Islands a pirate fiefdom. Half a world away, the island of Madagascar boomed as a cutthroat's lair, ruled by pirate potentates, a safe advance base from which the brigand fleets sallied forth to loot the Arab Mocha fleets and the Indian Mogul galleons. For years, the pirates cruised a regular "Pirate Round," as they called it, sailing from North America around the tip of Africa to pillage the Eastern Seas, then returning home when their holds were filled with swag or when the fancy struck them.

No one has ever attempted to calculate the amount of plunder that was taken during the Golden Age of piracy. But it was a treasure of national proportions. A pirate captain might seize a handful of ships in a single day and return from his cruise with loot worth hundreds of thousands of pounds—this in an era when the average merchant sailor did not see £500 in his entire lifetime.

In pursuit of their glittering prizes, the pirates performed prodigious feats of navigation and seamanship, engaged in some momentous battles and explored every facet of human experience.

They were often curiously immature. Aroused or in their cups, they were capable of unbelievable barbarities. They might allow insects to feast on an enemy's wounds, silence a man by sewing up his lips with a sail needle, or set fire to a shipload of screaming horses—or to a slave ship packed with manacled Africans. But there were moments, as Snel-

Prolific author and journalist Daniel Defoe, handsomely bewigged in this 1706 engraving, saw his General History of the Pyrates go into nine editions and four languages before he died. In time, there were more than 65 editions of the volume.

grave and others discovered, when they seemed almost touched by grace, when they could be moved by compassion, contrition, even love. Among themselves, aboard their ships and in their hide-outs, they were passionate advocates of a rude sort of democracy, with a high regard for justice and the rights of the individual, and a corresponding distaste for tyranny and the abuse of power. Crude and violent though they often were, they could be abundantly generous to those whom they liked and trusted, showering jewels and Arabian gold on the liquor traders and girls who oiled and sweetened their progress across the far-flung oceans of the tropic world. Shipmates who had lost eyes or limbs in piratical combat were allowed to live on board for as long as they chose; and many a peg leg clomped over the pirates' decks, earning a half share of plunder as a cook, no matter how little he knew of the culinary arts.

The pirates could be cowards, fleeing in their hundreds into the clammy security of the jungle at the mere sight of a Royal Navy sail hovering near their Indian Ocean base on Madagascar. But in the cannon's mouth, when they were cornered on the quarter-deck by a ring of steel or stood on the scaffold before a vast and jabbering crowd, they often faced death with steadfast courage and derisively ironic humor. Some would have been immortalized as martyrs and heroes to any other cause—men like Captain James Skyrme, who, his leg blown off by a shot, continued to direct his last battle on his bleeding stump till all was lost.

A few, a very few, succeeded at the game. Those who managed to get away with their ill-gotten gains settled down into exotic respectability as landowners in out-of-the-way colonies or became well-heeled bourgeois merchants in some civilized foreign nation near home. But most of the pirates failed to score high or, if they did, they frittered away their loot and ended their days destitute, either dead of disease or swinging from an Admiralty gibbet.

The names of the pirate leaders of the Golden Age are those of legend: Kidd, Blackbeard, Every, Tew, Low, Taylor, Roberts. In their own time, they were men of mystery whose lives were cloaked in the sea mists. They exerted a fascination—as they still do—on those familiar with their exploits. The pirates carried no scribes aboard their vessels. What is known of them comes from those, like Snelgrave, who in one way or another escaped their clutches, from the recollections of pardoned pirates and naval officers, from trial minutes and gallows confessions. The principal account—in some cases the only record—of the pirates was the work of a remarkable author-journalist of the day, who set himself the task of chronicling the Golden Age of piracy just as it ended.

In 1724, barely two years after the last great mass hangings of pirates, a book entitled *A General History of the Robberies and Murders of the most notorious Pyrates* was published in London and soon became a bestseller. The book dealt in depth with the pirates and was obviously based on such firsthand material as the transcripts of pirates' trials and interviews with pirates, their victims and their vanquishers. Four years later a second volume of the *General History* was published. The author of these volumes was alleged to be Captain Charles Johnson. It was later established beyond any reasonable doubt that Captain Johnson was in fact the great London novelist and journalist, Daniel Defoe, the author of such tales of seafaring life and adventure as *Robinson Crusoe* and *Captain Singleton.*

Defoe's books were intended for popular consumption. They were sensational and moralistic, and *A General History* is interlarded with a number of largely fictitious anecdotes. Yet for all these faults they are classics of the literature of the sea. His volumes on pirates purvey the authentic flavor of the pirate life, present a shrewd insight into the pirate mind, and are mostly correct in their principal details, as subsequent historical research has shown. Pirates, at their worst, wrote Defoe, were inhumane wretches "who could not be contented to satisfy their Avarice only, and travel in the common Road of Wickedness; but, like their Patron, the Devil, must make Mischief their Sport, Cruelty their Delight, and damning of Souls their constant Employment."

Everything about the pirates was larger than life, and their story is highlighted by images of dramatic vividness: the prow of Lieutenant Robert Maynard's sloop plowing through American waters toward Virginia with the severed head of Blackbeard hanging from the bowsprit; Captain Kidd, tortured by guilt and indecision, going slowly mad in the furnace heat of his cabin as he waits for prey at the mouth of the Red Sea; Henry Every, slipping home to Devon with a bagful of diamonds; the pirates of the Bahamas cheering their nemesis, Woodes Rogers, all the way from the beach to his fort; the body of the last great pirate, Captain Bartholomew Roberts, being dropped into the sea in his crimson coat and breeches and gilt finery; images of smoking cannon and ships in flames, of oaths and drunken laughter; the click of dice on a deck and the scream of a gale in the rigging, cries from the crow's nest, "A sail! A sail!"; the shudder of ship's timbers receiving a broadside; the screams of the maimed, and bone and brains in the scuppers; the clatter of golden doubloons, moidores and pieces of eight; a girl in a hammock in the hot Devil's Island noon or long Guinea night—and, at the end of many a life, a hemp noose rough on the sunburned skin of the neck. . . .

It has been said that piracy is humanity's third oldest profession, after prostitution and medicine. Indeed, records show it has existed wherever the rewards of the crime have been worth the risk of punishment.

Organized piracy flourished widely among the early civilizations of the Middle East. The coast of the Persian Gulf between Qatar and Oman was the haunt of generations of pirates who plundered the shipping of the Assyrian kingdoms and later harried the fleet of Alexander the Great. In the Mediterranean, piracy was accepted by merchants and seamen alike as an occupational hazard, and in the last hundred years of the Roman Republic, the pirates in the Mediterranean achieved such widespread power that they were able to sack some 400 towns along the Roman Main, hold Julius Caesar captive for six weeks, and even challenge the expansion of Roman rule.

No nation or nationality had a monopoly on piracy. The Cretans and the Vikings turned their hand to it; and for centuries the Barbary corsairs of North Africa plundered the shipping of the Mediterranean and even the open Atlantic. But it was the Europeans of the Atlantic seaboard—the French, the Dutch and most especially the British—who were to

Early practitioners of an ancient profession

Medieval pirate Eustace the Monk, a fall-away cleric believed to have black magical power, is executed after his defeat in the Straits of Dover in 1217. Matthew Paris—a monk in good standing—vividly recorded his demise with this dramatic sketch.

By the Middle Ages piracy was already an ancient occupation, and it experienced a remarkable upsurge in European waters as trade increased.

Among the most brazen brigands was Eustace the Monk, a renegade Flemish cleric who plundered French shipping for England's King John. But his greed led him to prey on English ships as well, and in 1212 he was forced to flee England.

Eustace then sold his services to the French and led an attempt to invade England. But the English sailors blinded the French by hurling lime at their ships and then followed up with a deadly rain of arrows. Eustace was captured and decapitated on the spot.

Another famed early pirate was the German Klein Henszlein, who operated in the North Sea until a fleet from Hamburg defeated him. He and 33 of his henchmen were paraded into the city, beheaded, and their heads impaled on stakes. The executioner, according to a contemporary account, was "standing in blood so deep that it well nigh in his shoes did creep."

The execution of the German pirate Henszlein and 33 of his men is illustrated in a flier printed in 1573. The executioner, says the flier, "flicked off" the heads in only 45 minutes —and then decapitated the pirates who were killed while resisting capture

develop piracy into its most refined form. The burgeoning of British maritime trade in Tudor times led to a corresponding increase in piracy in British waters. By the middle of the 16th Century there was hardly a fisherman of England who did not at least dabble in the "sweet trade," and the pirates openly displayed their plundered wares for sale on deck. Wales was virtually a pirate principality, and the inhabitants of the Cinque Ports on the southeast coast of England would sally forth to plunder any ship that happened to pass by. Noblemen like Sir Richard Grenville, the Earl of Pembroke, and Sir John Killigrew (the President of the Commissioners for Piracy) maintained control of pirate syndicates all around the British coast.

From time to time, pirates found it profitable to offer their services to nations at war, and in this role they operated as more or less legal naval auxiliaries under the general name of "privateers." The term applied to the crews of privately owned ships, specially commissioned by government letters of marque to attack and loot the shipping of an enemy. The practice of licensing privateers dated back to the 13th Century. Privateers had fought in every important war at sea since that time; nations considered privateering one of the most effective and least expensive ways of bedeviling the enemy.

In the 17th Century, Britain and France were almost constantly at war with Spain in the New World, seeking to break the Spanish monopoly of territory and trade, and privateers were in the vanguard of that struggle. Inspired by Sir Francis Drake's raids on the Spanish Main, English adventurers (and French and Dutch ones as well) continually harassed the Caribbean and Pacific seaboards of Spanish America, their greatest success being Sir Henry Morgan's 1671 raid on Panama, the richest town of the Spanish-American empire.

The distinction between these sea raiders and the pirates who followed them was as often as not in the eye of the beholder. The Spanish, in fact, flatly called them *piratas*. But Morgan and his cohorts regarded themselves as a special bread of privateer. They termed themselves buccaneers, or *boucaniers*; the term meant "smoker of meat" in French, and that is really what the early ones were—herdsmen and woodsmen on the Caribbean island of Hispaniola—before they turned their hand to sea roving. These men insisted that their activities were perfectly legal since all their depredations—no matter how piratical in character—were directed only against the Spanish.

The British and the French acquiesced in this view. Morgan actually became Lieutenant Governor of Jamaica. And to be sure, there was a grain of truth to the buccaneers' claim. The out-and-out pirates did not limit themselves to any one prey but habitually attacked ships of every nationality. They were, in an early definition by the Roman lawyer Cicero, *hostes humani generi*, enemies of the human race. Yet for all of this, the line between privateer, buccaneer and pirate was a fine one. What was one to make of Englishmen and Frenchmen who, as the buccaneers did, plundered Spanish ships with equal zeal in times of truce as well as during hostilities? Did that make them pirates one day and heroes of Britain and France the next?

In a sermon to his Boston congregation in 1704, the Reverend Cotton

Buccaneers, predecessors of the pirates in the Caribbean, cure meat in a smokehouse called a boucan, from which they took their name. The first buccaneers were more or less peaceful French and English squatters on the large Spanish-held island of Hispaniola; they took to the sea in response to Spanish efforts to oust them.

Cotton Mather, fiery preacher of Boston's North Church from 1685 to 1728, railed at Anglicans, Quakers, witches and, naturally, pirates. He beseeched condemned pirates to repent their evil ways, taking, as he said, "great pains to dispose them for a Return unto God."

Mather warned that "the privateering stroke so easily degenerates into the piratical, and the privateering trade is usually carried on with an unchristian temper and proves an inlet into so much debauchery and iniquity." Years later, when piracy as such had largely ceased to exist but there were still plenty of privateers, Admiral Horatio Nelson complained that "the conduct of all privateers is, as far as I have seen, so near piracy that I only wonder any civilized nation can allow them."

The particularly Caribbean form of privateering-cum-piracy known as buccaneering virtually died out after England made peace with Spain in 1689. By then many veterans of buccaneering had turned to outright piracy, and their ranks were soon swollen by all kinds of disaffected sailors anxious to improve their miserable lot by the acquisition of sudden riches from a captured prize.

From the Caribbean, these men ranged out into virtually all the seas of the world, and they found profits aplenty.

For it was a period of expansion in the international seaborne mercantile trade. By the end of the 17th Century, ports and trading posts had been established along most of the inhabited seaboards of the world, and a multitude of ships of all shapes, sizes and nationalities plowed along a complex network of shipping lanes, many of them bearing unbelievably valuable cargoes. There were Spanish treasure fleets laden with the priceless produce of the gold and silver mines of Spanish America; convoys of Portuguese merchantmen stuffed with the riches of Brazil; an endless stream of cargo boats shipping out the exports of the North American colonies to England; the ships of the Royal African Company and other European charter companies in Africa bringing out gold and ivory and slaves from the interior of West Africa; the Mecca pilgrim ships and the merchant fleets of the Grand Mogul of India carrying gold, precious stones and luxury goods between the Red Sea, the Persian Gulf and the mainland of India; the magnificent East Indiamen, blown by the monsoons across the Indian Ocean and round the Cape with their holds full of silks and jewels, spices and muslins acquired by the East India companies established along the Indian coast by various European nations. Such were the prizes that attracted a horde of pirates along the sea-lanes of the world during the Golden Age of piracy.

Yet pirate plunder was valuable only if its value could be realized—if it could be sold or exchanged in a ready market. And it was North America that provided the greatest market. During much of the Golden Age, the pirates operated with the active support and cooperation of the governors, merchants and populace of most of the North American colonies. In England pirates were hunted down remorselessly. But in American ports they were given protection and hospitality, ships, provisions, crews, fake privateer commissions and a place to sell their booty. For the American colonies made a profit out of piracy, just as the pirates themselves did. What is more, by condoning piracy the Americans struck a blow against British rule in a growing struggle that was to culminate in the American War of Independence.

Among the particular circumstances that turned the Americans into a nation of pirate brokers was the series of Navigation Acts passed by the English government beginning in 1651. Originally, their object was to

A catalogue of booty high and low

Though pirates coveted precious jewels, they wanted gold and silver even more. And they regarded coins, which were easily divided into equal shares, as the greatest booty of all. It is easy to imagine the roar of delight in 1716 when pirate Henry Jennings, cruising off the coast of Florida, came upon a Spanish galleon and found 350,000 pieces of eight.

However, pirates often went home with nothing. Calico Jack Rackam, on a two-year cruise in the West Indies, captured more than 20 ships, but most were fishing boats or small coastal traders. From one schooner all he got was "50 Rolls of Tobacco, and Nine Bags of Piemento."

The handwritten list at right catalogues the various goods confiscated from Edward Davis and two other pirates when they were apprehended off Virginia in 1688. Davis and his mates were about to retire after five years of plundering in the Caribbean and elsewhere. Besides coins and assorted silver plate weighing 142 pounds, they treasured "fower paire of silke stocking," "two papire Bookes" and "sevrall peeces of dampnifyed Ribbond."

The three spent a year in the Jamestown jail before being freed under a royal pardon. They then boldly petitioned the King for the return of their swag, claiming that it had been taken illegally. They eventually got most of it back, too—on condition they donate £300 to the founding of Virginia's College of William and Mary.

A 1688 list of pirate booty shows mundane goods to be as much a part of the swag as the legendary "peeces of eight" —silver Spanish coins worth eight reales that were often cut into pieces to make small change.

DUCAT (Denmark)

DAALDER (Holland)

MOHUR (India)

9 DENIERS (France)

LOUIS D'OR (France)

SHILLING (New England)

2 GUINEAS (England)

CROWN (England)

4 CRUSADOES (Portugal)

DOUBLOON (Spain)

PIECE OF EIGHT (Spain)

protect the British shipping trade from Dutch competition. The Acts stipulated that virtually no goods could be imported into England or her colonies except in British ships manned by British subjects. Moreover, most colonial imports and exports had to come from and go to England alone. The effect was to create a near monopoly of both shipping and trade by the mother country.

"The only use of the American colonies," Lord Sheffield once remarked, "is the monopoly of their consumption and the carriage of their produce." Historians disagree as to the net effect of this monopoly. It could be argued that American shipping, since it was colonial and therefore British, benefited from the Navigation Acts, particularly in the British West Indian colonies, from which the Spanish and Dutch were excluded. Nevertheless, many American colonials felt that they were being exploited, that they suffered from this enforced trade with England at prices fixed by English merchants, who habitually bought cheaply and sold dearly. On the one hand, the Americans could not prosper because the English market was too small to absorb all their agricultural products; on the other hand, they could not buy all the things they needed from the English. As a result, the Americans responded by encouraging smuggling and piracy. The tobacco planters of Virginia and Maryland disposed of their surplus tobacco by smuggling it out. And colonial merchants compensated for their lack of goods from the world market by buying them from the pirates.

In 1696 Edward Randolph, Surveyor-General of the Customs in New England, sent back a memorandum to London entitled *A Discourse About Pirates, With Proper Remedies to Suppress Them*. He wrote of the pirates: "In the 1670's I observed that they fitted out vessels of 60 or 70 tons and sent them without commission to the Spanish West Indies, whence they brought home great quantities of silver coins and bullion, with rich capes, church plate and other riches, insomuch that the Spanish ambassador complained thereof. But now these pirates have found out a more profitable and less hazardous voyage to the Red Sea, where they take from the Moors all they have without resistance and bring it to some one of the plantations in the continent of America or islands adjacent, where they are received and harboured and from whence also they fit out their vessels."

The illicit rapprochement between the American colonies and the pirates was widespread by the 1690s. With few exceptions colonial governors from New England to the Carolinas connived with the pirates. Rhode Island, Boston and New York became pirate depots. In Pennsylvania the Surveyor of Customs reported that the pirates behaved as if they owned the place. "They walk the streets with their pockets full of gold and are the constant companion of the chief in the Government. They threaten my life and those who were active in apprehending them; carry their prohibited goods publicly in boats from one place to another for a market; threaten the lives of the King's collectors and with force and arms rescue the goods from them. All these parts swarm with pirates, so that if some speedy and effectual course be not taken the trade of America will be ruined."

Who were these extraordinary men, the pirates? What kind of fellows were they? What did they look like? On December 20, 1699, Governor Francis Nicholson of Virginia, one of the few antipirate colonial officials at the time, issued a warrant for the arrest of the crew of the *Adventure*, who had recently landed in Virginia after a pirate cruise to the Red Sea. The list of wanted men included:

"*John Loyd*, of ordinary stature, rawboned, very pale, dark hair, remarkably deformed in the lower eyelid, about 30; *Thomas Hughes*, tall, lusty, rawboned, long visaged, swarthy, about 28; *Thomas Simpson*, short and small, much squint-eyed, about 10 of age; *James Venner*, short, well set, fresh-colored, pock-fretten, about 20; *Tee Wetherly*, short, very small, blind in one eye, about 18; *Thomas Jameson*, cooper, Scot, tall meagre, sickly look, large black eyes, 20; *William Griffith*, short, well set, broad faced, darkest hair, about 30; *Thomas Davis*, short, small, sharp-chinned, reddish hair, about 22; *Francis Reade*, short and small, reddish hair, about 18; *William Saunders*, of ordinary stature, well-set, fresh-colored, black hair, about 15."

On the basis of this sample, it would seem—from the names—that a number of the crew of the *Adventure* were of Welsh origin. A great many of the pirates of the Golden Age did come from Wales and the West of England—not surprisingly, since these regions then provided the majority of the seafaring men of Britain. Of the 52 members of Captain Bartholomew Roberts' crew hanged at Cape Coast Castle on the Gold Coast in 1722, nearly half came from Wales and the West. But the turnover of pirate crews was very high, and though the men of pirate ships as a whole came mainly from Britain and the American colonies, the admixture of other nationalities was considerable. Thus the pirate ship *Defiance*, while she lay off Rajapore, India, in 1703 mustered 164 Europeans, of which 43 were English, about 50 French, and the remainder Danes, Dutchmen and Swedes, together with 70 East Indians.

The one thing they all had in common was the sea. Indeed, when a pirate ship was hailed in mid-ocean by another passing ship, and asked who she was and whence she came, the traditional pirate reply was: "From the seas." This was a nice response: evasive, but accurate. For by far the majority of all pirates were professional sailors. Landlubbers, with the exception of surgeons and, sometimes, musicians, were not popular recruits on pirate vessels. If a man was going to be part of the pirate community, he had to be able to tell a marlinespike from a sounding lead, and fulfill all the normal requirements of a common seaman: furling, reefing and hauling about the ship.

Some of the pirates were deserters from Royal Navy warships. Other Navy men drifted into piracy through unemployment caused by the laying up of fighting ships at the end of foreign wars. "War is no sooner ended," John Graves, the Bahamas' collector for Customs wrote in 1706, "but the West Indies always swarm with pirates."

But the vast majority of pirates was drawn from the crews of ordinary merchant ships. These recruits were commonly taken from captured ships, either as volunteers or as forced men. Often they were mutineers who had taken over their own ship and turned pirate after killing or setting adrift their captain and any shipmates who did not wish to join them. Undermanned pirate ships increased their strength or replaced

losses caused by sickness, desertion and death in action with new men from captured cargo ships; or they reproduced themselves, like amoebae, by splitting in two: a section of the original crew might go off—"on their own account," as they called it—in a spare prize. Pirate crews were rarely crack teams of battle-hardened men welded together by years of service at sea together. They were, in every sense, a floating population, in a constant state of flux, never the same size or composition from one month to another, owing allegiance to nothing and no one, neither ship, nor captain, nor cause.

What made some men turn to piracy lay in the nature of their life at sea. A common grievance among sailors was the harshness of discipline on board merchant and Navy ships. A 17th or 18th Century sailor was subject to a whole repertoire of punishments and was the easy victim of sadistic or psychopathic officers; some made their men swallow cockroaches, or knocked their teeth out and forced them to gag on their own blood by jamming their mouths with iron bolts. Flogging was the most common punishment. The emotional impact of being flogged—quite apart from the physical damage—provided a powerful goad that drove men to piracy. Flogging could achieve an exceptionally barbarous level. Men could be flogged around the fleet, receiving six lashes alongside every ship. In 1704 Captain Staines of the *Rochester* had a sailor flogged 600 lashes with a tarred rope an inch thick. There is no record of whether or not the man survived; the odds are that he died.

Though most seamen might avoid such extreme punishments as keel-hauling (being scraped across the barnacles on a ship's bottom), running the gauntlet, being hanged from the yardarms, or being ducked from the yardarms or towed from the stern, few in their daily lives escaped some flick of a boatswain's tarred rawhide whip or the thwack of an officer's rattan cane. Nothing made mariners hate authority more—and hatred of authority was an essential characteristic of every pirate.

The brutality meted out to sailors—and returned by them when they turned pirates—was not something peculiarly nautical. All of life was brutal in those days. The Army was more brutal than the Navy and any barbarity at sea could be matched by greater barbarities on land. It was an age of legal tortures, when a man—or a woman, for that matter—might be subjected to the press (in which a prisoner's torso was loaded with weights until it was either crushed or the jailer was satisfied) or the thumbscrew, or branded on the face with a red-hot iron, or might be nailed by the ears in a pillory and stoned, or be tied to a cart and whipped through the streets. In 1685 an unfortunate named Titus Oates ran afoul of the authorities for fomenting political unrest. He was whipped from Aldgate to Newgate and then, two days later, from Newgate to Tyburn. "He received upwards of 2,000 lashes," a chronicler of the day reported. "Such a thing was never inflicted by any Jew, Turk, or heathen. Had they hanged him they would have been more merciful; had they flayed him alive it is a question whether it would have been so much torture." Miraculously, this man did live and later received a pardon and a pension from a different king. But such magnanimity was rare. Felony was punishable by hanging, and a public execution was an occasion for popular feasting and drinking.

As his mother weeps bitterly, a youth is sent away to sea where, as his two companions gleefully point out, the cat-o'-nine-tails awaits him and the gallows may prove his fate. The engraving is one of a moralizing series by Hogarth showing what could happen to an "Idle 'Prentice"— but life for the poor in 18th Century England was often worse ashore than at sea.

Gin Lane, where London's poor drank
themselves to death, exemplifies the
sort of pervasive degradation that drove
men to piracy in 18th Century England.
In this 1751 engraving by William Hogarth,
a besotted mother pays no heed to her
babe toppling over a rail, or to the
cadaverous drunk in front of her. In the
background a scowling pawnbroker
ponders goods offered by drinkers
desperate for cash, a suicide dangles from
a beam and a berserk cook prances
by with a child impaled on a spit.

It was a time of gross social and economic injustice in which the lower
classes, be they sailors or landsmen, were considered little more than
slaves to despotic masters. In 1688, by one scholar's estimate, 75 per cent
of Britain's national income went to barely 20 per cent of her population.
And while the gentry enjoyed their silks and carriages, the pale little
children of the poor were sent out at the age of seven to labor in the mines
and mills for a mere shilling a week; they commonly died there, too—of
fatigue, of cold, of heat, of some foreman's sadistic beating. Those who
survived such treatment were chained to a life of crushing labor and
marginal subsistence, lacking education, going without medical care
and facing years in a debtors' prison if they failed to produce so much as
a farthing to repay a usurer's loan.

It is no wonder that the pirate captain Charles Bellamy could turn to
the stubborn captain of a captured merchantman who refused to join his
pirate crew, and rage at him: "Damn ye, you are a sneaking puppy, and
so are all those who will submit to be governed by laws which rich men
have made for their own security, for the cowardly whelps have not the
courage otherwise to defend what they get by their knavery. But damn ye
altogether. Damn them for a pack of crafty rascals, and you, who serve
them, for a parcel of hen-hearted numbskulls. They villify us, the scoundrels do, then there is only this difference, they rob the poor under the
cover of law, forsooth, and we plunder the rich under the protection of
our own courage; had ye not better make one of us, than sneak after the
arses of those villains for employment?"

Yet if the all-pervasive injustice and harshness of the day mentally
prepared a sailor for some kind of change, it was the lure of money that
provided the strongest impetus. Sailors were not atrociously paid in
comparison with their social equals on land. A seaman commonly got
slightly more than £1 a month, whereas a laborer saw less than half that.
But unless a seaman rose to the rank of master and was able to buy a share
of his ship or his cargo—which happened rarely—he could not expect
much more than an impecunious working life and an austere old age.
Piracy could change this bleak prospect. In the great days of the Pirate
Round, scores of ships returned with booty amounting to £1,500, £2,000
and, at least once, £4,000 per man. This sort of money was almost beyond
belief in those days, equal to the annual income of the elite of England,
the great landlords of the peerage. It was double the income of most
merchants and bankers of London. By comparison, the governor of the
East India Company in Bombay earned a salary of only £300 per annum,
his senior agents £30, a clerk £5 a year.

For a particular kind of disaffected sailor the prospect of sharing in a
real haul was irresistible. The rewards outweighted the risks, and since a
man could be hanged for stealing a shilling, he had no compunction
about stealing a fortune. Bartholomew Roberts most succinctly summed
up the pirates' outlook:

"In an honest service there is thin rations, low wages and hard labor;
in this, plenty and satiety, pleasure and ease, liberty and power; and who
would not balance creditor on this side, when all the hazard that is run
for it, at worst, is only a sour look or two at choking. No, a merry life and a
short one shall be my motto."

The ships: predators, prey and protectors

The stages upon which the great dramas of the Golden Age of piracy took place were the sailing ships of the day. And the vessels the pirates sailed in, preyed upon and sometimes fought against shared many of the same attributes. This was inevitable, for the outlaw pirates had no shipyards to provide them with specialized pirate craft from the keel up. Instead, they went about their predatory business in a succession of captured merchantmen, which they usually altered to suit their purpose.

Naturally, the pirates prized power and speed—so much the better if both were combined in one hull. They particularly favored the predatory vessels depicted at right and on pages 34-35. In such ships they could bear down on their prey—merchantmen like those shown on pages 36-38. More often than not the pirates found such vessels vulnerable not only because they were heavily laden with cargo, but also because the poorly armed and barely motivated crews—their numbers usually kept to an absolute minimum by penny-pinching shipowners—were no match at all for the pirates' own screaming hordes.

The pirates, of course, did not have free reign of the sea. They were prey to others, mainly the roving fleets of the Royal Navy. The Navy's vessels were not great ships of the line, but lighter craft—sloops, frigates and snows, like those on pages 39-41. They were not so far different from merchantmen, or pirate craft, for that matter. However, their crews displayed fighting spirit, and any pirates foolhardy enough to slug it out with them usually met their doom.

Flagships of the brigand fleet

Distinguished by her two masts, rigged
primarily with fore-and-aft sails, and by the
narrowness of her hull, the schooner was
often used by pirates in North American and
Caribbean waters. Her great virtue was
speed, up to 11 knots in a stiff breeze, and at
90 to 100 tons as here, she was also big
enough to carry a crew of 75 to man her eight
cannon and four swivel guns. Another
feature, her shallow draft—five feet in this
example—enabled the pirates to navigate
shoal waters and hide in remote coves.

Suitable as the flagship of a pirate fleet, the
three-masted square-rigger was not
so swift and maneuverable as other vessels
commandeered by pirates. But she was
valued for her intimidating size—350 tons
and 110 feet along her main deck in
this example—and for her seaworthiness
on long voyages. When crewed by 150 to
200 pirates and mounted with 20 or more
cannon, plus numerous swivel guns,
she was on a par even with some naval
frigates. Moreover, her large cargo
capacity made her an excellent transport
for the collected swag of a pirate flotilla.

John Batchelor

Greatly favored by smugglers, the swift sloop was a near-ideal vessel for pirates. A rapier-like bowsprit almost as long as her hull enabled her to mount a parade of canvas that made her even more nimble than the schooner or brigantine; in favorable winds, a square topsail gave her an extra measure of speed, sometimes exceeding 11 knots. Though not so shallow in draft as the schooner —this large 100-tonner drew eight feet of water carrying 75 pirates and 14 cannon — the sloop could maneuver in the channels and sounds where the brigands hid.

Fast and sturdy workhorse of the day, the brigantine was also the chosen combat craft of many pirate captains. She was basically a two-masted vessel that carried on her mainmast either square or fore-and-aft sails, or a combination thereof, which made her immensely versatile; the square sails drove her best in quartering winds while the fore-and-aft sails were effective when sailing to windward. The vessel here was 80 feet long and at 150 tons was big enough to mount 10 cannon and carry a crew of 100.

Merchantmen for every trade

Biggest merchant vessel of her time, the
East Indiaman was built to carry the
wealth of the Orient and was the supreme
prize a pirate could hope to capture.
This great Dutch 700-tonner measured 160
feet along her main deck and 34 feet
at the beam. Between her ornate beakhead
and gilded stern she packed enormous
potential power: up to 54 cannon and a
crew of as many as 300. But she rarely
carried even half that number of guns since
they took up cargo space —and
therein lay her vulnerability to pirates.

Round-sterned, broad-beamed and flat-
bottomed, the Dutch flute made her
debut in the early 17th Century. The flute
was inexpensive to build, cheap to man
(only 12 in crew for this 80-foot 300-tonner)
and renowned for her cargo capacity —
half again that of similarly sized vessels
with sleeker lines. The English and
French quickly adapted the design, and
flutes ranged the world's sea-lanes
where they became routine prey for pirates.

In the days of sail commercial vessels were commonly called merchant ships, but mariners reserved the term for three-masted, square-rigged carriers. These were the large, passenger-and-cargo ships of the late 17th and early 18th centuries. With finer lines and more sails than the flute, this 280-tonner could sail from England to America in four weeks. Pierced for 16 cannon along her 80-foot length, she rarely mounted that many; her crew of 19 could barely handle three.

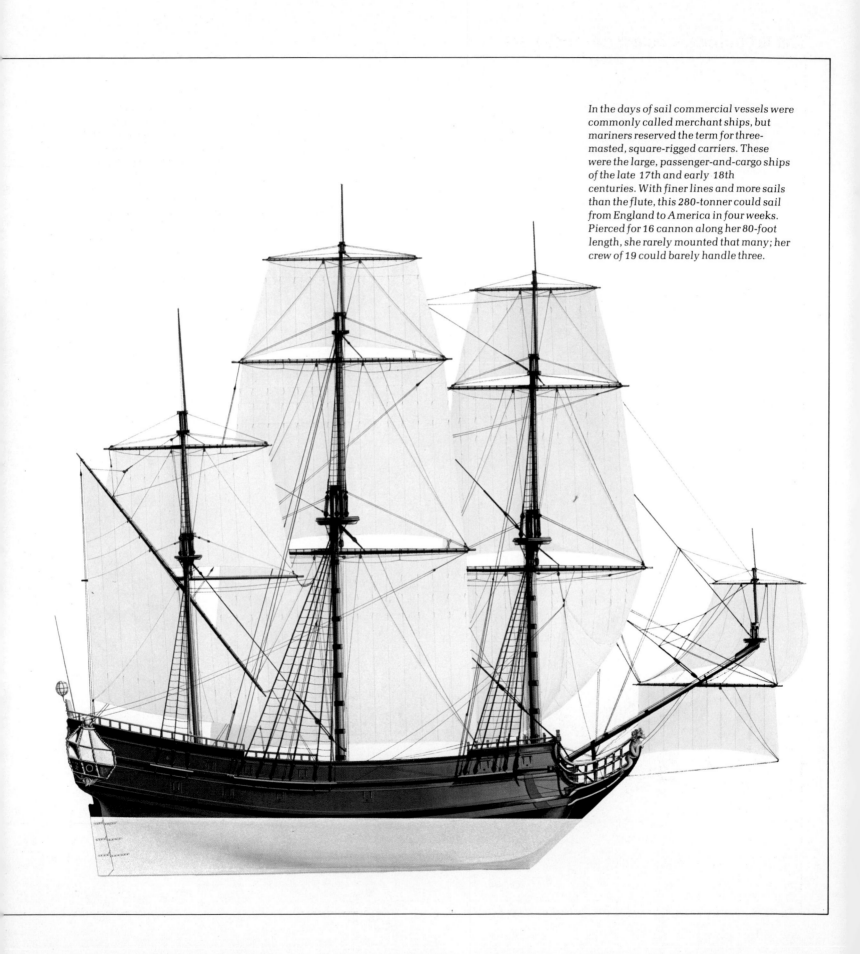

The Royal Navy's potent pirate-chasers

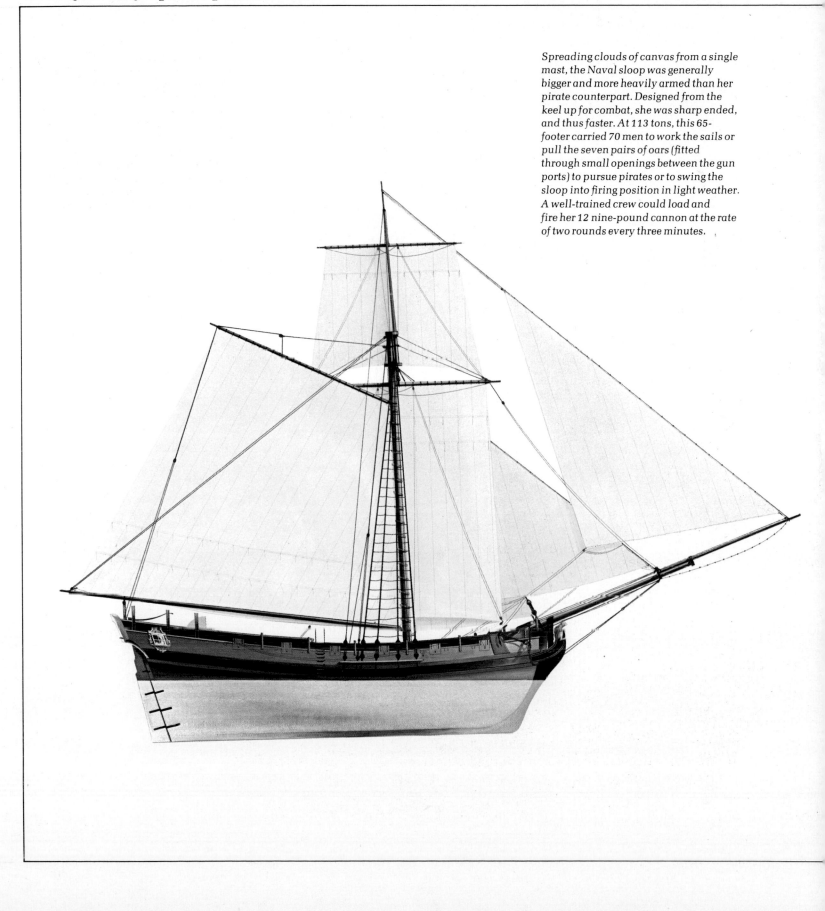

Spreading clouds of canvas from a single mast, the Naval sloop was generally bigger and more heavily armed than her pirate counterpart. Designed from the keel up for combat, she was sharp ended, and thus faster. At 113 tons, this 65-footer carried 70 men to work the sails or pull the seven pairs of oars (fitted through small openings between the gun ports) to pursue pirates or to swing the sloop into firing position in light weather. A well-trained crew could load and fire her 12 nine-pound cannon at the rate of two rounds every three minutes.

Somewhat similar to a merchant ship
in her three-masted, square-rigged profile,
the man-of-war was much more sturdily
built. At 360 tons and 26 guns, this 110-
foot frigate with its crew of 195 would have
served mainly as a scout in a major fleet
action (a ship of the line mounted at least
60 guns). But she was the backbone of
the West Indies Squadron dispatched to
convoy cargo vessels and to fight
pirates; her appearance on the scene was
usually enough to send the brigands fleeing.

Only the fore-and-aft trysail, flying
from a slender pole behind the mainmast,
distinguished the Navy snow from a
square-rigged brigantine. The Royal
Navy favored such a sail plan for this 90-
ton, 60-foot patrol vessel since it
allowed a square mainsail to be set at the
same time as the trysail, giving
added speed in light quartering winds.
With a crew of 80 she was formidable
enough with eight six-pounders resting
behind the canvas strung amidships over
the open bulwarks of the vessel.

Chapter 2

Followers of a brutal calling

43

Marooned on a desert isle, a condemned man awaits death in a re-creation of a terrible pirate punishment by the late-19th Century artist Howard Pyle.

"N o man will be a sailor," pronounced Dr. Samuel Johnson, the famed 18th Century man of letters, "who has contrivance enough to get himself into a jail; for being in a ship is being in a jail, with the chance of being drowned. A man in a jail has more room, better food and commonly better company."

Any pirate who had experienced the living hell of a London prison would have scoffed at Dr. Johnson. But there was a suggestion of truth in what he said. Even in the best of circumstances, life at sea in the 18th Century could be unbelievably severe. For the pirates it was in some ways better, some ways worse, than for the ordinary seaman. For the man seeking individuality, wealth and escape from oppression, life aboard a pirate ship offered many unique possibilities to offset the implacable demands of the sea.

Wooden sailing ships were damp, dark, cheerless places, reeking with the stench of bilge water and rotten meat. Whatever the weather, a wooden ship leaked; its planks could seldom be caulked so thoroughly that they let no water in. In heavy weather, seas beat down the hatchways, so that the lower deck was awash, and once wet the inside of a ship was difficult to dry. The men suffered badly from cramps, colds and catarrhs, made worse by a lack of dry clothes and by the ceaseless labor of hauling ropes and sails and manning pumps. When he went below, a sailor had only the forecastle—also called fo'c's'le—to go to; there in the wretched, candlelit gloom he might share a sopping blanket with a shipmate.

The pirates were luckier than most seamen in that they operated mainly in the warmer climes and thus avoided ordeal by cold. On the other hand they suffered from the terrible heat of the Red Sea and other tropic waters—and from excessive overcrowding. To man all the cannon and board their prey, a pirate ship often carried a crew three or four times larger than that of a merchantman. There were sometimes as many as 250 men jammed into a vessel rarely larger than 127 feet long by 40 feet on the beam. They slept packed side by side on the steerage floor, or lay, as one captured captain put it, "kennelling like hounds on the deck."

All crews did their best to combat pestilence. Merchantmen washed down the decks with vinegar and salt water. The pirates would even slosh the decks with plundered French brandy, if they had a lot of it and the mood seized them. Belowdecks, the usual drill on all vessels was to fumigate with pans of burning pitch or brimstone. But nothing could halt the accumulation of filth and the infestation of vermin during a long voyage. There were nooks and crannies that could never be cleaned or dried. Refuse collected in the bottom of the hull and became a breeding ground for beetles, cockroaches and rats by the scurrying hordes.

It was not unusual for a captain—pirate or merchant—to lose half his crew to disease during a voyage. Typhus and typhoid were endemic on board ship. Sailors also fell prey to scurvy, caused by a diet deficient in fresh fruit, especially citrus with its abundant Vitamin C. They suffered horribly as well from dysentery, malaria and yellow fever. Among the pirates, venereal disease was such a curse that crews boarding captured vessels were often more interested in ransacking the medicine chest for mercurial compounds to treat their syphilis than in searching for loot.

A seaman overturns a turtle in a 1724 engraving from the memoirs of an itinerant French priest who spent 12 years in the West Indies preaching among the pirates. The turtle was a perfect staple for pirates: immobilized on its back, it would stay put until its captor returned to reclaim it; in a ship's hold it could be kept alive until the cook slaughtered it.

Savory fare for sea wolves

By their very nature, the pirates could not keep to rules about provisions like those of the British Navy requiring "vittaulles well seasoned, both fleshe and fishe." For the pirates it was feast or famine—often the latter. But when the pirates went ashore or captured a merchantman with a well-stocked larder, they displayed a penchant for a hearty concoction called salmagundi.

The name is thought to be a corruption of the medieval French *salemine,* meaning salted or highly seasoned, and to have evolved to *salmagonde* by the gourmandizing Rabelais in the 16th Century. In any case, salmagundi was a dish of great versatility.

A cook might include as the basis of his salmagundi any or all of the following: turtle meat, fish, pork, chicken, corned beef, ham, duck and pigeon. The meats would be roasted, chopped into chunks and marinated in spiced wine, then combined with cabbage, anchovies, pickled herring, mangoes, hard-boiled eggs, palm hearts, onions, olives, grapes and any other pickled vegetables that were available. The whole would then be highly seasoned with garlic, salt, pepper and mustard seed and doused with oil and vinegar—and served with drafts of beer and rum.

Sometimes a ship of that era would carry a "petty tally," or small store of creature comforts, consisting of such things as sides of bacon and dried beef tongues, marmalade, currants and almonds. "For when a man is ill, or at the point of death," wrote Captain John Smith in his *A Sea Grammar,* "I would know whether a dish of buttered rice, with a little Cynamon, Ginger and Sugar be not better than Salt Fish or Salt Beef. And after a Storme, when poor men are all wet, and some of them have not so much as a cloth to shift them, shaking with cold, few of those but will tell you a little sherry or aqua-vitae is much better to keep them in health, than a little small Beer, or cold water."

The ordinary food was universally atrocious. The water stank, the meat and fish were rotten, the biscuits were infested with large black-headed weevil maggots. The men could bring themselves to eat only in the dark. But at least seamen and merchantmen had a reasonable expectation of something to eat, no matter how objectionable. For pirates, thirst and starvation were constant companions. The irregular nature of pirate cruises, with their sudden changes of course, their hazardous haunts in remote corners of distant oceans, often put the crews on desperately short rations. In 1691 an anonymous English pirate captain off Calicut, India, attempted to come to a gentlemanly agreement with the local English East India Company agent, and sent a note ashore, which was handed to a company employee:

"Though unknown to each other, yet being a countryman I presume to write to you to lett you know that we design to clean our ship at your haven, and get some wood and water, as well as provisions for refreshing our men, for which we honestly design to pay, as well as for one hundred weight of limes. I suppose I need not acquaint you who we are. We design no harm to any of our countrymen and it is only the troublesomeness of the times that sends us out on 'The Account.' And, upon the word of a soldier, if you come aboard our ship there shall be nothing offered you but what shall be civil, and you shall be safely put ashore.

"Your Unknown Friend"

A week later, as no reply had been received, the pirate changed his tune. He sent the master of a captured merchantman ashore with a message that he would keep the merchantman until he received confirmation that his request for supplies would be fulfilled. "Otherwise I shall come and take it. Send us a hogshead of rum and sugar equivalent for punch and also sufficient resin for our ship. A speedy answer is requested by one yet unknown, if you desire that he continue your FRIEND."

Soon afterward the needy pirates were driven off, still hungry and thirsty, by the appearance of three large ships coming from Bombay.

By the nature of their occupation, pirates suffered prolonged agonies of boredom, relieved mainly by playing dice and cards, and letting off guns when they could afford the ammunition. Drink, of course, was their greatest comfort—in particular, rum. But some pirates, those who could read, found solace in the Bible and prayer books. Considerable attention was given to a clergyman captured aboard the frigate *Onslow* in 1721 by Bartholomew Roberts; the pirate crew asked him to become their ship's chaplain. To "make Punch, and say Prayers" were to be his chief duties.

When the parson declined the offer of a position and a share of the booty, he was respectfully released by the pirates, for "however brutish they might be in other Things, they bore so great a Respect to his Order, that they resolved not to force him against his Inclinations."

From time to time on their interminable cruises and long layovers in port, the pirates livened things up with a unique game—the pirate pantomime, or mock trial. They lived with death as surely as they sailed under the death's-head emblem, and many of them were haunted by a vision of what would happen to them if caught—a court trial and probably the noose and the gibbet. To exorcise this vision of retribution, the pirates devised their own sham court. Each pirate played a part—judge, lawyer, juror, jailer, hangman—and in the resulting burlesque they came to terms with the unbearable prospect of a real court, a real execution.

A mock trial held by the crew of Captain Thomas Anstis in 1721 was reported by one of the participants to Daniel Defoe (and doubtless improved by him later). The court took place on an uninhabited cay off Cuba's coast. Pirate-judge George Bradley sat in a tree with a tarpaulin over his shoulders like a robe, a shaggy cap on his head like a wig, and large spectacles on the end of his nose. The pirate officers of the court assembled below, the criminals were led out, "making a thousand sour faces," and the pirate attorney-general opened the charges against them:

"ATTORNEY-GENERAL. An't please your Lordship, and you gentlemen of the jury, here is a fellow before you that is a sad dog, a sad sad dog; and I humbly hope your Lordship will order him to be hanged out of the way immediately. He has committed piracy upon the high seas, and we shall prove, an't please your Lordship, that this fellow, this sad dog before you, has escaped a thousand storms, nay, has got safe ashore when the ship has been cast away, which was a certain sign he was not born to be drowned; yet, not having the fear of hanging before his eyes, he went on robbing and ravishing man, woman and child, plundering ships' cargoes fore and aft, burning and sinking ship, bark and boat, as if the Devil had been in him. But this is not all, my Lord. He has committed worse villainies than all these, for we shall prove, that he has been guilty of drinking small beer, and your Lordship knows, that never was a sober fellow but what was a rogue.

"JUDGE. Heark'ee me, Sirrah—you lousy, pitiful, ill-looked dog; what have you to say why you should not be tucked up immediately and set a sun drying, like a scarecrow? Are you guilty, or not guilty?

"PRISONER. Not guilty, an't please your Worship.

"JUDGE. Not guilty! Say so again, Sirrah, and I'll have you hanged without any trial.

"PRISONER. An't please your worship's honor, my lord, I am as honest a poor fellow as ever went between stem and stern of a ship, and can hand, reef, steer, and clap two ends of a rope together, as well as e'er a he that ever crossed salt water. But I was taken by one George Bradley, a notorious pirate, a sad rogue as ever was unhanged, and he forced me, an't please your honor."

(There followed some repartee in which the actors took turns insulting one another. At last the judge loudly asked if dinner were ready.)

"ATTORNEY-GENERAL. Yes, my lord.

Making light of the dreaded Admiralty Courts, a pirate crew stages a mock trial of one of their fellows on a Cuban islet in late 1721. The robed and wigged judge perches in a mangrove tree, the bailiffs hold handspikes as staves of authority and the hangman stands by with a rope.

"JUDGE. Then heark'ee, you rascal at the bar; hear me, Sirrah, hear me. You must suffer for three reasons: first, because it is not fit I should sit here as judge, and nobody be hanged. Secondly, you must be hanged because you have a damned hanging look. And thirdly, you must be hanged because I am hungry; for know, Sirrah, that 'tis a custom, that whenever the judge's dinner is ready before the trial is over, the prisoner is to be hanged of course. There is law for you, ye dog! Take him away."

Game or no, these pirate pantomimes could be so realistic that they actually ended in free-for-all riots. In one recorded instance in 1717, a pirate playing the part of the accused was so carried away by the game that he believed it was a real kangaroo court and that he would actually be hanged. In a frenzy of rage and fear, he threw a hand grenade at the jury and with his cutlass hacked off the arm of the prosecutor, a pirate who called himself Alexander the Great.

One of the most remarkable characteristics of pirate life was the almost total absence of those features of ordinary society the pirates detested—overbearing authority, class distinctions, lack of a say in important matters. Unlike the privateer crews, who had the status of employees and worked for the captain who was appointed by the owners, the pirates shared their ship and worked for nobody. They elected their captain and they could depose him. "They only permit him to be captain," wrote Defoe, "on condition that they may be captain over him." Except in the heat of battle, major decisions were generally taken by a show of hands and if there was a sufficiently large dissident minority it left the ship and set out on its own account.

At its best, the pirate community was a kind of guild with no ideological ambition. At its worst it was anarchy with no form of self-discipline. Privilege was regarded as the first step toward autocracy and was treated accordingly. The pirate captain therefore had no constitutional authority and was entitled to no special privileges aside from a double share of the loot. Captain Bartholomew Roberts, one of the greatest pirate captains who ever lived, was allowed the use of the master's cabin, and a small amount of silver cutlery and china crockery. But this meant little. At any hour of the day or night a crewman could enter the cabin and help himself to Roberts' food and drink and use his cutlery and crockery; Roberts could not do a thing about it.

Only in battle did the pirate captain come into his own. Roberts' lieutenant, Walter Kennedy, who went off on his own account and was hanged in London in 1721, said at his trial at the Old Bailey: "They chose a captain from amongst themselves, who in effect held little more than that title, excepting in an engagement, when he commanded absolutely and without control." Defoe elaborated on this: "The captain's power is uncontrollable in chase or in battle, drubbing, cutting, or even shooting anyone who does deny his command."

Naturally, the pirates sought a captain who was judged particularly competent for the job—"one superior for knowledge and boldness," observed Defoe, "pistol proof they call it." If pirates could not abide tyrannical captains, they could not abide incompetent or unlucky ones either. While some pirate captains kept their appointments for years,

Emblems to strike terror on the seas

No one knows the origin of the name "Jolly Roger" for the pirate flag; it may have come from *joli rouge* (pretty red), a wry French description of the bloody banner flown by early privateers.

Whatever the derivation, the flags were meant to strike mortal terror in the hearts of the pirates' intended victims. They often featured skeletons, daggers, cutlasses or bleeding hearts on white, red or black fields. The skull and crossbones motif first appeared around 1700 when the French pirate Emanuel Wynne hoisted that fearful ensign *(below)* off the Cape Verde Is-

lands—with an hourglass to show his prey that time was running out.

Bartholomew Roberts brandished a double threat with two flags *(opposite, center and bottom left)*. One displayed the captain and a skeleton drinking a toast to death. On the other, Roberts gave vent to his vendetta against the islands of Barbados and Martinique by picturing himself astride two skulls labeled ABH and AMH—"A Barbadian's Head" and "A Martinican's Head." Around 1720 Roberts made good on a threat; he hanged the governor of Martinique from a yardarm.

CHRISTOPHER MOODY

THOMAS TEW

EMANUEL WYNNE

JACK RACKAM

STEDE BONNET

HENRY EVERY

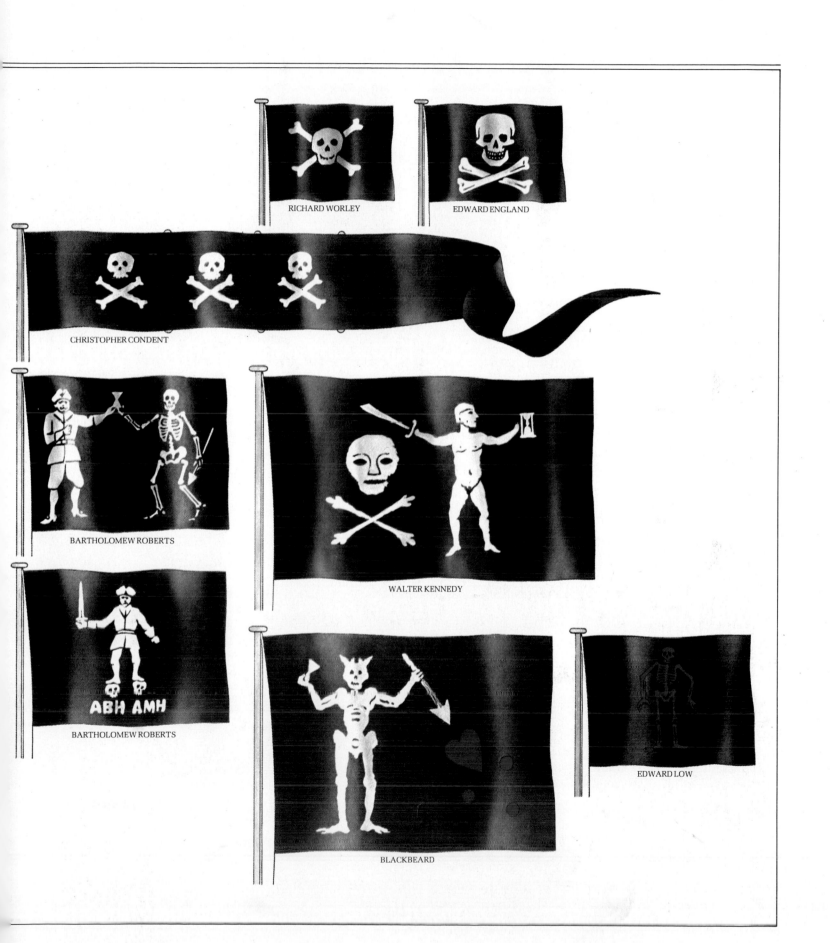

RICHARD WORLEY

EDWARD ENGLAND

CHRISTOPHER CONDENT

BARTHOLOMEW ROBERTS

WALTER KENNEDY

BARTHOLOMEW ROBERTS

ABH AMH

BLACKBEARD

EDWARD LOW

others were quickly removed: one ship had 13 captains within a few months. The pirates were only too well aware of the trouble a bad captain could get them into. The same Walter Kennedy, who was a spirited pirate lieutenant when he was with Roberts, proved something of a disaster on his own. Sailing his pirate ship back from the West Indies to his native Ireland, he strayed so badly off course that he ended up a creek in northwest Scotland.

Next to the captain the most important man on a pirate ship was the quartermaster. Defoe described him as "the trustee for the whole ship's company . . . like the Grand Mufti amongst the Turks to their Sultan, for the captain can do nothing which the quartermaster does not approve of. The quartermaster is an humble imitation of the Roman tribune, for he speaks for and looks after the interest of the company."

The quartermaster was the strong man of the ship. He was the ship's magistrate and empowered to punish minor offenses like quarreling or not looking after weapons properly, though serious offenses could only be tried by jury. He was the only man on a pirate ship who was allowed to administer flogging—though so detested was this form of punishment that it was allowed only when sanctioned by a majority vote of the crew. The quartermaster was also the first man to board a prize, and he was responsible for the selection and division of the plunder, and in charge of the ship's boat on any particularly difficult or dangerous enterprise. But he, too, was subject to the will of the community. He was chosen by majority vote and he could be deposed by it.

Besides the captain and the quartermaster, the pirates had all the other officers usual on a man-of-war—if they could get them. These officers were sometimes elected but more often appointed by the captain and the quartermaster. There was sometimes a lieutenant, who had no particular function except to assume command if the captain was killed. The sailing master was more important—it was he who was in charge of navigation and the setting of the sails. The boatswain was responsible for maintenance, ship's tackle and stores, and the day-to-day work of the ship. The gunner was in charge of the ordnance, gunnery training and the gun crews in action. Other invaluable specialist officers or "artists," as they were called, included the carpenter, the sailmaker and the surgeon. The surgeon on board a pirate ship often spent his time treating venereal disease among the crew members. Against the main causes of death and incapacity in tropic waters—yellow fever, malaria and dysentery—he was virtually helpless. During a battle he would be required to dress wounds and perform amputations. If there was no surgeon, the carpenter stood in for him: the tools were much the same.

The most popular ship's specialists were the members of the pirate orchestra. These were seamen who had been impressed from captured ships because of their ability as musicians. A pirate ship with a band was doubly blessed. The bandsmen were constantly on call to play a jig or a hornpipe at a pirate dance or to serenade the pirates as they took their communal meals. The bandsmen also served a more practical function—during a battle they were ordered to play nautical tunes and aggressive war notes on drums and trumpets to demoralize the enemy and encourage their own men. Captain Samuel Hyde, master of the East Indiaman

Dorrill, reported that on July 7, 1697, he was attacked by a pirate ship that bore down on him and came under his stern after making a great cacophony "with the music of Hautboys and Drums."

But if they were always on the lookout to press specialist officers, the pirates almost never forced ordinary seamen into service. They did not have to, since there were normally plenty of volunteers. And most pirates never forced a married man. When Edward Low captured Captain George Roberts, a bachelor, Low advised him to tell the pirate crew that he was married as "we have an article which we are sworn to not to force any married man against his will." When a man was forced into a pirate crew, he was usually issued a document by the pirate quartermaster certifying that he had been forced; this document could then be used as defense if he were ever put on trial for piracy. Sometimes seamen who volunteered to join the pirates asked the quartermaster to go through the motions of forcing them in the presence of their officers. The quartermaster was happy to oblige and do a blustery piratical turn for them, with much waving of cutlasses and mouthing of oaths. Alas, the authorities were aware of the ruse. At Admiralty trials in England, most specialists were acquitted as forced men, but ordinary seamen seldom so.

No matter who he was, when a man joined the pirate crew he had to sign the pirates' articles or rules, swearing over a Bible or an ax to obey them. The articles of Bartholomew Roberts' crew stipulated:

"I. Every man shall have an equal vote in affairs of moment. He shall have an equal title to the fresh provisions or strong liquors at any time seized, and shall use them at pleasure unless a scarcity may make it necessary for the common good that a retrenchment may be voted.

"II. Every man shall be called fairly in turn by the list on board of prizes, because over and above their proper share, they are allowed a shift of clothes. But if they defraud the company to the value of even one dollar in plate, jewels or money, they shall be marooned. If any man rob another he shall have his nose and ears slit, and be put ashore where he shall be sure to encounter hardships.

"III. None shall game for money either with dice or cards.

"IV. The lights and candles should be put out at eight at night, and if any of the crew desire to drink after that hour they shall sit upon the open deck without lights.

"V. Each man shall keep his piece, cutlass and pistols at all times clean and ready for action.

"VI. No boy or woman to be allowed amongst them. If any man shall be found seducing any of the latter sex and carrying her to sea in disguise he shall suffer death.

"VII. He that shall desert the ship or his quarters in time of battle shall be punished by death or marooning.

"VIII. None shall strike another on board the ship, but every man's quarrel shall be ended on shore by sword or pistol in this manner. At the word of command from the quartermaster, each man being previously placed back to back, shall turn and fire immediately. If any man do not, the quartermaster shall knock the piece out of his hand. If both miss their aim they shall take to their cutlasses, and he that draweth first blood shall be declared the victor.

"IX. No man shall talk of breaking up their way of living till each has a share of £1,000. Every man who shall become a cripple or lose a limb in the service shall have 800 pieces of eight from the common stock and for lesser hurts proportionately.

"X. The captain and the quartermaster shall each receive two shares of a prize, the master gunner and boatswain, one and one half shares, all other officers one and one quarter, and private gentlemen of fortune one share each.

"XI. The musicians shall have rest on the Sabbath Day only by right. On all other days by favour only."

Such articles to preserve the efficiency, unity, safety and welfare of a pirate crew varied slightly here and there. Those of Captain George Lowther made provision for the first man to sight a prize to be rewarded with the best pistols or other small arms on the ship, and required that "good quarter shall be given when called for." The articles of Captain John Phillips laid down that the punishment for striking another member of the crew, for smoking a pipe without a cap on it or for carrying a candle without a lantern in the hold, should be Moses' Law ("i.e. 40

MUSKET

BLUNDERBUSS

CUTLASS

stripes lacking one on the bare back''). Some articles prescribed, as a penalty for the murder of one pirate by another, that the murderer and the corpse should be tied together and both thrown overboard—the punishment the Royal Navy used for the same offense.

The pirates often provided a more just and effective society at sea than hereditary rulers did at home. When Harry Glasby, ''a reserved, sober man'' whom Roberts had forced to piracy because of his skill as a sailing master, was recaptured after jumping ship with a few others at Hispaniola—a capital offense under pirate law—his trial by his shipmates provided an interesting example of piratical judicial procedure.

The trial, as reported by Defoe, was held in the ship's steerage amid much puffing of pipes and quaffing of rum punch. The indictment was read out to the prisoners. The prosecution and defense had their say. The evidence was found to weigh against the accused, and sentence was just about to be passed when one of the pirate judges, Valentine Ashplant by name, taking his pipe out of his mouth, announced that he had something to say on behalf of one of the prisoners. What Ashplant said was short but impassioned: ''By God, Glasby shall not die. Damn me if he

To survive in close-quarters combat, a pirate had to be a walking arsenal. It is unlikely that he would have simultaneously carried the blunderbuss and musket shown here, but he would surely have carried a boarding ax for cutting nets and rigging, as well as a cutlass, a dagger and a pistol, which he would probably need on board.

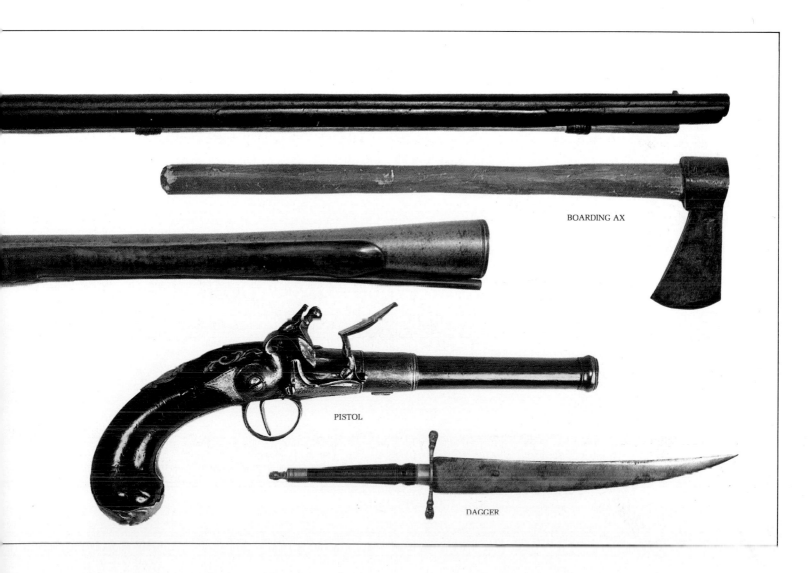

BOARDING AX

PISTOL

DAGGER

shall." He then sat down in his place and put his pipe back in his mouth.

Ashplant's motion was, however, loudly opposed by all the other judges, so he was forced to enlarge on his special plea:

"God damn ye, gentlemen! I am as good a man as the best of you. Damn my soul if ever I turned my back on any man in my life or ever will, by God! Glasby is an honest fellow, notwithstanding this misfortune, and I love him, devil damn me if I don't. I hope he will live and repent of what he has done; but damn me, if he must die, I will die along with him!"

Ashplant then pulled out a pair of pistols and pointed them at the learned judges. The evidence was overwhelming; they quickly changed their verdict and acquitted Glasby.

The rest of the accused were granted no such reprieve. Their only privilege was to choose their own firing squad from Roberts' crew. They were then tied immediately to the mast and executed.

Two other forms of pirate punishment have achieved great publicity: walking the plank and marooning. Walking the plank has long been considered synonymous with piracy. The inventor of this complicated method of precipitating prisoners to their watery grave is often said to be Major Stede Bonnet, a Barbados planter-turned-pirate. But not a shred of evidence has ever been produced to prove it, and there are virtually no recorded incidents of pirates forcing anybody to walk the plank.

The appalling punishment of marooning, on the other hand, was all too real a possibility. The offender was simply put ashore on a desert islet far from land and left there to die. Only a few survived. Among them were Captain William Greenaway and seven companions. Toward the end of 1718, unwilling to join the mutineers on their sloop and go pirating, Greenaway and the others were cast ashore stark naked and without provisions on Green Key, an uninhabited Bahamian island of ragged coral and dense scrub. What saved this particular group of maroons was the indecision of the pirates who marooned them.

At the last moment, just as they were about to sail away, the pirates relented a little. Returning ashore, they collected the maroons and carried them out to a captured sloop, which they turned over to the men. But first they fouled the main sheet and cut the foresail down so that it was no bigger than a jib, and then they slashed the rigging and sails to ribbons so that the sloop was next to useless.

The maroons were now in a worse position than before. Anchored a mile offshore without food or water, they would have perished if they had not found a broken hatchet blade on board. Greenaway, the only man who could swim, went ashore with the ax blade around his neck and cut down trees to make rafts. With the rafts the men ferried fruit, berries and cabbage palms onto the sloop.

After a week the castaways had mended the rigging and patched up a sail. But they had barely set off when, to their horror, they saw the pirates returning. They took to the rafts and paddled ashore, hiding in the brush—from which they watched in despair as the pirates chopped down the mast of their sloop and then sank the vessel in deep water. For eight days the maroons lived on berries, shellfish and sting rays, which they speared with sharpened sticks. Several times the pirates landed and called out to them but the maroons did not answer.

At last the pirates promised safe conduct, and Greenaway and his companions emerged from hiding. But it was a trick. The pirates forced Greenaway and two of his companions to join their crew and deposited the remaining five back on the cay. Then the pirates sailed off again.

For a fortnight, the abandoned men survived as best they could on the sparse provender their little island had to offer. Then the pirates returned. Incredibly—possibly at Greenaway's urging—they laid at the water's edge a large cask of flour, a bushel of salt, two bottles of gunpowder, two muskets, a store of shot, a good ax, a dozen knives, and some pots and pans. In addition, they left three hunting dogs of the kind used throughout the West Indies for catching wild hogs—the main source of a ship's provisions in those days. The maroons' worst hardships, if not their isolation, were over. They built themselves a hut. They ate roast pork. They settled down to a long wait for rescue by some passing ship.

But the ship that came was not a rescue ship. It was the pirates again. The pirates burned down the maroons' hut and ate their roast pork. Then they gave the maroons a bottle of rum and promised never to return. They never did. Instead they were soon afterward captured by Spanish authorities who, after Greenaway told his story, dispatched a rescue boat under a Bahamian named John Sims.

"Comfortable news!" Sims cried out to the maroons, who were hiding in the treetops for fear the pirates had returned. "Relief!"

So ended the ordeal of the men on Green Key, fortunate survivors of the diabolical pirate punishment called marooning.

By building a reputation for great cruelty, the pirates sought to intimidate their victims. Essentially, they were hit-and-run raiders, and their tactics were designed to that end. Speed and surprise were of the essence—and terror or the threat of terror was a basic weapon. Force was far from their favored way to gain an objective. They were well aware of what can happen to a man in a naval battle—the effect of a shower of oak splinters, flying like six-inch daggers; the butchery of the ship's surgeon or carpenter; the horror of gangrene in the tropics. They were not in any regular armed service; they were not fighting for King and Country or abstract causes or because they had to. They saw no reason to risk their lives for something they could not enjoy if they were dead.

Their ships were almost always fast sailers. They were selected for this quality, and were maintained to enhance it; ships were regularly careened to repair the ravages of the omnipresent teredo worm. Lurking among the cays of the Caribbean, or in the twisted tidal estuaries of the Carolinas, the pirates almost always spotted their prey before they themselves were discovered. In the open ocean they always kept a lookout who could scan 20 miles from the top of a 100-foot mast.

Once a ship had been spotted, it was thoroughly examined through a spyglass to determine what kind of vessel it was, its nationality, where it was likely to be coming from and where it was likely to be going, what cargo it might be carrying, what capacity for resistance it might have, and how it sailed. On the basis of this scrutiny the captain—or, as often as not, the crew by popular vote—decided whether to attack it or not. Since in those days it was not always easy to tell a heavily armed ship from a

Captain George Lowther and three crewmen take their ease ashore while Lowther's ship, the Happy Delivery (background), is being careened. This meant beaching and unloading the vessel, then hauling it over on its side in order to recaulk seams, burn off barnacles and replace planking that was infested by teredo worms (below). Careening was a hazardous business at best because it rendered pirates temporarily helpless.

The shells of teredo worms—mollusks that infest tropical waters—protrude from blocks of wood in this late-18th Century illustration. The worms tunnel through hulls below the water line, robbing vessels of speed and eventually seaworthiness. Since speed was the essence of pirate tactics, the crews had to coat hulls with a protective mixture of tar, tallow and sulfur at least three times yearly.

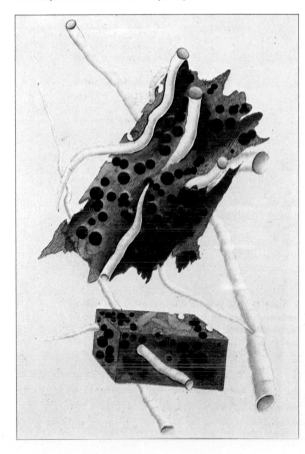

relatively unarmed one—some merchantmen had false gunports marked on their sides—pirates would often shadow their prey for several hours or even several days before striking.

At this stage of the chase the pirates never fired at their prize for fear of sinking her with all her plunder. They simply put a shot across her bows and waited for her to strike her colors. Usually that was the end of it.

The pirates were masters of psychology, and captured ship after ship without so much as a blow being struck, by frightening their prey into submission. Every sailor had his stock of pirate stories. The lurid tales of what happened to those who resisted or otherwise annoyed the pirates needed no embroidering. In 1695 a pirate captain named Dirk Chivers captured two East Indiamen in the Red Sea. The master of one of them, a Captain Sawbridge, irritated the pirates with his incessant reproaches. So they silenced him by sewing his lips up with a sail needle, and set the poor fellow ashore near Aden, where he soon died. Off the coast of Africa in 1719, a certain Captain Skinner surrendered to the pirates under the command of Edward England. When he came on board the pirate ship, Skinner was recognized by his former boatswain, with whom he had once pursued a bitter feud. "Captain Skinner! Is it you? The very man in the world I wished most to see. I am very much in your debt and you shall be paid in full and in your own coin." The boatswain had the wretched captain tied to the windlass, where he was pelted with broken bottles and severely cut. Afterward he was knocked about the deck by the pirates, until they were tired. Finally they told him that since he had been a good master he deserved an easy death. So they shot him in the head.

The most obvious symbol of pirate terror was the skull and crossbones flag, euphemistically named the "Jolly Roger." But the pirates had many other devices to remind their prey of who they were. While the pirate band produced horrendous noises, the pirates "vapored," as they called it, on the poop and afterdeck, which meant that they danced around growling and chanting war cries and waving their weapons and clashing their cutlasses—a chilling, ringing sound. If they spied the captain of the prize, they often singled him out for abuse. "You dog! You son-of-a-bitch! You speckle-shirted dog!" was how pirate captain John Russel hailed Captain George Roberts of the merchant sloop *Dolphin* as Russel stood by to board her in the Cape Verde Islands in 1722. "I will drub you, you dog, within an inch of your life—and that inch too!"

Some pirate captains with a gift for showmanship projected themselves as monsters; others appealed to sweet reason. In the Malacca Straits off Sumatra in July 1697, pirate captain Robert Culliford hailed the East Indian *Dorrill*, China-bound from Madras with a rich cargo and a great deal of specie. "Gentlemen," he said, "we want not your ship, but only your money. Money we want and money we shall have!"

Yet there were times when all threats failed, and a pitched battle at sea rocked the skies and bloodied the waters. Once fighting had broken out, merchantmen often fought to the bitter end, for the crew knew they could expect no quarter. They were many times remarkably successful; even an ordinary merchantship could turn itself into a floating fortress.

Ships in those days were broadly of two classes—galley built and frigate built. Galley-built ships were flush decked, with a wooden cabin under the quarter-deck of massive construction, loopholed for small arms. Frigate-built ships were well decked, with an open space between the forecastle and the after part of the ship, sometimes known as the aftercastle. Both the forecastle and the aftercastle were fronted by heavy wooden beams with loopholes for muskets and small guns and a heavy door to close in the defenders. These were the "closed quarters," to which the defenders could retire if the pirates boarded the main deck amidships and in which they could hold out almost indefinitely.

One of the most gripping accounts of a battle with pirates was written by Richard Salwey, a seaman on the English ship, the *Bauden*, attacked while sailing to India. The *Bauden* was a small frigate, only 170 tons, with 16 guns and 68 men, of whom 38 were landlubbers, soldiers on their way to the East Indian Company garrison in Bombay.

At 6 a.m. on October 26, 1686, off the island of St. Jago, the *Bauden* sighted a strange sail three leagues westward. This turned out to be a French pirate vessel, the *Trompeuse*, 300 tons, 30 guns and 250 men. The *Bauden*'s commander, Captain John Cribb, prepared to defend his ship. He ordered the guns to be double-loaded with shot, the decks cleared, the foreyards slung in chains to prevent their being cut away and two powder chests set up on the forecastle, and one on the poop. To hinder the pirates boarding his ship he had the decks smeared with butter and strewn with dried peas and wooden boards with tenpenny nails sticking up through them. He had four 6-pounder guns run out on the quarter-deck and a swivel 6-pounder set up in the closed quarters with which he could sweep the deck if the pirates came on board.

At noon, the pirate ship, flying French colors, ranged down on the *Bauden*'s starboard quarter. One of the pirates climbed out onto his ship's bowsprit and ordered the *Bauden*'s captain to come aboard his vessel. Captain Cribb refused. He said if there was any business to discuss, the visitors could come onto the *Bauden*, to which a pirate replied in broken English that that was exactly what they were going to do.

"Welcome," Cribb answered, "win her and wear her." A volley of small-arms fire from the pirates greeted this remark, and Cribb and Salwey ducked into fortified closed quarters. The rest of *Bauden*'s crew fired a volley from the waist of the ship and withdrew according to plan, half into the stern, half into the forecastle.

The men of the *Bauden* were now in closed quarters. From the forecastle they brought their big guns to bear on the pirates' bow. The pirate ship then turned and rammed her bowsprit into the *Bauden*'s mainmast rigging, whereupon the *Bauden* discharged her steerage guns. The impact made the pirate ship veer astern, so that her bowsprit became entangled in the *Bauden*'s rigging. The pirates then lashed their bowsprit to the *Bauden* and some of them began to crawl along it onto the merchantman, while others crept up the *Bauden*'s sides. All the while, the guns of both ships blasted away at point-blank range. Once on board the *Bauden* some of the pirates climbed up the shrouds in an attempt to cut down the yards. They failed because Captain Cribb had lashed the yards with chains, and many of the pirates were shot down into the sea, while the rest retreated back to their own ship.

None of the pirates dared to board via the *Bauden*'s quarter-deck be-

The awful death that never was

Of all the popular legends about pirates—their hoards of buried treasure, their ubiquitous parrots and eye patches and their penchant for rum spiked with gunpowder—none looms larger in mythology than the vision of pirates forcing their victims to a watery grave by walking the plank.

There is only one obscure account of any such thing happening. The story may or may not have been true, and in any case it had nothing at all to do with pirates. In 1769, long after the Great Age of piracy, an ordinary seaman named George Wood, who was on his way to his hanging for mutiny, reportedly revealed to the chaplain at Newgate that he and his mutinous mates had forced a number of loyal crewmen "to walk on a plank, extended from the ship's side, over the Sea, into which they were turned, when at the extreme end."

Whether this alleged confession had anything to do with subsequent fictionalized accounts of pirates and the plank is highly debatable. Nothing was made of it at the time, and it soon disappeared into the dust of history.

How, then, did the myth come about?

As early as 100 B.C. pirates preyed on Roman shipping in the Mediterranean, and those brigands played a cruel game with their captives. They would fall to their knees when the Romans identified themselves as subjects of the emperor and with great sarcasm beg for mercy, ending by telling their victims that they were now free "to walk home." But the only place the Romans could walk was over the rail and into the sea. Whether these ancient pirates ended the charade by pitching their victims overboard is not known. It is certain, though, that 17th and 18th Century pirates routinely fed to the sharks any captives who displeased them or for whom they could find no further use.

From such episodes, it required only a brief flight of imagination for an author—or an illustrator like pirate buff Howard Pyle, whose engraving is shown below—to take the whole thing one step further and depict a bunch of fiendish pirates goading a hapless and blindfolded captive to the end of a plank, and the end of his days.

From an 1887 Harper's Monthly, this scene is Howard Pyle's conception of how pirate victims walked the plank.

cause of the gun that was trained on it. Instead they concentrated their fire on the closed quarters in an attempt to kill Cribb. The pirate guns blasted three great shots through the *Bauden*'s sides. The last shot smashed into a powder chest, which exploded with a great boom. The pirates gave a loud shout and redoubled their efforts. They swarmed onto the merchantman's poop with poleaxes and tried to cut down the ensign staff pole. But the *Bauden*'s crew, aiming their muskets through the loopholes of the thick beams protecting their closed quarters, poured a withering fire on the pirates, who were forced to retreat again.

By this time, the fight had been going on for two hours. Cribb had been severely wounded in the groin when he emerged from the closed quarters to encourage his men. He now went out again and was hit a second time, the bullet passing through his right breast and coming out of his back and causing his death within half an hour. Seaman Richard Salwey was wounded not long afterward but he was able to fight on. The pirate captain had been killed, too, and his vessel had taken so many shots that it was leaking badly.

Two more hours passed, during which the combatants remained lashed together and pummeled each other with shot. At last the *Bauden*'s crew swept the pirate vessel with a 9-pounder loaded with a maiming mixture of partridge and double chain shot. This blast caused havoc when it struck the pirate ship and a terrible outcry could be heard from the men on board. They had had enough. They cut loose from the *Bauden* and sheered off.

As the pirate ship moved awkwardly away, sailing with one side high to keep water from flooding in through the shot holes, the men of the *Bauden* ran up onto the poop in great excitement. They began to beat their drum and gave their enemy a farewell shout of "What Cheero!" By their reckoning at least 60 pirates had been killed. As for the *Bauden*, her portside had been shot through, and much of the rigging had been damaged by more than 1,000 rounds of shot. Eight of the crew had been killed, including the captain and his chief mate, and 16 wounded, among them the gunner, the quartermaster, the boatswain—and the author. "I, the writer of this, Richard Salwey, have received besides bruises, one small shott which went in a little below my small ribs and struck down to my bladder above five inches where it still remains in my body. But, blessed be God, I feel no pain save on change of weather."

It was rarely that pirates were beaten off with quite such a bloody nose. If they did engage in battle, they usually won the encounter. Perhaps the most resounding of all pirate engagements was between the East Indiaman *Cassandra* and the pirate ships *Fancy*, under Captain Edward England, and *Victory*, under Captain John Taylor, off Johanna Island near Madagascar in August 1720.

The *Cassandra*, mastered by Captain James Macrae, and a companion East Indiaman, the *Greenwich*, under Captain Richard Kirby, had put in to Johanna to obtain fresh provisions for their crews. This was an island noted for its springs of fresh water, and was used by all seafarers—pirates and merchantmen alike. Captains Macrae and Kirby had just topped off their water casks and were about to sail out again when the

A repertory of psychopathic torments

During the three weeks English Captain William Snelgrave spent as a prisoner of pirates in 1719, he watched with horrified fascination the treatment meted out to a French master less fortunate than himself. Because the Frenchman did not strike his colors when first fired upon, Snelgrave recollected, "they put a Rope about his Neck and hoisted him up and down several times to the Main-yard-arm, till he was almost dead."

Such was pirate cruelty—wanton, capricious and almost childish in its willfulness. The lash, the rope and fire were favorite instruments of torture, and the pirates could inflict hideous barbarities—like stuffing a man's mouth with oakum, a hemp caulking material, and setting it ablaze. Nothing was too much. As these early-19th Century illustrations depict, a pirate felt free to act out whatever sadistic—or merely wild—thought might enter his head.

Two pirates, one of them wielding a cat-o'-nine-tails, goad their mounts—a pair of captured Portuguese monks—aboard a ship off the coast of Brazil in 1718.

Lashed to the capstan aboard a vessel off the coast of Africa in 1718, a prisoner is pelted with broken bottles by the pirate crew—before being shot dead.

On a pirate vessel in the West Indies
in 1723, the pirates subject their victim to
"sweating"—forcing him to run around
and around the mizzenmast, by jabbing
him with pointed tools and weapons.

Off Newfoundland in 1723, a pirate, in
a relatively benign mood, forces a
teetotaling prisoner to down a full quart of
rum virtually in one gulp. The poor
fellow at first had demurred —until the
pirate, whipping out his pistol, told him
to choose either the booze or a bullet.

Fancy appeared, flying a black flag at the main-topmast, a red flag at the fore-topmast and the cross of St. George at the ensign staff. Macrae in the *Cassandra* engaged the pirate vessel immediately. When a second pirate ship, the *Victory,* appeared, Macrae asked the *Greenwich* to come to his assistance. But the *Greenwich* declined to fight. Instead, Kirby slipped out of the bay—even though Macrae actually fired at him to make him stop—and half a league away brought his ship about to watch the battle.

Captain Macrae of the *Cassandra* was furious. "He basely deserted us," he reported to the East India Company afterward, "and left us engaged with barbarous and inhuman enemies with their Black and Bloody flags hanging over us and no appearance of escaping being cut to pieces. But God in his good Providence provided otherwise; for notwithstanding their superiority, we engaged them between three and four hours, during which the biggest received some shot between wind and water which made her keep off a little to stop her leaks. The other endeavored all she could to board us by rowing with her oars. But then by good fortune, we shot her oars to pieces, which prevented them coming aboard and so saved our lives."

By 4 o'clock most of the *Cassandra*'s officers and men posted on the quarter-deck had been killed or wounded, and the *Fancy* had crept sufficiently close to fire a broadside at her. Since Kirby in the *Greenwich* still refused to intervene, there was nothing left for Macrae and his men to do but run the ship ashore and try to flee into the jungle. The *Cassandra* drew some four feet more water than the *Fancy,* but the *Fancy* hit the shallows first; she was thus prevented from boarding her prey. There, in the shoal water just offshore, the two ships began pounding away at each other even more fiercely, and threatened to blow each other out of the water. "All my officers and most of my men behaved with unexpected courage," wrote Macrae later, "and as we had considerable advantage by having our broadside to his bow I believe we should have taken both, for we had this one sure, had Captain Kirby then come in."

But Captain Kirby did not come in. "The other pirate, still firing at us," Macrae went on, "supplied his consort with three boatloads of fresh men. About five in the evening the *Greenwich* stood away, leaving us struggling in the very jaws of death. Which the other Pirate, that was now afloat, seeing, got out a rope and was hauling under our stern. By this time many of my men being killed and wounded and no hopes left from all being murdered by enraged, barbarous conquerors, I ordered all that could to get into the long boat under cover of the smoke from the guns. So that, what with some did in the boats, and others by swimming, most that were able got ashore by seven o'clock. When the Pirates came aboard they cut three of our wounded men to pieces. I with a few of my people, made what haste I could to the African King's house some 20 miles from us and there arrived next day almost dead with fatigue and loss of blood, having a musket ball wound in the head."

So Macrae lost his ship and £75,000 worth of valuables in its hold at the cost of 13 of his own men killed and 24 wounded and some 90 to 100 pirate casualties. What happened next is no less remarkable. The pirates offered a £2,000 reward for Macrae's arrest, but after 10 days this bold man reckoned that their wrath might be sufficiently abated for him to return and attempt to negotiate for the return of his ship and cargo. It was courageous almost to the point of foolhardiness, and many of the pirates were in favor of killing him on the spot. The pirate captains, England and Taylor, were strongly divided on this point—England for and Taylor against sparing Macrae's life. Fortunately for Macrae, he was known and respected by several of the pirates, who had served with him in the past.

At a critical moment a fierce-looking, heavily whiskered pirate seaman, with a wooden leg and a belt stuffed with pistols, stomped up the deck swearing like a parrot; taking Macrae by the hand he swore that he knew the captain, he had sailed with him once, and was very glad to see him. "Shew me the man that offers to hurt Captain Macrae," he roared, "and I'll stand to him, for an honester fellow I never sailed with." This unnamed member of Taylor's crew was to gain immortality many years later as the inspiration for *Treasure Island*'s Long John Silver.

The pirates allowed Macrae to go free in the badly damaged *Fancy* with a skeleton crew and half his original cargo. The *Cassandra* they kept as a replacement. After a terrible voyage of 48 days, becalmed for much of the time, Macrae and his men eventually reached India, starving and almost naked. For his courage against the pirates, the East India Company promoted him and he eventually rose to be the governor of Madras. The pirate captain England was soon deposed by Taylor because of his clemency to Macrae, and was turned out of the company. With a few others likewise banished, England succeeded in reaching Madagascar in an open boat, where he lived on the charity of other pirates at St. Augustine's Bay and died a pauper not long afterward.

As for Taylor, he was fated to succeed in the greatest single piratical coup in the whole of the Golden Age of piracy. This incredible event took place a year later, in 1721, on Quasimodo Sunday, April 26, when Taylor, on board the captured *Cassandra*, sailed into the roadstead of St. Denis on the island of Bourbon in the Mauritius island group. With him was the *Victory*, under the French pirate La Buze. Anchored in the harbor was a Portuguese East Indiaman, *Nossa Senhora do Cabo* (Our Lady of the Cape), undergoing repairs after being dismasted in a gale during her voyage from Goa, the Portuguese enclave in India.

The *Cabo* was heavily laden with the luxuries of the East—with Indian and Chinese silks and textiles, porcelain and exotic products of all kinds. But what made the *Cabo*'s cargo so inordinately precious was the enormous consignment of diamonds on board. There were pounds upon pounds of the glittering gems. Most belonged to the retiring Viceroy of Goa, Dom Luis Carlos Ignacio Xavier de Meneses, fifth Count of Ericeira. The Count had obtained the diamonds in private trading and was taking them back to Portugal to restore the depleted family fortune.

As the two strange ships entered the roadstead, the Count of Ericeira prepared to salute them imagining that once they had dropped anchor they would salute him in return, as was customary. Instead the strangers kept on coming and ranged up alongside the *Cabo*, one on either side so that she was sandwiched between. They then struck the English flags they had been flying and hoisted black flags with white skulls and crossbones on them. And instead of firing their guns in salute, they opened up with a broadside and devastating fire into the helpless East Indiaman.

Portuguese nobleman Luis de Meneses, Count of Ericeira and Marquis of Lourical, lost a king's ransom in diamonds to pirates while returning from India in 1721. In fact, some diamonds destined for his king were among the loot, and the Count, whose fortune was lost, was banished from court for 10 years.

The *Cabo* was virtually defenseless, for there were only 21 cannon and 34 muskets to share among the crew of 130. Against the Portuguese were ranged 200 fearsome cutthroats armed to the teeth with cutlasses and blunderbusses. Hurling grenades onto the *Cabo*'s deck, the pirates swarmed on board. There was not much chance to resist, and 13 crewmen immediately deserted to the pirates. But the gallant Count, conspicuous in his scarlet coat, made a desperate last stand on the quarterdeck. When his sword was broken in two in hand-to-hand combat, he continued to lash about until Captain Taylor roared out the order to give quarter and the fighting stopped.

The Count of Ericeira's bravery earned him the pirates' respect. They treated him with courtesy and gave his broken sword back to him, though its hilt was encrusted with gold and diamonds. They even offered to return some of his personal effects, but he proudly refused, saying he would permit no distinction between himself and his companions. So the pirates shrugged and tore up his precious Oriental manuscripts and ancient books to make wadding and cartridge paper for their guns. After the Governor of Bourbon had paid the pirates a ransom equivalent to £400, the pirates rowed the ex-Viceroy ashore in a specially decorated boat to the accompaniment of a viceregal 21-gun salute and three loud cheers of "*Vive le Roi!*"

Taylor and his mates could afford to be generous. After they had set sail with their new prize, they counted up the profits of their piracy. The Count of Ericeira's diamonds alone were worth upward of £500,000 in the currency of the day; the silks, porcelain and other goods aboard the *Cabo* came to another £375,000. With plunder taken earlier in the cruise the sum total came to more than £1,000,000. At the share-out, each of the pirates received more than £4,000 plus 42 small diamonds per man. One of the pirates was given a single large diamond reckoned to be the equivalent of 42 small ones; but he was so upset about this that he took a hammer and smashed the stone to bits in a mortar, boasting afterward that he had obtained more than 42 diamonds as a result.

Most of the newly enriched pirates got away with their loot. A number of them settled down in Madagascar; others accepted a French pardon and retired on the island of Bourbon. The remainder, about 140 men, sailed away with Taylor. Refused an English pardon by the Governor of Jamaica, they sought a Spanish one instead. In July 1723, they dropped anchor in Porto Bello, an important Spanish port on the Isthmus of Darien, now Panama. John Taylor and his crew, all British or American, stepped ashore as free men, pardoned by the King of Spain, doubtless on account of the tremendous value of the pirates' spending power to the economy of the colony.

Taylor subsequently spent the rest of his active life as a well-to-do officer commanding a Spanish patrol vessel in Central American waters. Neither he nor any of his men were ever brought to justice.

His victim did not fare so well. The Count of Ericeira was sentenced to be banished from the Portuguese Court in Lisbon: it seems that many of the diamonds taken by Taylor's men belonged to the King and Queen of Portugal, the Royal family and many Lisbon merchants; it was 10 years before he was allowed back into the Royal presence.

Chapter 3

A pirate path to the fabled Orient

aptain Thomas Tew made what amounted to a triumphal progress. No sooner had his vessel, the eight-gun *Amity*, docked in his native Newport, Rhode Island, in April 1694, than the citizens of that nautical town were seized with delirium. Tew, heretofore a man of modest reputation, was suddenly the cynosure of all eyes, lionized by the gentry in their handsome frame houses on the hill overlooking the harbor. The shopkeepers, merchants and tavern owners down near the docks frantically elbowed one another in their haste to provide his free-spending crewmen with all the liquor, women and other necessaries demanded by mariners who had spent more than 15 months at sea.

When the people of Newport had exhausted their welcome, Tew and his family traveled to New York. There he was feted and dined by the Royal Governor, Colonel Benjamin Fletcher, who described the captain as "what they call a very pleasant man; so that at some times when the labours of my day were over it was some divertisement as well as information to me, to hear him talk." Mrs. Tew and the two Tew daughters attended gala functions at the Governor's mansion, dressed in rich silks from the Orient and glittering with diamond jewelry that the captain had brought back with him. The Tews, in short, were the cream of East Coast society, prominent (if recently arrived) members of a colonial aristocracy of wealth and accomplishment.

Back in Newport after his sojourn in New York, Captain Tew began to ready the *Amity* for another cruise, thereby causing a second wave of hysteria. The sight of the *Amity* being refitted in the harbor caused quite a commotion, a witness reported, with "servants from most places of the country running from their masters, sons from their parents," all of them eager to join in Tew's next cruise. Even proper young men from Newport's most respectable families tried to sneak aboard the *Amity*, while preachers labored from the pulpit to restrain them with hoarse threats of the lash and hell fire.

What roused the preachers' ire—without reducing the citizens' plaudits or society's approval—was the source of Tew's new-found wealth and fame: he had captained one of the most electrifyingly successful cruises in the history of piracy.

When the *Amity* had docked in Newport after a 22,000-mile rampage along the coasts of Arabia and India, she had carried a dazzling fortune: £100,000 in plundered gold and silver, plus a king's ransom in elephant-tusk ivory and spices, coffers of jewels and bales upon bales of smooth and shiny silks. Each crew member had been awarded a share that was worth the munificent sum of £1,200. Little wonder that every discontented—or merely foot-loose—young man in the environs of Newport

Eastern riches are offered to Britannia in this 18th Century ceiling painting of London's East India Company office. India presents pearls as China waits with porcelain and tea. Looking on are Mercury (right) and Father Thames (lower left); an East Indiaman (center) symbolizes the treasure fleet—and the pirates' prey.

yearned to sail with Tew on a second piratical voyage. As for being held back by conscience, they had nothing to worry about: it was considered no sin to rob infidels.

Tew had not only made an immensely profitable voyage; he had also pointed the way to apparently boundless future riches available for the taking in the Red Sea and the Indian Ocean, domains of the sheiks and Moguls. In the wake of Tew's exploits, stories of the high adventure and fabulous treasure that could be found in the East produced a kind of Red Sea fever on the North American seaboard, in England and among mariners in the Caribbean.

To be sure, pirates had been preying on shipping in the Eastern Seas for years. There had always been native Indian pirates in well-armed vessels prowling about the Arabian Sea, and early in the 17th Century they were joined there by pirates from Europe. Dutch and French ships cruised in the Mozambique Channel. Portuguese pirates lurked in Table Bay, Danish pirates sailed south on the "pirate wind." Early English pirates had royal support, and they sailed with a special commission from James I and Charles I that licensed them to plunder "from the Cape to China and Japan, including the Red Sea, Persian Gulf and the Coromandel Coast." But the pirates had been relatively few in number, and their plunder was modest by comparison with Tew's grand score. Now dozens of onetime privateer captains and shady or disaffected merchant skippers turned to piracy. Thousands of apprentices, indentured servants, bankrupt shopkeepers and debtors passed along the news that riches were to be found in the Red Sea (money there, one of them was quoted as saying, was "as plenty as stones and sand"). They rushed to sign on the fast-multiplying pirate ships—although the more experienced captains tended to regard such lubberly volunteers with a jaundiced eye. The leading merchants of the North American port cities—Boston, Newport, New York and Philadelphia—were no less stricken with visions of vast treasure, and they eagerly bankrolled the pirate captains in exchange for a share of the anticipated loot.

The large island of Madagascar became a virtual pirate kingdom. It was an ideal advance base, 250 miles off the east coast of Africa, within easy striking distance of the Red Sea and Indian Ocean. Scores of traders—most of them retired pirates—profited handsomely catering to the day-to-day needs of the brigand crews. A few amassed such wealth and power that they became potentates ruling over large areas of the island with hundreds of slaves and subjects at their beck and call.

But it was no tropic idyll for the pirates. Disease, native uprisings, the vagaries of wind and weather took a heavy toll of them ashore as well as at sea. And as the pirates, including Tew, learned to their pain, there were times when the Moorish treasure ships fought ferociously to defend themselves. Yet to the pirates, the rewards to be reaped from the Pirate Round were worth every risk.

Captain Tew's first venture had been an example to all. That pioneering voyage in 1692 had gone smoothly from the start. Tew, an experienced privateer, had been offered a share in the 70-ton sloop *Amity* by a group of merchants and officials in Bermuda. He paid for his share of the ship in December 1692, recruited a like-minded crew of 60 men, and

Captain Thomas Tew, recently back from an astoundingly successful pirate cruise to the Eastern Seas, regales New York's Governor Fletcher with tales of his adventure in this engraving from an oil by illustrator Howard Pyle. The Governor's open cooperation with pirates—he even gave Tew a gold watch—eventually led to his recall in disgrace in 1698.

persuaded the Governor of Bermuda, Isaac Richier—who had no more scruples about dealing with piratical folk than New York's hospitable Governor Fletcher—to sell him a privateering commission, authorizing Tew to raid a French trading post on the west coast of Africa. Such commissions to prey on the French, with whom the English were then at war, were as important a part of a pirate captain's equipment as his quadrant, for they enabled him, if caught, to claim that he had merely been plundering the king's enemies—which was perfectly acceptable, indeed praiseworthy.

Armed with this license to steal, Tew and the *Amity* headed east across the Atlantic. The ship had been at sea only a few days when Tew gathered his crewmen and outlined his plan. To no one's surprise, he proposed abandoning the ostensible purpose of the voyage, on the ground that raiding a French outpost would not be very profitable. Instead he suggested making one daring drive for riches in the East. As piracy's famed chronicler Daniel Defoe put it, "He was of Opinion, that they should turn their Thoughts on what might better their Circumstances; and if they were so inclined, he would undertake to shape a Course which should lead them to Ease and Plenty, in which they might pass the rest of their Days. That one bold Push would do their Business, and they might return home, not only without Danger, but even with Reputation. The Crew finding he expected their Resolution, cry'd out, one and all, 'A gold Chain, or a wooden Leg, we'll stand by you.'" At that, Tew shaped a course toward the Cape of Good Hope. Once there he rounded Africa and headed for the Indian Ocean and the Red Sea.

In all the months that followed, Tew came across only one real prize. But one was enough. This was a vessel belonging to the Great Mogul of India. She was on a run between India and the Arab ports on the Red Sea, and despite the presence of 300 Indian soldiers, offered virtually no resistance to Tew's musket-shooting, cutlass-wielding pirates when they boarded her in the Red Sea. Not a single pirate was killed in the engagement. When it was over they scoured the merchantman and found a treasure equal to their wildest dreams.

Once he had his booty aboard, Tew sailed his ship southward, fetching up at St. Mary's, a tiny island off the Madagascar coast. There he shared the loot according to the standard formula employed by pirates, one share per man, two shares for the captain and one and a half shares for such valuable crew members as the quartermaster and the ship's surgeon. Tew also careened his ship at St. Mary's. By December 1693, he was ready to sail for home. He arrived in Newport without incident the following April. Nothing could have been easier.

By November 1694, Tew was ready to go to sea once more. But he was not so lucky this time. He again took the precaution of obtaining a privateering commission—this one from New York's corrupt Governor Fletcher, who was only too happy to oblige—for £300. Commission in hand, Tew set sail for the Red Sea. In September 1695, he was killed while the *Amity*'s crew was attempting to board a second Indian merchantman. As related by Daniel Defoe, Tew's demise was a gory one: "In the Engagement a Shot carry'd away the Rim of Tew's Belly, who held his Bowels with his Hands some small Space."

Four East Indiamen are approaching Johanna Island, close to
Madagascar, in this 1670s sketch. With its abundant fresh water,
Johanna was a favorite stop until pirates began lurking there.

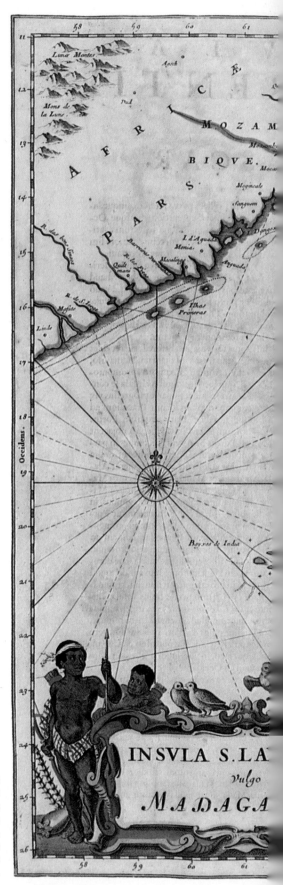

A Dutch map drawn around 1665 shows
with remarkable fidelity the coastline
of Madagascar and the places that became
pirate lairs: St. Mary's Island (Isle
Ste. Marie), Port (Fort) Dauphin, Bay of St.
Augustine (Baye St. Augustin), Diego
Suarez (Soarez) and Bay of Antoguil (Baye
d'Antongil), later known as Ranter Bay.

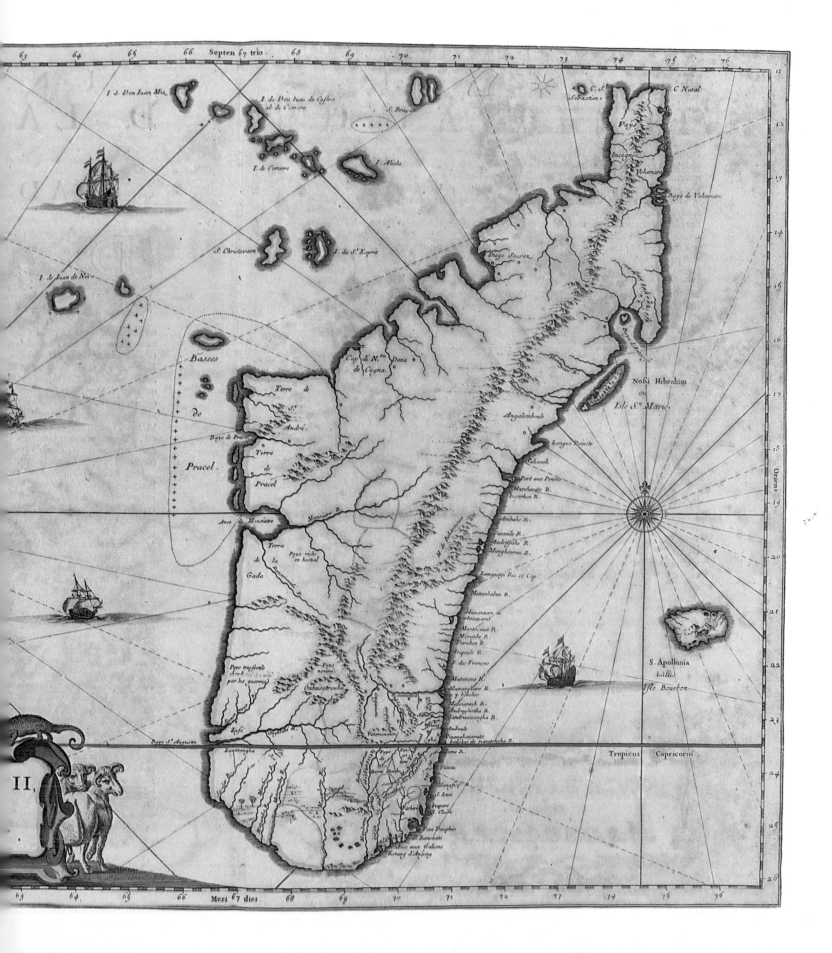

I. d. Don Iuan Mix

I. de Don Iuan de Castro
ali de Comoro

S. Braça

C. S.
Sebastien
C. Natal

Pays

I. de Comoro

I. Aliola

Incognea

Vohemar

Baye de Vohemaro

S. Christo avon

I. du S. Esprit

Diego Soarez

I. de Iuan de Novo

Basses

Capo de N.ra Dona
de Cugna.

Terre de
S.t
André

Baye de Pracel

Terre
de
Pracel

Pracel.

Ance de Maniare

Manniare R.

Terra
de la
Gada

Baye riche
en bestal

Noßi Hibrahim
ou
Isle S.te Marie.

Angalemboule

Longue Pointe

Sahauch

Port aux Prenis

Marehangte R.
Imoirhon R.

Ambahi R.

Vacaule R.
Andraſahe R.
Mangheurou R.

Limgnoiſi Ria et Cap.

Mananhaban R.

Mananenari ou
Intaneari

Mareheaus R.
Moronbe R.
Parahon R.
Itapoule R.

P. des Franceys

Pays des
nomine

Onhattotronha

Matatana R.
Mancaghare R.
y Echelas
Mahanach R.
Andragshitha R.
Sandramampha R.

Anabode

Pays trafferale
par les guerrer

Pays
nomine

Vinangſanarats
benchas de maratanoha R.

Bare S. t Augustin

Laiptangha

Pays
Fon

Fune R.

Manafil R.
S. Luce
Itapere
S.t Claire

Zofo

Manafif R.

S. Apollonia
briller
Isle Bourbon

Tropicus Capricorni

II,

The news of Tew's death, when it reached across the ocean, caused scarcely a moment's reflection among the crews fitting out for the Pirate Round. Such was the wealth of the treasure fleets in the Indies and so generally weak was their protection that pirates "going on the account" multiplied by leaps and bounds all through the 1690s. Many of the "Moorish" vessels, as the pirates dubbed all non-European shipping, actually belonged (like Tew's prize) to the Great Mogul of India. There had been six Great Moguls of the same family who passed on the rule of India, father to son, from 1526 to 1707. Under them, India was united, trade flourished and wealth accumulated. Much of this wealth came from commerce with their fellow Moslems in the Middle East. Mogul fleets crossed the Indian Ocean from the west coast of India to the Persian Gulf and the Red Sea carrying gorgeous fabrics, ivory, spices and precious stones. From Red Sea ports such as Mocha, the Indian goods were transported by caravan across the Nubian Desert to the Nile, and thence to Cairo, Alexandria and the Mediterranean. On the return voyage to India the Mogul ships carried the proceeds of their trading—largely gold and silver, and in enormous quantities. Outbound or inbound, the Moorish vessels were good prey, especially since the power and unity of the Mogul's rule was in decline and his navy could offer no serious resistance to the pirates.

Nor were the Mogul fleets the only tempting targets. A number of the European ships sailing these Eastern waters belonged to the East India companies of Britain, France and Holland. The largest and richest was the British East India Company, which had been chartered by Queen Elizabeth I in 1600. By the 1690s, the British East India Company had well-established trading posts at Madras, Calcutta and Bombay—all three destined to grow into large and important cities. The company's ships, like the outbound Moorish vessels, were crammed with silks, ivory and jewels—and with coin garnered from the sale of English goods in India. The East India Company had its own naval force, but it was miserably inadequate, at one time forbidden to use gunpowder during training except on special occasions (to get the gunners accustomed to firing, "lest in time of action they should start at the noise or the recoil of their arms"). Nor was there any effective Royal Navy presence east of the Cape of Good Hope. When Britain was at war with Spain or France—as was the case almost continuously between 1688 and 1713—the Royal Navy was needed elsewhere. In periods of peace, niggardly Naval budgets idled ships and men.

The British East Indiamen were joined on the route from India and the East by Portuguese vessels sailing from Goa, Portugal's trading outpost in India, and by Dutch ships taking valuable cargoes home from Ceylon and other Dutch trading areas in Asia. The pirates thus could profitably range over an immense triangle of ocean. They could sail northward toward the mouth of the Red Sea and there lie in wait for the Mogul's ships. Or they could sail northeastward some 2,000 miles to raid coastal shipping on India's Malabar Coast. Or finally they could intercept Dutch, Portuguese and English ships near Réunion Island off the Madagascar coast. The lure of the Eastern Seas was irresistible to pirates, noted a 1701 East India Company pamphlet on piracy, "for the news of

Aurangzeb, the Indian Mogul whose vast wealth attracted the pirates, receives a courtier as his son stands by. All three wear thick strands of pearls, and clothes decorated with diamonds, emeralds and rubies. A European visitor observed that some of the Mogul's rubies "weigh apparently 200 carats and more."

the rich booties stirred up the old buccaneer gang to direct their course to the East." Once there, so "successful and undisturbed" was their pirating, the pamphlet went on, "that whole companies both from England and our American colonies flocked thither."

What is more, most of the pirates got away unscathed and unpunished—at least in the beginning. With royal governors, merchants and the general populace all more or less sympathetic, the rare pirate brought to trial in the colonies usually could count on a "not guilty" verdict from a jury of his peers. Now and again one or two unfortunate crewmen were hanged, but to the pirates it was well worth running that slender risk for the chance of winning the fortune of a lifetime.

The demand for the exotic goods that the pirates brought home grew so great that New England shipyards did a thriving business building and fitting out vessels for piracy. Indeed, the Red Sea run worked like a legitimate business; pirate crewmen who were regularly employed on it became sufficiently domesticated to marry and bring up children. One New York merchant, Frederick Philipse, actually did run piracy like a business and made so much money from this and other ventures that he became the richest man in colonial New York.

The greatest problem with the Red Sea trade was the enormous distance involved, and this, in turn, spawned a number of advance bases where pirates could put in for rest and reprovisioning. At first the pirates used the sun-baked little island of Perim, or Bab's Key, at the entrance to the Red Sea. Perim's location was ideal but it was waterless, and the pirates soon turned to the large tropical island of Madagascar—and its satellites, such as Johanna, one of the Comoro Islands between Madagascar and the African coast. Madagascar was more remote from the Red Sea and India's Malabar Coast than Perim, but it was superlative from every other point of view. It had excellent harbors where the pirates could lay up, careen their ships and repair their rigging. It offered abundant fresh water and ample provisions, which included essential antiscorbutics such as limes. The native black population on Madagascar was on the whole friendly, and in any case the indigenous tribes were too busy squabbling among themselves to be capable of launching a concerted action against the white interlopers.

One of the first pirates to set up as a trader in the Madagascar area was Adam Baldridge, who fled there from Jamaica after he had killed a man in 1685. Baldridge established his business on the islet of St. Mary's, where Tew shared out his loot. Its bottle-necked harbor was one of the most superbly defensible anchorages on the Madagascar coast. Here Baldridge built an immense castle-like mansion on top of a hill—a landmark for pirates far out at sea—behind a stockaded fort with a battery of 40 guns overlooking a group of warehouses. The fort protected the ships careening in the harbor from attack by other pirates or by ships of the East India Company's haphazard naval force. St. Mary's soon became the pirates' favorite base, with a burgeoning population of brigands who had chosen to live in the East rather than return home. Life on an Indian Ocean island offered a comfortable existence in an easy climate, personal freedom and all the ingredients that made a pirate's life worth living—

The proper burgher who was a pirate broker

Some of the richest hauls in piracy's Golden Age were found far from the treasure routes, on the dry land of the market place. Probably the greatest profiteer of all was a New Yorker by the name of Frederick Philipse: church patron, landholder, respected governor's councilor—and, with help from son Adolph *(right)*, chief broker for the Madagascar pirates.

Arriving in Nieuw Amsterdam from Holland about 1647, Philipse went to work as a carpenter for Governor Pieter Stuyvesant; from the start he showed himself a shrewd lad. When he married, he chose a widow who brought him a dowry of ships and land—and when she died, he found another wife just like her. In time, he parlayed his parcels of land into a baronial estate stretching for 21 miles along the Hudson. Meanwhile, his shipping business grew extensively, as it traded his farm-produced flour and other goods.

For such an entrepreneur, the riches from pirate trading proved irresistible. In the 1690s his vessels supplied the Madagascar pirates with almost everything they needed and returned laden with cargoes of slaves and booty.

For years, Philipse was in cahoots with colonial officials, who ordered customs inspectors "not to be strict what goods come to Frederick Philipse." Then, in 1698, a change of governors brought trouble for him. Some of his ships were seized, including one with a cargo valued at £20,000. Philipse was dismissed from the Governor's Council on suspicion of dealing with pirates, but records do not show that he was prosecuted. He died in 1702, unrepentant and one of the richest men in New York.

One of pirate-trader Frederick Philipse's legitimate businesses was based primarily on the two grist mills below the manor house on his 90,000-acre estate on the Hudson River north of Manhattan.

Adolph Philipse, the elder of Frederick's two sons, was an important partner in his father's pirate dealings; at one point he personally supervised the transfer of contraband at sea to evade trade rules.

A church-going pillar of the community, Frederick Philipse presented this silver communion cup to the Old Dutch Church of Sleepy Hollow, built about 1697 with funds that he and his wife Catharine donated. Philipse's name is engraved on the cup in its original Dutch spelling.

#	Item	Amount
1	To 26 barrils of beer at 60 p/8 pr barril	1560
2	To 15 barrils of wine at 60 p/8 pr barril	0900
3	To 2 pipes of wine 100 a pipe	0800
4	To 72 gall of wine	0240
5	To 927 gall & ½ of rum at 4 p/8 & ½ pr gall	4173
6	To 10 Barrils of Salt at 15 p/8 pr barril	0150
7	To 10 Barrils of peace at 20 p/8 pr barril	0200
8	To 10 dozen of black hafted knives ½ a p/8 a k	0060
9	To 12 Shoomakers knives at 1 p/8 ½ pr knive	0018
10	To 1 dozen of thimbles	0006
11	To 20 dozen ½ of Sizars 1 p/8 a paire	0246
12	To 6 Pound & ½ of thread	0030
13	To ¼ of a pound ditto	0001
14	To 5 pound Colloured thread	0027
15	To 6 dozen of horn Combs	0072
16	To 2 dozen & ½ of Ivory Combs 2 p/8 pr Com	0060
17	To 2 pair taylers Sizars	0010
18	To 3000 Needles	0100
19	To 12 all blades	0002
20	To 6 groce of buttons	0050
21	To 1 dozen tobacco boxes 3 p/8 a box	0036
22	To 2 Reem of paper	0058½
23	To 100 pair of pumps 2 p/8 a pair	0200
24	To 114 hatchetts	0200
25	To 19 hundred of Sugar 15 p/8 pr hundr	0285
26	3 hatts 10 p/8 pr hatt	0030
		9514

A ledger sheet from records of the Philipse family's dealings with the pirates of St. Mary's in the 1690s lists, among other things, beer and wine at 60 pieces of eight per barrel, "hatts" at 10 pieces per hat and tailors' scissors at five pieces a pair; however, "black hafted knives" were only one-half piece per dozen. The total for 26 items came to 9,514 pieces of eight, or roughly £2,380.

women, liquor and convivial company. At one time 1,500 such sailors had settled on St. Mary's alone.

The canny Baldridge was soon the absolute ruler of St. Mary's, and since the perpetually warring natives respected the power of Baldridge's armory of European firearms, he also became the patriarchal ruler of several nearby native tribes. He even held a personal court to settle disputes, and his fame for dispensing justice spread throughout Madagascar, so that Africans came from the remotest settlements on the main island to beg the "King of the Pirates" on bended knee to help them ransom their wives and children from slavery to rival tribes.

Baldridge made a handsome living by supplying pirate vessels with food, ammunition and other necessities. He obtained cattle and island produce (and sometimes slaves) from tribal chiefs who were grateful for his help in their incessant tribal wars. Baldridge then traded the cattle and other provisions for plunder brought into St. Mary's by the pirates; his warehouses were usually piled to the roof with muslins, calicoes, ivory and other luxuries. These Baldridge exchanged in turn for manufactured goods—rum, guns, gunpowder, tools, clothing, spices and other necessities of the pirate profession—shipped direct to him in vessels employed by American businessmen expressly for this purpose.

It was a good trade for both Baldridge and his American suppliers. Rum bought at two shillings a gallon in New York could be sold to the pirates of St. Mary's for three pounds a gallon. Wine that was purchased at £19 a pipe—the equivalent of about 120 gallons—could be sold at St. Mary's for £300 a pipe.

In a detailed, factual little journal, Baldridge logged his commercial transactions, and his lists stand as an inventory of the pirates' requirements. The entry for August 7, 1693, records that the ship *Charles*, a pirate trading vessel from New York, arrived carrying "44 paire of shooes and pumps, 6 Dozen of worsted and threed stockens, 3 dozen of speckled shirts and Breaches, 12 hatts, some Carpenters Tools, 5 Barrells of Rum, four Quarter Caskes of Madera Wine, ten Cases of Spirits, Two old Stills full of hols, one worme, Two Grindstones, Two Cross Sawes and one Whip saw, three Jarrs of oyle, two small Iron Potts, three Barrells of Cannon powder, some books, Catechisms, primers and horne books, two Bibles, and some garden Seeds, three Dozen of howes." For this entire shipment, Baldridge paid 1,100 pieces of eight, 34 slaves, 15 head of cattle and "57 barrs of Iron."

There were other pirate bases on Madagascar—St. Augustine, Diego Suarez, Port Dauphin, Charnock's Point, Mathelage—but it was the lure of St. Mary's above all that was celebrated in the chanties of the time:

Where is the trader of London town?
His gold's on the capstan
His blood's on his gown
And it's up and away for St. Mary's Bay
Where the liquor is good and the lasses are gay.

The lasses were almost always local Malagasy girls. The pirates of St. Mary's and the other bases were very partial to these women and boasted they had "as great a seraglio as the Grand Seigneur of Constantinople."

A pirate on Madagascar enjoys an island belle's company as his ship lies at anchor, while a lookout (top left) scans the horizon in this drawing for an 1840 book on piracy. Madagascar women were noted for comeliness and complaisance, and many pirates took local wives.

Baldridge himself kept a harem of Madagascar girls at his big house, and there he continued to dwell in riches and comfort until local citizens, angered because he had sold a large number of their compatriots into slavery, forced him to flee St. Mary's in 1697. He fetched up safely in New York, where he lived to a ripe old age.

Years went by before another pirate trader rose to similar eminence. Then in 1720 John Plantain arrived in Madagascar; he soon proved himself an even more successful entrepreneur than Adam Baldridge and became, in effect, lord of the entire island. He made his headquarters at Ranter Bay, a harbor north of St. Mary's. Plantain was born at Chocolate Hole, Jamaica, to English parents, and had gone to sea at 13; by the age of 20 he was a full-fledged pirate and was serving on a Rhode Island-based sloop called the *Terrible*. After a couple of seasons of successful piracy in the Gulf of Aden at the mouth of the Red Sea, Plantain retired to Ranter Bay, where, with two other ex-pirates, a Scot named James Adair and a Dane named Hans Burgen, he built a stockaded fortress. The living area was sumptuous and included quarters for a bevy of local girls, to whom Plantain gave English names such as Moll, Kate, Sue and Peg. Plantain dressed his harem in silks, and a number of the girls had diamond necklaces—as was befitting to the consorts of the King of Ranter Bay, as Plantain called himself.

Despite all this wealth, Plantain was unhappy. He coveted a half-caste woman named Holy Eleanora Brown—Brown because that was the name of her dead English pirate father, and Holy because she could recite the Lord's Prayer, the Creed and the Ten Commandments. Unfortunately Holy Eleanora was the granddaughter of a neighboring tribal chieftain named King Dick, who would not give her up. So Plantain declared war on King Dick and armed a large force of tribesmen with lances and with firearms that he had bought with his pirate booty. With English, Danish and Scottish colors flying, Plantain's force met King Dick's army and defeated it, killing a number of English pirates who fought on the side of the chief. After further skirmishing, Plantain captured King Dick himself, burned down his village and took Holy Eleanora captive. She was, it turned out, already pregnant by one of the English pirates killed in the battle. This infuriated Plantain, who vented his rage by ordering King Dick put to death; nevertheless, he took Holy Eleanora back to Ranter Bay, where she became his favorite wife and bore him a number of children.

Plantain's success against King Dick gave him even larger ambitions: he resolved to become sovereign of all Madagascar. Sometime in the 1720s, he led his motley force against Port Dauphin, capital of another powerful native chieftain whose name has escaped history. After an 18-month siege—Port Dauphin had been armed with batteries of cannon by the pirates who used the place as a haven—Plantain's forces again won out and he proclaimed himself King of Madagascar.

By this time, however, Plantain had made numerous enemies, in no small measure because of his practice of torturing and killing captured tribesmen. Fearing for his life, he had two pirate shipwrights fit out a small sloop for him. Taking along Holy Eleanora and his children, and all the plunder the sloop would carry, he made for Johanna Island off

Madagascar's northwest coast. There he managed to loot an Indian-owned ship, then pushed on into the Indian Ocean. Old accounts of piracy in the Eastern Seas differ as to where Plantain eventually settled, but it seems likely that he made a landfall on the Malabar Coast and ended his days in India.

But few pirate traders on Madagascar were as aggressively ambitious as Baldridge and Plantain. Most were content to live a life of tropic ease, luxuriating in the island's benign climate, trading with incoming ships as the mood suited them, maintaining good relations with the local chiefs and eventually ending their days on Madagascar. Such men were customarily buried with full honors by their fellow pirates. Captain John Halsey of Boston, who had relieved Indian merchant vessels of some £50,000 before his retirement to Madagascar, was interred with great solemnity after dying of a fever. A flag was flown at half-mast, the prayers of the Church of England were read over his body and his coffin was

Desperate tales of life as a Madagascar slave

Tribesmen await survivors of the Degrave, wrecked off Madagascar in 1703.

"I was not fourteen years of age when these miseries and misfortunes befell me," Robert Drury wrote in 1726, beginning the story of his ill-fated voyage to the Eastern Seas, which ended in 13 years of captivity among the natives and pirates on Madagascar.

Drury was a passenger sailing home to London on board the East Indiaman *Degrave* when she sprang a leak and foundered off the southern coast of Madagascar in April 1703. The lad was one of only four survivors of the shipwreck to escape slaughter by the natives on shore. He was taken instead as a slave and passed from one black ruler to another until he was finally rescued, and returned to England in 1717. There, some years later, he published *Robert Drury's Journal*, a fascinating account of his bondage that was probably ghost-written for him by that master of adventure and tireless recorder of pirates, Daniel Defoe.

Actually, Drury's tale of enslavement by local black rulers may have been, as some scholars suspect, a mask to disguise years spent among the is-

land's European pirates, possibly as one of them. Drury's *Journal* speaks knowingly of several brigands, including one Nick Dove, by coincidence a *Degrave* survivor who had joined a pirate crew and had become "vastly rich" from plundering Moorish ships. Another pirate of Drury's acquaintance was John Pro, who was a Dutchman living "in a very handsome manner," eating off pewter plates, sleeping in a curtained bed and owning "many cattle and slaves. Nicholas Dove was nothing so rich."

Nevertheless, Drury had obviously spent much time among the Madagascar natives. He learned their language, so forgetting his own, he said, that he needed an interpreter when he first met Europeans again. He also learned to follow the Madagascar slave ritual of obeisance—licking the soles of his master's feet.

Drury went on war parties and cattle raids with the natives. He argued religion with them. He scoffed at their *owleys*, or totems, and they, in turn, scoffed at his Bible stories. If only Noah survived the Flood, they asked him, was Noah black or white?

For most of his captivity, Drury said,

covered with his ship's jack, on which were laid his sword and pistol. As many guns as the years of his age (46) were fired in salute and four volleys of firearms were discharged over his grave. He was buried in a garden of watermelons, which was subsequently fenced off to stop the wild pigs from rooting up his corpse.

Of all the thousands of pirates who sought their fortune and lived and died in the Eastern Seas, none was more famous in his own lifetime than Henry Every, an English captain known as John Avery or Long Ben Avery. He was the subject of a vastly popular play called *The Sucessful Pirate* at London's Theatre Royal, was the prototype for the hero of Defoe's picaresque 1720 novel *The Life, Adventures & Piracies of Captain Singleton,* and was the source of endless gossip and rumor in England and Ireland alike. According to some contemporary pamphlets, he had offered to pay off the national debt in exchange for a pardon. Accord-

he was slave to a cruel king, Mevarrow, who had two boys castrated for stealing cows and repeatedly threatened to shoot Drury—on one occasion for not licking his feet. It was not until he fled across rivers that were swarming with crocodiles that he was able to find refuge under a much more lenient master, the crippled King Moume. After two and a half years with Moume, Drury attempted to escape by pleading with a visiting English slaver to buy him his freedom. But the captain ignored Drury's plea and the ship sailed off with another castaway, Will Thornbury, rather than Drury. It was from Thornbury's conversation in a London tavern, however, that Drury's father at last learned that his son was alive on Madagascar and sent William Mackett, who was the captain of the slaving ship *Drake*, to rescue him.

For a man so recently "freed from slavery," as he claimed, Drury showed remarkably little compassion for the blacks being carried off Madagascar by the shipload for sale in the West Indies and America. Before he sailed for home in 1716, Drury served as go-between in Mackett's slaving transactions with a local chieftain. And a year

after his return to London, he was heading for Madagascar on another slaving expedition.

Drury returned from this voyage a man of means. He stopped briefly in Virginia, where he traded his slaves for tobacco, which he then sold at a handsome profit in London. Yet nine years later, when he published his *Journal*, Drury had been reduced to the lowly job of porter at East India House. What had happened? Had some subsequent slaving or piratical venture gone awry? History does not record the answer, although Drury may have given it to those who answered the invitation appended to his *Journal*:

"I am every day to be spoken with in Old Tom's Coffee-house in Birchin Lane, where I shall be ready to gratify any gentleman with a further account of anything herein contained, to stand the strictest examination, or to confirm those things which to some may seem doubtful."

No more winning an invitation to buy a drink for a man who was down on his luck could have been written.

Their captors kill all except four survivors of the shipwreck for attempting to escape.

ing to others, he had settled down in Madagascar with the Great Mogul's beautiful daughter, where he lived in great royalty and state surrounded by his many children.

The truth was rather different. Many of Every's men were eventually caught and hanged in England, and it is possible that Every himself died a pauper in a cottage in Devon. But the legend of his wealth persisted and was the single greatest factor in publicizing the Eastern Seas as a pirate's El Dorado at the end of the 17th Century.

One account of the time describes Every as "middle-sized, inclinable to be fat and of a jolly complexion." It goes on to say that he was "daring and good tempered, but insolent and uneasy at times, and always unforgiving if at any time imposed upon. His manner of living was imprinted in his face, and his profession might easily be told from it. His knowledge of his profession was great, being founded on a strong natural judgement, and sufficient experience advanced by incessant application to mathematics. He still had many principles of morality which many subjects of the King have experienced."

As with most pirates, little is known for certain of Every's early life. He seems to have been born near Plymouth, England, about 1653 and to have been sent to sea as a boy. He then appears to have drifted from honest seamanship to deliberate piracy via a variety of maritime pursuits. Different accounts, some undoubtedly fictional, have him serving as a Royal Navy tar present at the 1671 bombardment of the Mediterranean pirate base of Algiers, as a buccaneer on the Spanish Main, as captain of a logwood freighter in the Bay of Campeachy, and as a pirate in 1691 and 1692 under Captain "Red Hand" Nicholls. It is definitely known that he was a slaver employed by the Royal Governor of Bermuda along Africa's Guinea coast. As a slaver, he seems to have been even more devious than most other practitioners of that sordid craft. A Royal Africa Company officer reported in 1693: "I have no where upon the coast met the negroes so shy as here, which makes me fancy they have had tricks play'd them by such blades as Long Ben, alias Every, who have seiz'd them and carry'd them away."

Every was in his early forties when he turned full-time pirate and embarked on the devastating cruise of the Eastern Seas that was to make his reputation as one of the most villainous pirates of the Western world. This cruise began innocently enough, in the spring of 1694, when he embarked as sailing master, or first mate, aboard a Bristol ship called the *Charles II*, carrying 46 guns and chartered as a privateer by the Spanish government to intercept French smugglers in Spain's Caribbean colonies. It seems more than likely that Every and some of his old companions signed on with the deliberate aim of hijacking the *Charles II* and taking her on a pirate cruise in the Indian Ocean. She was a fast, well-armed ship, ideal for the purpose. In May, shortly after the ship put into the Spanish port of La Coruña to take on passengers and stores, Every laid his plan for a mutiny. Most of the crewmen needed little persuasion to join him, for they had received no pay for eight months and expected little plunder from the French.

The idea was to take the *Charles II* when her commander, a certain Captain Gibson, was drunk. The captain, Defoe reports, was "mightily addicted to Punch" and usually spent his evenings on shore drinking himself into a stupor in some dockside dive. But on the appointed night he did not go ashore; instead he took his usual drop on board and was snoring in his bunk when the hour approached. This did not deter Every and his mutineers. They secured the hatches, stealthily weighed the anchor and put out to sea with so little fuss that they aroused the suspicion of neither the captain nor any of the nonmutineers asleep in their hammocks. They were out on the Atlantic swell before Captain Gibson was awakened by the motion of the ship and the noise of working tackles up on deck. The captain rang the bell in his cabin and Every and two of his mutineers went down and entered. They found the captain half-asleep and in a kind of fright.

"What was the matter?" Captain Gibson asked.

"Nothing," Every replied.

"Something's the matter with this ship. What weather is it?"

"No, no," answered Every. "We're at sea, with a fair wind and good weather."

"At sea!" The captain was beside himself. "How can that be?"

"Come," Every crooned, "don't be in a fright. Put on your clothes, and I'll let you into a secret."

While the befuddled captain sought to clear his head, Every explained the situation to him.

"You must know that I am captain of this ship now," he said, "and this is my cabin; therefore you must walk out. I am bound to Madagascar, with a design of making my own fortune, and that of all the brave fellows joined with me."

When Captain Gibson recovered his senses he began to understand the implications of what Every was telling him. He had two options, Every told him. He could either join the mutiny and, if he gave up drinking, become Every's lieutenant, or he could be put ashore. Captain Gibson was either unwilling to turn to piracy or unwilling to give up the bottle; whatever the reason, he and five or six others chose to leave the ship and make for the land as best they could in a ship's boat.

And so the *Charles II*, renamed the *Fancy*, under a new captain and flying a new flag—four silver chevrons on a red background—set course for the Eastern Seas around the Cape of Good Hope to Madagascar. There, for the best part of the next two years, Every pursued and broadsided and boarded and plundered and ravaged for all he was worth, till his name was known from Mocha to the Cape to the Bay of Bengal. Every began his piracy off the Cape Verde Islands in the Atlantic, where he halted three English ships and relieved them of their provisions and whatever else he and his men coveted. After rounding the Cape, Every made for the island of Johanna where he careened the *Fancy* and stripped off some of her upper work so she would sail more swiftly—fast enough to evade any pursuer. Hardly had Every made these changes when a French pirate ship entered the harbor. Every quickly seized the French ship, which turned out to be loaded with loot taken from Moors in the Red Sea. The French crew of 40 joined Every's crew, as did 12 other Frenchmen who had been shipwrecked on Johanna. The *Fancy* was now a formidable pirate vessel.

It was at Johanna that Every wrote a curious document in the form of an open letter that he left with the local native chief, asking him to deliver it to the first English ship that came in. To read it is to hear the authentic voice of the Arch Pirate (as he came to be known):

"To All English Commanders.

"Let this satisfy that I was riding here at this instant in the ship *Fancy,* man of war, formerly the *Charles* of the Spanish Expedition who departed from La Coruña 7th May 1694, being then and now a ship of 46 guns, 150 men and bound to seek our fortunes. I have never as yet wronged any English or Dutch, or ever intend whilst I am commander. Wherefore as I commonly speak with all ships I desire whoever comes to the perusal of this to take this signal, that if you or any whom you may inform are desirous to know what we are at a distance, then make your ancient"— that is, the ship's flag—"up in a ball or bundle and hoist him at the mizen peak, the mizen being furled. I shall answer with the same, and never molest you, for my men are hungry, stout and resolute, and should they exceed my desire I cannot help myself. As yet an Englishman's friend,

"At Johanna, 18th February 1695

"Henry Every

"Here is 160 odd French armed men at Mohilla who waits for opportunity of getting any ship, take care of yourselves."

This curiously muddled compound of patriotism and piratical bravado was duly handed to the captain of an English East Indiaman a few days after its author had sailed from Johanna for the rich pirate hunting ground of the Red Sea. The letter did not have the desired effect. Every's depredations swiftly earned him a place at the head of the wanted list, where he remained for the rest of his life. He was one of the few men specifically declared outside all the various Acts of Grace promulgated from time to time by the British government to pardon pirates at large and thus rid the seas of them.

In August 1695, the *Fancy,* arriving at the mouth of the Red Sea, was joined by five other pirate vessels, including four from the American colonies. Every was put in temporary supreme command of this formidable criminal fleet.

At first the pirates had little luck; practically the entire annual convoy of treasure ships heading eastward toward India, 25 ships in all, managed to slip by during the night. The next morning, however, Every saw action enough. Trailing behind the body of the treasure fleet came the *Gang-i-Sawai,* a vessel so vast and powerfully armed that it ventured to sail with only one escort, the smaller *Fateh Mohamed.* Every's swift *Fancy* gave chase and caught up with the *Fateh Mohamed,* and the pirates boarded her. Evidently impressed with the *Fancy's* 46 guns and her villainous-looking crew, the *Fateh Mohamed's* sailors put up little fight. Making a rapid search of their prize, Every's men found some £50,000 in gold and silver aboard.

Hoisting all sail, Every then pursued the fleeing *Gang-i-Sawai.* This formidable vessel carried 62 guns and 400 to 500 musketeers as well as 600 passengers, among them some high-ranking officials of the Great Mogul's court returning from a pilgrimage to Mecca. The Indian historian Khafi Khan considered the *Gang-i-Sawai* to be the greatest ship in all

Henry Every, who with Thomas Tew was one of the first pirates to operate in the Indian Ocean, commands from shore as his crew on the Fancy (foreground) attacks a Mogul treasure vessel, in this 1734 engraving. Though Every was in the thick of the fight, he did not participate in the brutalities later inflicted on the crew and passengers of the captured ship.

the Mogul's dominions. She was carrying a cargo of 500,000 gold and silver pieces and was within eight days of her destination at Surat in India when Every caught up with her. Considering that she was much bigger than the *Fancy*, carried more guns and had more than four times the complement of soldiers and sailors, the *Gang-i-Sawai* must have seemed a forbidding proposition. But as soon as she opened fire on the pirates, one of her great guns burst and the fragments killed three or four of the gunners. This caused great confusion on board, which was not improved when a well-placed shot from one of the pirates' guns snapped the mainmast and left the Indian ship unmaneuverable. Greatly encouraged, the pirates came alongside, drew their swords and boarded the *Gang-i-Sawai*—no mean feat, as presumably they had to climb up her sides in order to do so.

According to one of Every's crew, Philip Middleton, the Indians put up a strong resistance, fighting through the ship for two hours and killing many of Every's men—perhaps as many as 20. But the Indian historian, Khafi Khan, clearly saw it all as a disgraceful performance. "The English are not bold in the use of the sword," he wrote. "If any determined resistance had been made they had been defeated." However, the Indians lacked the necessary leadership, since the *Gang-i-Sawai*'s captain, Ibrahim Khan, had fled belowdecks as soon as the pirates came on board, and rushed to the side of some Turkish girls he was transporting from Mecca to be his concubines. He put turbans on the girls' heads hoping to make them look like men. This panic measure came to nothing; the girls fell into the pirates' hands anyhow.

It was considered normal in those times for whites to brutalize people with darker skins, since most were "heathens" anyway. Even so, the people on board the *Gang-i-Sawai* were treated with extraordinary barbarity. Men and women alike were tortured to make them confess the whereabouts of their valuables on the ship. The men were then butchered. The women were savagely raped, some of them dying of their resulting injuries; even the aged wife of a high-ranking official, related to the Great Mogul, was abused in this way. (It was this relative of the Mogul who became the inspiration for the subsequent story about the beautiful princess whom Every married.) Some of the women threw themselves overboard rather than submit to the pirates, and some killed themselves with daggers.

From the *Gang-i-Sawai* the pirates took great quantities of gold, silver and jewels, and a saddle set with rubies intended as a present for the Great Mogul. When they had finished their plundering of the *Gang-i-Sawai* and the *Fateh Mohamed*, they set the ships loose, but without the surviving women, who were kept on board the pirate vessel until the men tired of them. The Indian ships eventually returned to Surat to give the news, but what happened to the women is not known. They were either thrown overboard or put ashore at Réunion, where the *Fancy* eventually landed to share out the plunder.

The Indian owners later estimated their losses at £600,000, but this was probably an exaggeration intended to improve their compensation from the East India Company, whose entire business was in jeopardy unless it made good the losses caused by English and American pirates.

The president of the East India's trading post at Surat put the loss at £325,000, which was probably nearer the mark. This was not divided among the crew of the *Fancy* alone; some of the other pirate ships in Every's little fleet also joined in the share-out. Each man's share of the plunder amounted to more than £1,000, plus a quantity of jewels. There were some younger pirates aboard—boys between 16 and 18—and they got £500 each. And then there apparently were some even younger ones; they received £100 each, with which, the pirates said, "to apprentice themselves to an honest trade ashore"—an interesting reflection on the pirates' view of their profession. As for Every, he received the normal pirate captain's allowance of two shares.

Now that they had made their fortune, the members of the pirate fleet split up. One ship went to the Persian Gulf, another to Ethiopia, a third to Madagascar. Every had always intended to sail straight for New Providence in the Bahamas, since he had no base or connections in the North American colonies. But some of the crew wanted to go to Brazil and came near to mutiny before Every got his way.

Despite Every's efforts, more than 50 hands left the ship to settle down as prosperous colonists on the tropic island of Réunion. To fill their place, Every—reverting to his old profession—took aboard a consignment of 90 African slaves and in April 1696, set sail with a crew of 113 for the long voyage to the Bahamas. Along the way he put in for provisions at the Portuguese island of São Tomé, where he paid for the goods with the 17th Century equivalent of a rubber check—a Bill of Exchange drawn on the Bank of Aldgate Pump, witnessed by John-a-Noakes and signed by Timothy Tugmutton and Simon Whifflepin, English names so outrageously false that they suggest Captain Every was as gifted with a sense of humor as he was with a flair for villainy.

The pirates slowly ate and drank their way across the Atlantic to the Caribbean. When they arrived at the Danish island of St. Thomas, they further fattened their purses by putting some of their stolen goods up for sale at bargain prices. The populace clamored to buy the booty. Pére Labat, a Jesuit priest, wrote appreciatively in his journal: "A roll of muslin embroidered with gold could be obtained for only 20 sols and the rest of the cargo in proportion."

At the Bahamas, Governor Nicholas Trott welcomed the pirates with open arms. He could afford to be magnanimous, for they had greased his palm with 20 pieces of eight and two pieces of gold per man, besides loading him with ivory and other goods, the whole worth £7,000. In the end they even gave him their ship, the *Fancy*. Trott entertained Every and his men at his own home. Philip Middleton, who served aboard the *Fancy*, records, however, that the good Governor's hospitality extended only so far. When one of the pirates accidentally broke a glass, the Governor charged him eight sequins, worth £3.16s, a sum that would have kept a pirate in beef for a year back home in England.

That convivial party around the table of a colonial governor was probably the high-water mark in the fortunes of Henry Every and his merry crew. Still flush with the excitement of their prodigal wealth, they forgot for the moment the problems that confronted them as felons back in England. For they still could not walk the streets of home without run-

Fierce doings along the Malabar Coast

British ships pour a devastating fire into the major pirate fortress on Severndroog Island as a powder magazine goes up in flames.

The Westerners who plied the Pirate Round were not the only sea rovers to ravage shipping in Eastern waters. Native pirates had infested the Indian Ocean and Red Sea since the beginning of commerce. But most of them were only smalltime brigands—until the late-17th Century, when a fearsome dynasty of pirates made themselves masters of the Malabar Coast.

The sire of the clan, Kanhoji Angria, first began plundering Indian Ocean shipping in the 1690s. By 1715 he ruled a chain of 26 forts on the coast south of Bombay, from which his fleets preyed on the cargo carriers of the various East India companies.

"He takes all private merchant vessels he meets," wailed the British East India Company's factors to their superiors in London. And every European trader breathed a heartfelt sigh of relief when Kanhoji finally died in 1729, leaving his five sons to quarrel over who would succeed him.

For 14 years, while the internecine struggle raged, East India shippers enjoyed a respite. But in 1743, the eldest son, Tulaji Angria, emerged as his father's heir and the pirates swooped down on shipping once again.

So immense were the depredations that in 1755 the British dispatched a squadron under Commodore William James to deal once and for all with Tulaji. On April 2 James attacked Severndroog, one of the strongest links in the pirates' chain of fortresses. Guarding the harbor mouth was an island fort mounting 50 cannon. Three mainland forts—one with 44 guns and two of 20 guns each—protected the quay and warehouses in which pirated cargoes were unloaded and stored.

Of the four British vessels under James's command, only one—the Protector, with 40 guns—could be classed as a man-of-war. The others were small auxiliaries mounting fewer than 20 guns between them. But with this tiny fleet James fought a heroic battle. Hugging Severndroog's shore so closely that few of the island's guns could be brought to bear, the Protector kept up a steady cannonade from her main battery. For two days, the bombardment continued, then a powder magazine exploded inside the island fortress, and the pirates frantically abandoned it. Next morning, James pounded all three mainland forts into submission.

Tulaji escaped, taking refuge in his Gibraltar-like bastion at Gheria. But he was finished. In February 1756 other squadrons captured the fort and took him prisoner. Today, on Shooter's Hill in London, stands the 63-foot tower of Severndroog; on it is engraved: "This far-seen monumental tow'r Records the achievements of the brave, And Angria's subjugated pow'r, Who plundered on the Eastern wave."

COMMODORE WILLIAM JAMES

ning the risk of being thrown into jail and strung from the nearest gibbet. And the obliging Governor Trott could not help them on that score—he was not empowered to issue pardons.

Nor would William Beeston, the Governor of Jamaica, where the pirates next sailed. On June 15, 1696, he wrote a self-righteous note regarding the pirates to the Council for Trade and Plantations in London:

"They are arrived at Providence and have sent privately to me, to try if they could prevail with me to pardon them and let them come hither; and in order that I was told that it should be worth to me a great gun (i.e. £24,000), but that could not tempt me from my duty."

Stranded back in the Bahamas, Every's crew broke up, and so did the *Fancy*. Though they had given her to the Governor, the pirates still lived on board. Drunk or beyond caring, they allowed the vessel to be driven ashore in a gale; she became a total loss except for her guns, which Governor Trott persuaded the crew to salvage and mount in an earthwork to repel an expected French attack. Soon afterward Every's company dispersed. A few slipped secretly into America and vanished—one married the daughter of Governor Markham of Pennsylvania—and some probably drifted into the dockside pool of unemployed brigands in the pirate ports of New England. One stayed at New Providence, having gone insane when he lost all his jewels on a wager. One was eaten by a shark off Jamaica. Most of the others, including Every, who now changed his name to Benjamin Bridgeman, clubbed together to buy sloops in which to sail home to the British Isles, an unusual and desperately dangerous hideaway for the Pirate Roundsmen of that time. It was at this point that their troubles began.

The test of a true criminal is how he disports himself *after* a successful crime. The master criminal will keep a low profile at all times and modify his life style only with great discretion. Every's men proved that they were far from master criminals. In June 1696, when the first of their sloops, the *Isaac*, landed on the other side of the Atlantic, the members of the crew quickly drew attention to themselves by their conspicuous spending and drunken vainglory. The people of Westport, County Mayo, in Ireland, were astonished that a small sloop should have nothing but chests of silver and gold as cargo, and became profoundly suspicious when the sailors on board her offered "any rates for horses: £10 for nags not worth ten shillings." The sheriff quickly arrested a number of them. One of Every's men, John Dann, had quilted his gold—£1,045, all in half sovereigns, plus 10 guineas—into his jacket, which must have weighed close to 20 pounds as a result. He was caught in Rochester, near London, when the chambermaid at the inn where he was staying discovered this preternaturally heavy garment and slipped away to tell the mayor. In London and Bristol, jewelers and goldsmiths reported strange sailors who tried to sell gems and foreign coins, and in this way more of the pirates were rounded up. All told, 24 of Every's men were arrested. Six were eventually hanged and most of the rest were deported to Virginia as convict laborers.

But not Every. In the sense that he was never caught, Every proved a master criminal. After he had landed his sloop at Dunfanaghy, 30 miles northwest of Londonderry in Ireland's County Donegal, he left his com-

The head office, or "factory," of the Dutch East India Company at Hooghly, on the Bay of Bengal, included warehouses, residences and gardens tucked behind stout walls. Camped outside (upper right) in this 1665 view is the entourage of an Indian dignitary who has come to barter. Throughout the 17th Century, booty for the pirates increased as the Europeans tapped the rich Indian market.

A hand-wringing 1704 Parliamentary proposal for dealing with piracy invokes the specter of Madagascar pirates propagating a whole new generation of freebooters who would bring disrepute — not to say commercial loss — to England with their heinous crimes. Occasionally, the Crown authorized royal pardons to wean pirates from their evil ways, but in the end a policy of extermination turned out to be the only effective deterrent.

(1)

REASONS

For Reducing the

Pyrates at Madagaſcar:

AND

PROPOSALS *humbly offered to the Honourable Houſe of Commons, for effecting the ſame.*

THAT certain Pyrates having ſome Years ſince found the Iſland of *Madagaſcar* to be the moſt Proper, if not the only Place in the World for their Abode, and carrying on their Deſtructive Trade with Security, betook themſelves thither ; and being ſince increaſed to a formidable Body are become a manifeſt Obſtruction to Trade, and Scandal to our Nation and Religion, being moſt of them *Engliſh*, at leaſt four Fifths.

That *Madagaſcar* is one of the Largeſt Iſlands in the World, and very Fruitful, lies near the Entrance into the *Eaſt-Indies*, and is divided into a great many petty Kingdoms independant of each other, ſo that there is no making Application to any Supream Monarch (or indeed any elſe) to Expel or Deſtroy the Pyrates there.

That upon a general Peace, when Multitudes of Soldiers and Seamen will want Employment ; or by length of Time, and the Pyrates generating with the Women of the Country, their Numbers ſhould be increaſed, they may form themſelves into a Settlement of Robbers, as Prejudicial to Trade as any on the Coaſt of *Affrica*.

For it's natural to conſider, That all Perſons owe by Inſtinct a Love to the Place of their Birth : Therefore the preſent Pyrates muſt deſire to return to their Native Country ; and if this preſent Generation ſhould be once Extinct, their Children will have the ſame Inclination to *Madagaſcar* as theſe have to *England*, and will not have any ſuch Affection for *England*, altho' they will retain the Name of *Engliſh* ; and conſequently all thoſe ſucceeding Depredations committed by them will be charged to the Account of *England*. Notwithſtanding they were not born with us, ſo that this ſeems the only Time for Reducing them to their Obedience, and preventing all thoſe evil Conſequences.

It muſt therefore be allow'd to be a very deſirable and neceſſary Thing, that they ſhould be ſuppreſſed in Time ; and that if it ever be effected, it muſt be either by Force or Perſwaſion.

A2

panions and dropped out of sight. Later one of his captured crew said Every had been planning to make for Scotland. Another said that he had seen him in Dublin and heard him say "he would go to Exeter, being a Plymouth man." A third said he was living in London and had been joined by Mrs. Adams, the wife of Every's quartermaster on the *Fancy*; she had been seen getting into a stagecoach at St. Albans "on her way to Captain Bridgeman."

Thereafter all trails run cold. Daniel Defoe, writing more than 20 years later, has a very picturesque end for the Arch Pirate. According to his account, Every went to the town of Bideford, in Devon, and negotiated with some merchants for the sale of his swag, which was all in diamonds except for a few gold chalices. The merchants put down a small deposit, took the diamonds and refused to pay the balance. From time to time they sent Every a pittance to live on, but when he asked for the money they owed him, they threatened to expose him. In the end he was reduced to penury and even beggary, and died "not being worth as much as would buy him a Coffin," cursing the merchants as being "as good Pyrates at Land as he was at Sea."

Whether Every lived the life of a squire or died the death of a pauper, there is no doubt of the impact of his spectacular coup. As with Tew a few years before, word of Every's success was the subject of every tavern conversation, every shipboard conspiracy. A share in the riches of the Great Mogul fleet fired the imagination of every disgruntled jack-tar, every hopeless and oppressed swabber on board ship. The Eastern Seas become ever more infested with pirate vessels; no roadstead or trade route, from the Mozambique Channel and the Red Sea Straits to the Arabian Sea and Coromandel Coast, was safe from them.

But if pirates were more active, their opponents were no less so. Every's capture of the *Gang-i-Sawai* had caused such a furor among the minions of the Great Mogul that feelings against the English ran high. There was a sharp retaliation against the East India Company. The company's trading posts at Surat, Broach, Agra and Ahmedabad were closed down and an armed guard of Indian troops was stationed to keep watch over the company's goods and money. The company's officers were thrown into prison, where they were kept in irons, three men to a cell; some were beaten so badly that they died; one was stoned to death. Not until there was conclusive proof that the company was innocent of collusion with the pirates were the officers released.

The East India Company men were not in a good mood. They had no sooner shaken the filth of the Indian jails from their clothes than they were writing letters of protest in the strongest possible terms to the government in London. The ravages of the English pirates threatened the very existence of the British East India Company. The company offered a reward of £500—to which the crown added another £500—for each remaining member of Every's crew. The company asked the government for special powers to arrest all pirates within the area of their charter and to set up special courts of Admiralty in which to try the pirates. The request was turned down. The company then pleaded for the Royal Navy to be sent to help them.

Instead of the Royal Navy, they got Captain Kidd.

Dazzling treasures of the Peacock Throne

The pirates operating in the Red Sea and the Indian Ocean understood well enough about the European trading companies whose heavily laden East Indiamen they plundered whenever the opportunity presented itself. But of their other favored prey, the "infidel" Moslems whose craft plied back and forth carrying pilgrims and treasure between the Mogul Empire in India and the holy city of Mecca in Arabia, the pirates knew next to nothing—only that their ships sometimes held amazing booty in gems, gold and silver.

Actually, India's Mogul rulers were themselves interlopers, Moslem invaders in a largely Hindu land. As fierce and nomadic horsemen, claiming descent from Genghis Khan and Tamerlane, they had thundered down into India from the mountains around Kabul in 1526. Yet crude though they were at first, these terrible warriors proved to be apt rulers. Under the Moguls, India was unified for the first time in its history, and the country entered an age of unparalleled artistic splendor. The exquisite miniatures on this and the following pages from a royal album suggest the opulence and refinement of court life under Shah Jahan, the fifth Mogul and builder of the Taj Mahal.

Christendom had no monarchs whose treasure could even begin to compare with that of the Moguls. Shah Jahan's magnificent Peacock Throne was studded with rubies, garnets, diamonds, pearls and emeralds, and covered by a bejeweled canopy (right). Its gems represented but a small part of the Moguls' collection. In November 1665 the sixth Mogul emperor, Aurangzeb, permitted the prize jewel in his collection—the Great Mogul diamond, later known as the Koh-i-noor, or Mountain of Light—to be inspected by an itinerant French jewel merchant named Jean-Baptiste Tavernier. Tavernier calculated its weight at 280 carats. On the same day, he watched with amazement as Aurangzeb accepted annual tribute of still more jewels from his subjects. "In diamonds, rubies, emeralds, brocades of gold and silver, and other stuffs," Tavernier wrote "the Emperor received in presents more than 30,000,000 livres"—a royal haul almost four times the £700,000 personal income that one of Aurangzeb's kingly contemporaries, William III of England, would be granted by Parliament a few years later.

Yet it was under Aurangzeb that Mogul rule slipped into a slow but fatal decline. He was a harsh and bloody-minded tyrant who had succeeded to the Peacock Throne by beheading two of his brothers and imprisoning not only his father, Shah Jahan, but also three of his own sons and his eldest daughter. He reimposed a detested Moslem religious tax on India's Hindu majority and found himself bedeviled by Hindu uprisings. Despite the expenditure of vast sums of money, Aurangzeb could not put down the rebels. In time, the decline of imperial power touched the seas, as poorly protected Mogul fleets became prey for pirates.

The depredations of the pirates infuriated Aurangzeb. Not only was much treasure lost; it was sacrilege of the worst sort to attack a shipload of Mecca-bound or returning pilgrims. Since most of the pirates were English or American colonials, the British East India Company bore the brunt of the Mogul's wrath. At one point, Aurangzeb accused the company of being in league with the pirates, and imprisoned 50 Englishmen, including the company's manager, until that worthy could convince the Mogul of their innocence. Nevertheless, Aurangzeb issued an edict making all European traders, including the unhappy Dutch and French, responsible for the safety of Mogul vessels. The companies, which were gradually and painfully learning to convoy their own ships, responded by sending heavily armed East Indiamen to sail with the Mogul fleets.

These convoys—and the intercession of the British Navy—did much to drive away the pirates by the time Aurangzeb died in 1707 at the age of 89. Thirteen more Moguls followed him to the throne but their might waned so rapidly that in 1739 a Persian army invaded India and carried away the Peacock Throne as booty.

As the years went on, the Moguls were reduced to a role as puppets of the British East India Company. In 1858, even their nominal reign came to an end as India passed under British sovereignty. The Koh-i-noor diamond, no longer its former size—over the intervening years it had been cut down to 186.5 carats—was added to the British crown jewels. And the Mogul name survived only as an English word signifying a person of great might and wealth.

From his Peacock Throne (worth six million pounds in the currency of the day), Shah Jahan inspects an emerald topped with a pearl as courtiers wait. The Emperor, who ruled from 1627 to 1658, was said to be so fascinated by precious gems that not even the most suggestive dancing girls could distract his gaze.

94

One of two miniatures of the 1633 wedding of Shah Jahan's favorite
son, Dara Shukoh, shows sitar players heading the procession
as bejewelled elephants follow, carrying women beating drums and
cymbals. On foot (right) are attendants bearing flowers.

In the other miniature, courtiers carrying gifts follow in the nuptial parade, with nobles of the Mogul's court on horseback (center) while trumpeters on elephants bring up the rear. The cost of these festivities —in modern equivalents —was millions of dollars.

Kneeling under a pearl-encrusted canopy, Shah Jahan receives a
group of mullahs—patriarchs learned in Islamic law and
theology. Ostentatious even in his religion, Shah Jahan once sent a
huge gem-studded candelabrum to Mecca for the Prophet's tomb.

Guests at Shah Jahan's evening entertainment, the mullahs sit
by the light of golden candelabra in the royal dining hall.
They knelt before a sumptuous feast of delicacies laid out on golden
platters. Tiny cups for tea or sweet ices were placed beside them.

Nobles of the imperial court watch attentively as Shah Jahan seats himself in the scales preparatory to distributing his weight in gold to the populace. The ceremony took place twice annually —on the Mogul's birthday and on the first day of the new year.

New Year's celebrations in Shah Jahan's court also included ceremonial dances such as these, performed by women in diaphanous dresses, to the music of flutes and sitars (lower right) and drums and trumpets from the balcony (upper right).

Chapter 4

The fateful cruise of the "Adventure Galley"

uring the afternoon before he was put to death, Captain William Kidd—ship's master and navigator of the Eastern Seas, naval hero and "well-beloved" agent of King William III of England, New York merchant and man of property, faithful husband and devoted father of two, but now, alas, a convicted pirate and murderer—was visited by one of the more sanctimonious bores of Newgate prison, the Chaplain and Ordinary, Paul Lorrain. This busy divine gained his living in the present world and his hopes of salvation in the next by wringing confessions from condemned felons and publishing the juicy tidbits in moralizing booklets, which he peddled in the coffeehouses of London.

The prospect of imminent death being what it is, the Reverend Paul Lorrain usually had little difficulty extracting repentance from the miserable wretches in his charge. But Captain Kidd was different. "I found him very unwilling to confess the crime he was convicted of," complained Lorrain. Which is not surprising, since the 56-year-old Kidd did not believe he had committed any crime at all. However, the chaplain was not one to give up a challenge lightly. On the day of the execution, he was in Kidd's cell early, and hauled him up to his chapel both in the morning and in the afternoon. "I was afraid the hardness of Captain Kidd's heart was still unmelted," he recalled. "I therefore apply'd myself with particular exhortations." It seemed to work, for Kidd "readily assented and said that he truly forgave all the world: and I was in good hopes that he did so."

But the chaplain was in for a shock. Between the time Kidd left the prison chapel and the time he passed through the prison gates on the way to the place of execution at 3 p.m., some charitable soul slipped him a considerable quantity of alcohol. When Kidd emerged through the great arch of Newgate, he was reeling drunk and oblivious to the howls of execration from the mob waiting outside.

At the front of the macabre procession in an open carriage came the Admiralty's deputy marshal, bearing over his shoulder the silver oar that symbolized the authority and power of the Admiralty. Behind him came the marshal himself, the powdered and bewigged Mr. Cheeke, on whom had fallen the responsibility of arranging the execution and the disposal of the bodies. Finally, flanked by constables, came a black-draped tumbrel carrying the condemned men—Kidd, his shipmate Darby Mullins and another pirate not involved with their case. Amid the roar of the London mob, the cortege moved off at a walking pace, clattering over the cobbles of Cheapside, past the Royal Exchange and the Aldgate pump, with the square keep of the Tower of London on the right, above the dark expanse of the Thames. The solemn pomp of the procession was intended to instill respect for the law among the citizens. But execution day was fete day in London, and Hangman's Fair at Wapping was celebrated as an occasion for orgies of all kinds. A great, raucous crowd followed Kidd to his killing place. Low-class whores and harpies lined the smelly little streets among the run-down tenements and hovels and cheap taverns, and they closed in behind the procession and screamed out for Arabian gold and rings and gems and pieces of eight   for pirates sometimes threw a few pieces of treasure to the crowd when they were on

In his wig and jabot, William Kidd appears more patrician than piratic in this 1701 portrait. But the old mariner was on trial for his life, vilified by his Admiralty prosecutors as an "Arch-Pirate and the common Enemy of Mankind." The painting, by an unknown artist, is based on a sketch hastily limned at Kidd's trial by court painter and pirate enthusiast Sir James Thornhill. Supposedly framed in timbers from Kidd's ship the Adventure Galley, the picture bears swatches of velvet, silk and gold lace (lower left) snipped from the last suit Kidd wore.

their way to be hanged—while others bawled out a ballad specially composed for the occasion, *Captain Kidd's Farewell to the Seas:*

My name was Captain Kidd, when I sail'd, when I sail'd,
And so wickedly I did, God's laws I did forbid,
When I sail'd, when I sail'd.
I roam'd from sound to sound, And many a ship I found,
And them I sunk or burn'd, When I sail'd.
I murder'd William Moore, And laid him in his gore,
Not many leagues from shore, When I sail'd.
Farewell to young and old, All jolly seamen bold,
You're welcome to my gold, For I must die, I must die.
Farewell to Lunnon town, The pretty girls all round,
No pardon can be found, and I must die, I must die,
Farewell, for I must die. Then to eternity, in hideous misery,
I must lie, I must lie.

It was two hours before the procession reached Execution Dock at Wapping on the edge of the Thames mud flats. The gallows, awash at its base at high tide, now stuck up out of the mud. Beside the scaffold stood the Reverend Paul Lorrain. He had gone on ahead in order to greet the prisoners. But when he set eyes on Kidd he saw, to his unspeakable grief, that the captain was inflamed with drink, "which had so discompos'd his mind that it was now in a very ill frame and very unfit for the great work now or never to be perform'd by him." The captain would still not confess his crimes or ask forgiveness. "He expressed abundance of sor-

Ornate dormer windows and stepped gables mark William Kidd's large brick house at the corner of Pearl and Hanover streets in Manhattan. Visitors were impressed by the Oriental carpet, fine furniture and abundance of silver plate that Kidd had amassed as a successful merchant captain before his downfall.

row for leaving his wife and children," recalled Lorrain. Indeed, "the thoughts of his wife's sorrow was more occasion of grief to him than that of his own sad misfortunes." The constables prodded Kidd onto the scaffold and the hangman fitted the noose round his neck. The crowd waited, noisy and gleeful. Lorrain sang a penitential psalm and said a short prayer and then the hangman pushed the unrepentant drunk, William Kidd, into space.

But if Captain Kidd had one outstanding characteristic in his life it was bad luck, and bad luck did not desert him now. For he had dangled only briefly from the gallows' arm before the rope snapped under his weight, tumbling him down into the mud. A great shriek went up from the crowd. Confused and stunned, Kidd was manhandled up a ladder and tied to the gallows tree a second time. The indefatigable Lorrain, seizing his chance, clambered up the ladder behind him and, balanced in this precarious position, tried one more time with urgent pleas to get the poor old sailor to repent his sins. So the old salt, not knowing exactly where he was or what was happening, gasped it out and the chaplain, at last satisfied, climbed down. Then the hangman yanked away the ladder and the judicial murder was complete.

At the time of his death in 1701, and for generations after, Captain Kidd was popularly regarded as a maritime gangster of the most evil sort, the apotheosis of a cutthroat pirate. But nobody endured a worse reputation with less reason. No pirate of the day spilled less blood—or captured fewer prizes, though not entirely by design. If he was a *cause célèbre*, it was because of political intrigue rather than actual crime. For the complex story of Captain Kidd's foray into the Eastern Seas is inextricably linked with the shadowy figures of some of the noblest men of the British realm. And in the end they betrayed him.

Little is known of the first 45 years of William Kidd's life. He was a Scot, possibly born at Greenock, probably in 1645. He presumably took to the sea when he was a boy and he may have emigrated to America in his early 20s. In any case, by the early 1690s, he was a man of substance in New York. He had his own merchant ship and had distinguished himself as a privateer captain in the king's service against the French in the West Indies in 1689. Returning home, he married a lovely English woman, Sarah Oort, who had outlived two previous husbands though she was still only in her early 20s. Through his marriage Kidd acquired New York property, which one day would be worth a fortune—86-90 and 119-121 Pearl Street, 52-56 Water Street and 25-29 Pine Street. Within a few years Kidd was not only rich but respected; he held a pew at Wall Street's Trinity Episcopal Church; he was interested in politics and he counted himself among the confidants of the Governor of New York, Colonel Benjamin Fletcher.

In the mid-1690s, following the wildly successful pirate cruises of Thomas Tew and Henry Every, the Eastern Seas were alive with pirate vessels. Month by month the toll of the Great Mogul's shipping mounted; month by month the position of the East India Company deteriorated as outraged native rulers laid the blame on the Company's English managers. At last, in 1695 the King agreed to relieve New York's Governor

THE EARL OF ROMNEY
Master General of Ordnance

THE EARL OF ORFORD
First Lord of the Admiralty

SIR JOHN SOMERS
Lord Keeper of the Great Seal

THE DUKE OF SHREWSBURY
Secretary of State

The Earl of Bellomont (left) met Kidd in London in 1695 and offered the ambitious sea captain an enticing opportunity: a privateer's commission authorizing him to attack Red Sea pirates— and French traders as well—and to pocket a bit of the plunder. But there were aspects of the deal that troubled Kidd, and he might have backed out had his secret partners (above) not been some of England's most powerful men. "Lord Bellomont assured me again and again," Kidd later wrote, "that the noble lords would stifle all complaints."

EARL OF BELLOMONT
Governor of New York and New England

Fletcher, who was by then notorious for his dealings with Tew and other pirates. In his place as governor of both New York and New England, the King appointed the Earl of Bellomont, an Irish peer with a powerful sense of duty. His was the task of smothering piracy on the American coast from New Jersey to Maine. At the same time, the government hoped to attack the pirates in the East. But England's war with France meant that there were few ships to spare for pirate chasing. And this was when Captain Kidd came on the scene.

In the summer of 1695, Kidd arrived in London with his sloop *Antegoa* after a trading run from New York. Here he chanced to meet Colonel Robert Livingston, a prominent New Yorker who presented him with a grandiose scheme for ending Red Sea piracy and making a profit into the bargain. Livingston's idea was to dispatch a specially built privateer ship under a specially qualified privateer captain with the backing of a syndicate of influential men who would recoup their investment with the profits from captured pirate booty. Like all enterprises doomed to failure, this one was flawed at its heart. While it purported to be a praise-worthy act of international policing, it was in fact merely a device for making a financial killing of astronomical proportions. For the real target was not so much the pirates but the prodigious plunder presumed to be in their ships. There was thus at the outset an ambiguity, a confusion of aims that was eventually to prove fatal to the man who was placed in command—William Kidd.

Kidd seemed the ideal choice for this venture. He was an honest, reliable merchant sea captain. At the same time, as a former privateer in the King's service, he was a fighting sailor who knew the ways of pirates. Forthwith, Livingston hustled Kidd off to see the new governor of New York, Lord Bellomont, at his London home on Dover Street. Bellomont thought it all a splendid idea. He quickly put Livingston in touch with four of England's most powerful men, all close friends of the King: Sir John Somers, Lord Keeper of the Great Seal, and subsequently Lord Chancellor; the Duke of Shrewsbury, Secretary of State; Sir Edward Russell, First Lord of the Admiralty, later Lord Orford; and the Earl of Romney, Master General of Ordnance. These gentlemen were only too pleased to put money into the venture, provided, of course, that their names were not mentioned. Even the King promised to put up £3,000 though in the end he never did.

In October 1695, Livingston, Bellomont and Kidd signed the Articles of Agreement. Bellomont was responsible for finding four fifths (£6,000) of the cost, this sum coming from the four anonymous noble backers. Livingston and Kidd together put up one fifth. As was customary, the first 10 per cent of any booty would go to the Crown. The remaining 90 per cent would be split three ways—60 per cent for Bellomont's backers, 15 per cent for Kidd and Livingston and only 25 per cent for the crew—not the usual 60 per cent of a privateering agreement. There was to be no share-out of the spoil during the cruise, only at the end when it had been properly condemned by an Admiralty court. If there should be no booty, Kidd and Livingston were to pay back every farthing their backers had put into the venture.

A few months later, Kidd was issued two special commissions to overlay this private venture with an official veneer. One was a letter of marque, which empowered Kidd to capture any ships or goods belonging to Britain's enemy, France. The other was a commission from the King, issued under the Great Seal of the Crown of England, empowering Kidd to seize pirates, in particular four named pirates including Tew, and their ships and "Merchandizes, Money, Goods and Wares." The commission referred to him as "our Trusty and well-beloved Captain William Kidd." But it also contained a prophetic warning: "We do hereby jointly charge and command you, as you will answer the same at your utmost Peril, That you do not, in any manner, offend or molest any of our Friends or Allies, their Ships or Subjects."

None of these arrangements was particularly advantageous to Kidd. To raise his part of the expenses he had to sell his ship and a third of his interest to a London speculator. What he would get in return was dubious: there were few French in the Eastern Seas, and the chances of any crew of his capturing elusive pirates were slim at best. The whole enterprise was vague and equivocal.

To give him his due, Kidd had tried to wriggle out of it at the start. He knew how fine was the distinction between privateering and piracy. He knew that it was usual for privateer crews to mutiny and turn pirate if there was no plunder. He was prosperous enough already. But Livingston and Bellomont put great pressure on him. They took him along to the impressive houses of their noble backers. They suggested that it would be disloyal to refuse the King's commission. As Kidd later protested to one of his backers, Bellomont "added threats to his wheedles." Kidd felt himself powerless to oppose the all-powerful English establishment. "I thinking myself safe with a King's commission and the protection of so many great men," wrote Kidd later, "accepted, thinking it was in my Lord Bellomont's power as Governor of New York, to oppress me if I still continued obstinate. Before I went to sea I waited twice on my Lord Romney and Admiral Russell. Both hastened me to sea, and promised to stand by me."

Captain Kidd's vessel, the *Adventure Galley,* was launched at Deptford on the Thames in December 1695, and was well adapted to his mission. An armed ship of 287 tons mounting 34 guns, she carried a large amount of sail and in addition was pierced for 23 pairs of oars for maneuvering when becalmed. Great care was taken to select a reliable cadre for the crew, men who would not, when confronted with pirates, turn pirates themselves; nearly all these first 70 men were married, with settled families in England (the remaining 80 or so were to be recruited in New York on Kidd's farewell visit home). But Kidd's precautions turned out to be in vain. On March 1, 1696, within a day of setting sail from London, occurred the first and perhaps the most crucial of a whole series of setbacks that were to dog his voyage from beginning to end.

As the *Adventure Galley* slid down the Thames, Kidd unaccountably failed to salute a Navy yacht at Greenwich, as custom dictated. The Navy yacht then fired a shot to make him show respect, and Kidd's crew, who were handling sail up on the yardarms, responded with an astounding display of impudence—by turning and slapping their backsides in deri-

Bearing a somber portrait of King William III, Kidd's privateering commission, dated December 11, 1695, licenses him to attack any French merchantman that he encounters. This letter of marque led the unfortunate Kidd to believe that he enjoyed complete royal protection.

sion. Shortly thereafter, a press gang from a large man-of-war boarded the *Adventure Galley* and forcibly carried off nearly all of Kidd's hand-picked crew for service in the Navy, replacing them with a ragtag collection of Navy rejects.

It was the kind of calamity that never should have occurred. In the first place, Kidd should have been far too seasoned a captain ever to permit gratuitous insults to the Royal Navy—unless he had become giddy with power over his king's commission. And while there was never any actual proof that the press gang was in retribution, the entire incident was typical of Kidd's abysmal lack of judgment—and luck—for the brief remainder of his life.

Kidd arrived in New York in July and did not leave until September. The sale of a French fishing boat he had captured as a lawful prize during the Atlantic crossing conveniently provided funds with which to purchase the provisions necessary for a long cruise to the Indian Ocean. But filling out the remainder of the 150-man crew was not so easy. New York was still a hotbed of piracy—the starting and finishing point of the Pirate Round. Kidd's proposed cruise against pirates in the Eastern Seas was not likely to prove a popular proposition to seamen whose friends were pirates or who were pirates themselves. To attract any sort of crew at all, Kidd was forced to raise their share of the profits to 60 per cent, though he does not appear to have informed his sponsors of this change. He eventually set sail with a full complement of 150 men—one of them his brother-in-law, Samuel Bradley—but it was a sorry lot he had picked himself. Even Colonel Fletcher, who was still governor, pending the arrival of Lord Bellomont, had a low opinion of them. "Many flocked to him from all parts," he wrote to the Board of Trade, "men of desperate fortunes and necessities, in expectation of getting vast treasure. It is generally believed here that if he misses the design named in his commission, he will not be able to govern such a villainous herd."

It took the *Adventure Galley* five months to reach the pirate island of Madagascar. The voyage does not seem to have reduced the arrogance that the Great Seal of the King's commission had apparently induced in Kidd. He had already affronted the Royal Navy in the Thames. He was to do so again off the Cape of Good Hope. On December 12, 1696, about 100 miles northwest of Capetown, he fell in with a Navy squadron under Commodore Thomas Warren. Kidd demanded from the commodore some new sails to replace ones he had lost in an Atlantic storm. The commodore curtly refused. Kidd then told him that his commission entitled him to aid, and if the Navy refused it he would seize the sails from the first merchant ship he encountered. Angry words were exchanged and Commodore Warren threatened to press 30 of Kidd's men the next morning. So Kidd, in the calm of night, sneaked away with the use of his galley's oars, and sailed into the Eastern Seas without calling at Capetown, where he would certainly have been arrested. Kidd was just as untactful with the East India Company. At Johanna Island he was joined by an East Indiaman flying a Navy pennant. Kidd told the East Indiaman's captain to strike the pennant, as only he, Kidd, had the right to fly a Navy flag, by virtue of his royal commission. The East India crewmen were so suspicious of Kidd that they kept their guns trained on him throughout his stay and warned him to leave harbor before they boarded him. Kidd had thus earned a most dubious reputation before he had even set off on his Indian Ocean cruise.

After taking on water at Johanna, Kidd made for the nearby island of Mehila, in the Comoros, where he had the ship careened, and where, in the space of a single week, 50 of his men sickened and died of disease, a catastrophe that both Kidd and his surviving crew seem to have treated as a perfectly ordinary event of life at sea.

It was now more than a year since the *Adventure Galley* had first set sail from the Thames, and neither Kidd nor his surviving crew had earned a penny. Provisions were running low and those who had been recruited in New York began openly to advocate piracy. On April 27, 1697, Kidd set sail northward to the Red Sea. From this point onward, the trap that Kidd had unwittingly laid for himself could be said to be well and truly sprung.

In July 1697, the *Adventure Galley* dropped anchor off the small island of Perim in the narrows at the mouth of the Red Sea. This was a favorite ambush spot for pirates, for the big convoys of Arab and other merchant ships from Mocha, chief port of the Yemen coffee trade, provided rich pickings. It was an appropriate spot, therefore, for Kidd to lie in wait, either for pirates or enemy, meaning French, prizes. Several times, Kidd sent a small boat through the straits to Mocha. On the third reconnaissance it returned with news that 14 or 15 ships appeared ready to sail. But for three weeks Kidd rode at anchor, waiting for them to come

Costumed more like a courtier than like a seagoing cutthroat, Kidd kicks his family Bible into a sandy grave in this 1837 depiction of one of the legends about the star-crossed captain. The story has it that Kidd launched his piratical career by burying the book near Plymouth Sound.

through the narrows. Day after day the sun burned down out of a cloud-less white sky; the humidity reached saturation point; and the cooling southwest monsoon wind died, leaving only a stifling stillness upon a fiercely glittering sea.

Kidd must have reviewed his options time and again. He was in an equivocal position. He had been sent out to capture pirates and had been given a letter of marque empowering him to take French vessels as well. But since it was customary for vessels to fly whatever flag they deemed convenient at the moment, it was not always easy to discover a ship's true identity. Indeed, it was sometimes impossible until the other crew chose to reveal its allegiance. What would happen if he set off in pursuit of a strange sail, and that ship resisted him? Suppose he pressed the matter, and lives were lost in the ensuing action? Suppose then that his target ship turned out to be neither pirate nor French, but Dutch—or, infinitely worse, English?

On the other hand, what would happen if he played it safe, and in so doing came home empty-handed? How would he then fulfill the oner-ous financial requirements of his contract? Clearly he had to be aggres-sive; he had to take prizes. But suppose he could find no pirates or Frenchmen? What then?

What would be the position if he captured and plundered Moorish vessels? By a strict legal definition that would be piracy. But the authori-ties back home had in the past winked at the practice, and Moorish ships were customarily regarded as fair prey by the captains of Christian priva-teers. Where *was* the dividing line between privateering and piracy anyway? Kidd himself was fundamentally averse to piracy. But his rapa-cious crew was not, and it was bringing intense pressure on him to take a prize—nationality be damned. And who, in that waste of Red Sea water on the other side of the world so far from home and government, cared what he did, or would ever know?

Late in the evening of August 14, the fleet sailed out of Mocha, and Kidd took the first step along his fatal path. He went after it. There is conflicting evidence as to what took place the next morning. The fleet was neither pirate nor French, and it is certain that some ships flew English or Dutch colors, and that they opened fire on Kidd. It is certain, too, that Kidd fired back. But what Kidd's intention was has never been made clear. Edward Barlow, master of the *Sceptre*, one of the well-armed English East Indiamen escorting the convoy, observed Kidd's maneu-vers and formed his own conclusions.

At first, Barlow did not notice Kidd until someone reported that there was one vessel too many in the convoy. By this time the *Adventure Galley* was right in the middle of the Mocha fleet. "He showed no col-ours," wrote Barlow in his log, "but had only a red broad pennant out without any cross on it," which the *Sceptre*'s master took to signify an order to surrender or no quarter given. Kidd appeared to have singled out a large Moorish merchant ship as a target. Feeling him out, Barlow in the *Sceptre* let Kidd come on until he was nearly abreast before he hoisted his English colors and fired two or three guns at the *Adventure Galley*. By this time, the *Adventure Galley* was alongside the Moorish ship and Kidd leveled a broadside at her, hitting her in the hull and sails and rigging. The *Sceptre* immediately gave chase and the *Adventure Galley* hastily retreated under sail and oars. By next morning, Barlow recorded, the *Adventure Galley* was out of sight and gone for good.

Kidd had taken neither prize nor plunder in the Red Sea, and his prestige among his men sank lower still. There seems now to have been unbearable pressure on him to which, step by step, he appears to have given way. By the end of August when he was off the Malabar Coast of India north of Goa, the *Adventure Galley* met with a small Moorish barque, manned by Moors under an English captain named Parker, and with a Portuguese mate on board. Technically, the Moorish barque was not a legitimate prize. But Kidd had already proved himself a wobbly sort of King's agent by firing on the Moorish vessel escorted by the *Sceptre*. This time he allowed his crew to board the barque, and they brought back a bale of pepper and a sack of coffee that he let them keep for their own mess. For his part, Kidd forced the English captain to join him as pilot and the Portuguese mate as "linguister," or interpreter— valuable assets on such a strange cruise in such strange seas.

One might think that in the empty vastness of the Indian Ocean a ship could get away with virtually anything without detection. But the ports where a ship could be reprovisioned were few, and their seafaring populations regularly traveled back and forth, spreading every story. By mid-September, when Kidd put in for wood and water at Karwar, a port on the Malabar Coast between Calicut and Goa, word had spread of his activities. Two English officers of the East India Company trading "factory" boarded the *Adventure Galley* and demanded the release of Parker and the Portuguese. Kidd had the men locked in the hold and vigorously denied their existence, and eventually the officers left. But two of Kidd's crew, not liking the turn of events, jumped ship at this point and later made depositions to the East India Company station in Bombay that Kidd was "going on an ill design of piracy."

From Karwar, the chief factor of the East India Company wrote that Kidd was a "very lusty man" and exceedingly hard on his men: they went in awe of him because of his special commission from the King, and he was always threatening to knock their brains out with a pistol butt. "They are a very distracted company," the factor continued, "continually quarrelling and fighting amongst themselves, so it is likely they will in a short time destroy one another, or starve, having only sufficient provisions to keep the sea for a month more."

When Edward Barlow, of the Mocha convoy, reached Karwar on October 15, the whole coast was talking about the pirate chaser who had turned pirate. At Calicut, Barlow noted in his log, Mr. Penning, the local East India Company manager, refused to provide Kidd with wood and water—even when Kidd informed him that "he was sent out by the King of England." It was almost as though the ambiguity of Kidd's original contract, and the conflicting pressures from his sponsors and his crew, had produced in him a split personality—that he genuinely believed himself to be still a dutiful servant of the Crown while appearing to others to act to the contrary.

The cruise continued, and Kidd wandered across the empty ocean. Finally, in early November, he overhauled a cargo ship sailing north-

A fighting ship for a wayward captain

When she was launched in 1695 at the Thames River shipyard of Deptford, Captain William Kidd's ship *Adventure Galley* was the latest in fighting vessels. Designed for speed, maneuverability and firepower, the *Adventure Galley* was equally suited as the privateer for which she was intended or as the pirate ship she soon became.

She was a hybrid vessel, combining a modern hull and sail rig with the ancient concept of oar power; under full sail, with 3,200 square yards of canvas, she could make a swift 14 knots; without wind but with two or three pirates straining at each of her 46 oars, she could still move at three knots, even though she was heavy for a ship of her size (since she was built for combat she had larger, more closely spaced ribs than a merchantman).

Aside from the captain's cabin, in which councils of war were held, and a nearby cubby for the first mate, the interior of the *Adventure Galley* was spartan in the extreme. There were no crew quarters as such; at night the 150 or so men crammed into her 124-foot hull curled up wherever they could; they relieved themselves by clambering onto the bowsprit. There was no galley—just a gigantic stewpot and a bricked-in hearth used only in calm weather and located far from the powder stores. Fire was the terror of every crew. No smoking or open flame was permitted belowdecks; light for the powder room emanated from a lantern shining through a heavy glass window in the tin-lined lightroom.

In the hold, the shot locker, with its six tons of shot for the 12-pounder cannon, and the huge water casks, each weighing a ton, were located amidships to help ballast the ship. Hoisting the stores aboard was very difficult: it took 40 men to work the giant capstan; a major job, such as raising the 3,000-pound anchor with its 6,000 pounds of cable, could take an hour or more.

1. GREAT CABIN
2. QUARTER-DECK
3. FIRST MATE'S CABIN
4. MAGAZINE LIGHTROOM
5. MAGAZINE
6. PROVISIONS
7. CAPSTAN
8. SHIP'S PUMPS
9. SHOT
10. UPPER DECK
11. WATER CASKS
12. SHIP'S STORES
13. LOWER DECK
14. GALLEY
15. FO'C'S'LE DECK

ward along the coast. There was great excitement on board the *Adventure Galley* at the prospect of a big prize, but when she came up within a league of the merchantman, Kidd saw she was flying English colors.

William Moore, the gunner on the *Adventure Galley,* proposed that they plunder the vessel anyway. Kidd refused to consider it. "I dare not do such a thing," he said.

"We may do it," cried Moore. "We are beggars already."

The English ship proved to be the *Loyal Captain,* outward bound from Madras to Surat. All her papers were in order and Kidd let her go. This infuriated his crew. A few brought out their small arms, but Kidd faced them down. He had not come here to take any Englishmen or lawful traders. "If you desert my ship," Kidd told them, "you shall never come aboard again, and I will force you into Bombay, and I will carry you before some of the Council there."

The mutiny fizzled out. But not the rancor. On October 30, 1697, Captain Kidd and gunner Moore had their final confrontation. According to a teen-age deck hand named Hugh Parrott, the quarrel began as Moore, who had been ill, sat grinding a chisel on deck. When the captain appeared, Moore shouted at him:

"Captain, I could have put you in the way to have taken the ship, and have never been the worse for it."

According to Parrott, this put Kidd "in a passion"—so much so that the lad took refuge belowdecks. Other hands remained up top. Moore continued to upbraid the captain.

"You have brought us to ruin, and we are desolate," he railed.

"Have I brought you to ruin?" cried Kidd. "I have not done an ill thing to ruin you. You are a saucy fellow to say those words."

According to a sailor named Palmer, Kidd did not say "saucy fellow" but "lousy dog." To which gunner Moore screamed, "If I am a lousy dog, you have made me so!"

All agree about what happened next. The captain, now beside himself with fury, yelled: "Have I ruined you, you dog?" And with that he seized an ironbound bucket (worth eightpence of lawful English money, his prosecutors were to point out later) and crashed it against Moore's head, a little above the right ear.

The gunner's shipmates carried Moore below as the captain cried out after them: "Damn him! He is a villain!"

Moore died the next day of a fractured skull.

A stunned and sullen peace descended on the wretched *Adventure Galley.* Weeks went by. Then at the end of November, four leagues from Calicut, they sighted a sail. Kidd bore down on the vessel and ordered French colors to be run up—a ruse to make the stranger do the same. Sure enough, the ship hoisted a French flag in return. The ship was the *Maiden,* bound for Surat with a cargo of cotton, quilts, sugar and two horses. Her captain and two officers aboard were Dutchmen; all of the seamen were Moors. The Dutch skipper explained to Kidd that his ship was Moorish, and he also produced a French pass—indicating that she sailed under French auspices. Kidd evidently believed that this French pass made the *Maiden* a legitimate prize. "By God, have I catched you?" he cried. "You are a free prize to England!"

The Sceptre, a 36-gun vessel belonging to the British East India Company, gave Kidd's Adventure Galley a scorching baptism of fire in 1697 when the pirate captain cut into its convoy of Moorish treasure ships. "Had not our ship happened to have been in their company, he had certainly plundered all the headmost ships of all their wealth," surmised the captain of the Sceptre.

Kidd turned the Moors loose in the longboat, and with the connivance of the Dutchmen, he sold the cargo ashore for cash and gold, which he shared out among his men—an act in direct contravention of his contract. He renamed the captured ship *November* after the month of her capture, and took her along with a prize crew on board.

This was the first money the crew had touched since the *Adventure Galley* had left London nearly two years before. But it was not money they were entitled to. True, the Dutch captain had handed Kidd a French pass. But the pass was meaningless, since shipowners routinely obtained a pass from every nation operating in the area, and the captain had a number of other passes in his possession. The *November* was actually Indian-owned, and though it was customary for privateers to take prizes on even flimsier pretexts, according to the strict letter of the law Kidd had committed piracy.

Something must have clicked in Kidd's tortured mind at this stage in his voyage. It would seem he had finally decided that the lowly men who shared his leaking vessel were a more immediate threat than the few great men to whom he owed allegiance in Whitehall half a world away—and that, though forced to do wrong, he remained morally right. For he was now to commit piracy again and again.

Three days after Christmas 1697, Kidd seized a Moorish ketch off the Malabar Coast, and took some tubs of candy and a sack of coffee. Twelve days later he plundered a Portuguese ship of a quantity of East India Company goods, and some gunpowder, opium, rice, iron, beeswax and butter. So far Kidd's plunder added up to little more than the contents of an Indian general store. But on January 30, 1698, he took his most fateful prize. The *Quedah Merchant* was a 500-ton merchantman belonging to Armenian owners and commanded by an English captain named Wright. Outward bound from Bengal to Surat with a rich cargo of silks, muslins, sugar, iron, saltpeter, guns and gold coin, she was making heavy weather off the Indian coast 10 leagues north of Cochin when she was spotted from the lookout of the *Adventure Galley*. Crowding on sail, Kidd pursued her for four hours. When he finally came up with her he fired across her bows and hoisted his French flag. Kidd ordered the merchantman's master to come on board the *Adventure Galley*, yet it was not Captain Wright who arrived, but an old French gunner posing as the captain. Whereupon, to the Frenchman's great surprise, Kidd ran up the English flag and claimed the vessel as a prize.

And so it seemed at first. The old gunner handed him a pass signed by the Director General of the Royal French East India Company in Bengal only a fortnight before. But as with the *November*, the fact that the *Quedah Merchant* carried a French pass did not make her a French ship. Her Armenian owners were on board and offered to ransom the ship for nearly £3,000, an offer Kidd scorned as insufficient. Instead, he sold some cargo onshore for £10,000, divided the proceeds among the crew, and sailed to Madagascar with both the *November* and the *Quedah Merchant* as prizes. It was only when they had been sailing for five or six days that the true identity of the *Quedah Merchant*'s master was revealed. Captain Wright was brought before Kidd and Kidd was horrified to discover that he had unwittingly broken even his own rules and

captured an Englishman's command. Only now, perhaps, did he become fully aware of the extent to which he had compromised himself. He summoned the crew and addressed them from the quarter-deck.

"The taking of this ship would make a great noise in England," he told them. He proposed that they should hand the *Quedah Merchant* back to Captain Wright. But his crew would not hear of it, and so the three ships continued on their course.

On April Fool's Day, 1698, the tiny fleet finally reached Madagascar. Ironically, the harbor they entered was the pirates' haven of St. Mary's Island. And for the first time in his two-year cruise, the pirate catcher was confronted with a pirate ship.

Riding at anchor in St. Mary's was the *Mocha Frigate*, a captured East Indiaman, whose captain, Robert Culliford, had turned pirate after serving on a privateer. Even now Kidd was torn between his duty and his destiny. Although he had gone pirate, he still dreamed of catching pirates. He urged his men to seize the *Mocha*. They howled with derision. They told him they would rather fire 10 shots at him than one at the pirates, and began to share out the spoils of the *Quedah Merchant*. Curi-

Wild with rage, Kidd hurls a bucket at his mutinous gunner, William Moore, as they cruise off the coast of India. This melodramatic 19th Century engraving cast Kidd as vicious blackguard, Moore as his innocent victim. Eyewitnesses never agreed upon who was to blame, but Moore's death provoked a murder charge that eventually sent Kidd to the gallows.

ously, it was a privateer share-cut, for Kidd got a full 40 shares of the plunder, not the usual two shares accorded a pirate captain. After that, however, all but 13 of his men deserted to Culliford, including Robert Bradinham and Joseph Palmer, who later testified for the prosecution at Kidd's trial, sealing his terrible fate. They sacked and burned the *November*. Next, they clambered all over Kidd's remaining two ships, stripping them of guns, small arms, powder, shot, anchors, cables, surgeon's chests and anything else that took their fancy. They burned Kidd's log, threatened several times to murder him, and almost certainly would have done so had he not barricaded himself in his cabin. There, Kidd was totally trapped and finally compromised.

It is not recorded how long Kidd remained in his cabin. But at some juncture during those sweaty tropical weeks in St. Mary's, he capitulated to the pirate captain Culliford. "Before I would do you any harm," he finally swore, "I would have my soul fry in hell-fire."

Kidd's surrender had the desired effect: his life was spared, along with that of his brother-in-law (a sick man since the epidemic 15 months before) and the handful of men who had stayed loyal to him, while the *Quedah Merchant* was allowed to remain afloat with a fair share of booty still on board. In mid-June, Culliford's *Mocha*, her crew grown to 130 and her guns up to 40 at Kidd's expense, sailed out into the Indian Ocean and Kidd began to prepare for his return to England.

The first voyage of the *Adventure Galley* had proved to be her last. Half full of water and resting on a sandbar in the shallows, she could sail no farther. Kidd had her stripped and her hull burned for its iron. He then fitted out the bulky *Quedah Merchant* for the voyage home and began the difficult task of recruiting a crew from the nautical flotsam drifting around the islands. He had plenty of time, for he had to wait five months before the northeast monsoons could blow him around the Cape. At last, on November 15, 1698, the *Quedah Merchant* weighed anchor in St. Mary's harbor. Kidd seems to have had no qualms about the wisdom of returning home. His family awaited him; he had property to attend to; and he undoubtedly believed that he still had enough cargo in goods, jewels, silver and gold to square accounts with his powerful sponsors.

Captain Kidd was only three days out from St. Mary's when the East India Company wrote a letter from its headquarters in Surat to the Lords Justices in London in which a number of extreme accusations of piracy were leveled against him. The charges fell on receptive ears. To Kidd's high-placed backers—Lord Somers, now Lord High Chancellor; Lord Orford, First Lord of the Admiralty; Lord Shrewsbury, Lord Chief Justice; and Lord Romney, Privy Councillor—it had long been obvious that their opportunist effort at merchant-venturing was a dismal flop. There had been no decrease in the incidents of piracy. As for Kidd, there had been no news but uncomplimentary rumor. Now, it seemed, their worst fears were confirmed.

The response of the Lords Justices was vigorous and immediate. They ordered a Naval squadron, on the point of sailing to the Indian Ocean, to capture Kidd. At the same time, the Admiralty dispatched a circular letter to the governors of the American colonies ordering them to apprehend Kidd so that "he, and his Associates, be prosecuted with the utmost

Rigour of the Law.'' Finally, with the object of isolating Kidd, a free pardon was offered to every pirate east of the Cape except Kidd and two other captains, one of whom was Henry Every.

The news spread like smoke throughout England. A first-class political scandal erupted as Tory opposition politicians ripped into the four Whig Lords who had sent Kidd off in the *Adventure Galley*. William Kidd had become an archcriminal guilty of the most unspeakable crimes, and in the eyes of the government, the East India Company, the press and the general public he was found guilty before he had set foot on land, or so much as uttered a word.

Such was the situation when, early in April 1699, Kidd made his landfall at Anguilla in the Leeward Islands and sent his boat ashore. It returned with devastating news. In every port of the colonies, in virtually every quarter of the known world, Kidd and his crew had been declared pirates, to be arrested on sight.

For four hours the *Quedah Merchant* rode at anchor. Some of the men wanted to scuttle the ship against a reef and then disperse rather than sail into a port that was under English control. But Kidd would not run. He had been away too long. He was too old for an outlaw's life of exile. He would see the thing through. He had powerful friends in London and New York and he had the two French passes from the vessels he had plundered, so he was not a pirate—or so he believed. He decided to make for New York, where he reckoned he could count on the protection of the new governor, Lord Bellomont, one of the first supporters of the *Adventure Galley* cruise.

As Kidd sailed north, it was obvious to all that the *Quedah Merchant* had to be replaced. She was too big and distinctive to avoid detection, too barnacled and seaworn to outsail pursuit. In the Mona Passage on the southeast coast of Hispaniola, they came upon a becalmed trading sloop, the *Antonio*. The *Antonio* was neat, fast and anonymous. Kidd bought her from her owner-skipper for 3,000 pieces of eight and moored the *Quedah Merchant* under guard up the Higuey River in Hispaniola. He transferred much of the *Quedah Merchant* booty, including his own personal treasure—gold bars, gold dust, silver plate, precious and semi-precious stones, fine silks—to the *Antonio*. And then with a crew of 12, the rest opting to remain, he sailed boldly for New York.

On June 10, the *Antonio* rounded Long Island and anchored in Oyster Bay. Kidd had been away nearly three years. He had voyaged more than 42,000 miles, a distance greater than the circumference of the earth. The ship in which he had sailed was a ruined hulk on a tropic island; all but a handful of his crew were dead or pirating in the Eastern Seas. And he was an outlaw. Kidd's desperate gamble for life and freedom now entered its most critical stage. Everything depended on winning over Lord Bellomont, and to do this Kidd pinned his hopes on his two French passes. From Oyster Bay, therefore, Kidd sent a letter to an old friend and neighbor of his in New York, a lawyer named James Emmott, asking him to come out to the ship. Emmott arrived in a day or two, spoke with Kidd, then hastened to Boston, where Bellomont had his headquarters. Emmott saw Bellomont late on the night of June 13, proposed that he should grant Kidd a pardon and handed him the French passes.

Bellomont, who had received unequivocal orders to arrest Kidd, was in a difficult position. His own career was in the balance, and he dared not make any move that would cause Kidd to flee. On June 19, he sent a letter to Kidd by the hand of the Boston postmaster, Duncan Campbell, a friend of Kidd, in which he inveigled the captain into port with a masterpiece of double-dealing.

"I have advised with His Majesty's Council and shewed them this letter," wrote Bellomont, "and they are of the opinion, that if you can be so clear as you (or Mr. Emmott for you) have said, then you may safely come hither. And I make no manner of doubt but to obtain the King's pardon for you, and for those few men you have left who I understand, have been faithful to you, and refused as well as you to dishonour the Commission you have from England. I assure you on my word and honor, I will perform nicely what I have promised."

Confided Bellomont in a letter to London: "Menacing him had not been the way to invite him hither, but rather wheedling."

Kidd, overconfident, perhaps, as a result of his exchanges with Bellomont, now played his hand badly. Instead of bringing in his cargo for condemnation by Admiralty court, he appeared to regard it as his private property. To Bellomont's wife he unwisely sent as a "gift" a number of baubles, including a magnificent enameled box with four diamonds set in gold. Left and right he handed out largess, hoping to ingratiate himself with everyone. Yet he was not so foolish as to discard all precautions. Sloops came and went, carrying away treasure to friends for safekeeping. Finally, in the orchard of Gardiner's Island at the eastern tip of Long Island, he buried the bulk of his swag—including a chest containing gems and a box of gold—and duly obtained a receipt from the proprietor of the place, John Gardiner. Captain Kidd's treasure was now cunningly dispersed in a number of widely scattered caches. If he went free, he could pick them up later; if he was taken in custody, they would be a useful bargaining point.

Kidd's wife, Sarah, and his two daughters joined Kidd on board the *Antonio* at Block Island. The girls had been only three and four years of age when he left; he had missed nearly half their childhood. After such a long separation it was a heartfelt reunion, given added poignancy by the terrible circumstances of the occasion. Sarah Kidd had suffered through the hue and cry over her husband for months; she could hardly have shared his optimism as to the outcome. The family stayed on board all the way to Boston. They were to enjoy only two weeks together before being parted forever.

The Kidd family landed in Boston on July 2, 1699, and took rooms in a boardinghouse. Kidd unwisely sent another bribe to the Governor's wife, Lady Bellomont, this time £1,000 worth of gold bars sewed up in a green silk bag. She immediately sent them back. The next day, Kidd was interviewed by Bellomont, sitting in Council in his house. The Captain was coldly asked for a detailed account of his movements since leaving England. He replied, somewhat truculently, that his crew had destroyed his log. The Governor and Council ordered him to prepare a report. Kidd either could not or would not. Finally on July 6, all patience at an end, the Council voted for Kidd's immediate arrest. The police searched high

Captain Kidd's treasure island

As their captain looks on, two of Kidd's crewmen bury their hoarded treasure close to Cherry Harbor beach on Gardiner's Island in this dramatic 1894 re-creation by illustrator Howard Pyle.

John Gardiner, the self-styled "Lord of Gardiner's Island," often dealt with the pirates and privateers who passed his tiny fiefdom in Long Island Sound. So he was not surprised one evening in 1699 when the sloop *San Antonio* dropped anchor in Gardiner's Bay. But he was somewhat puzzled by her captain. Mysterious and cagey, William Kidd attempted to barter some water-damaged muslin and silk for a barrel of Gardiner's cider, and haggled endlessly over the paltry items. He then sailed away, leaving Gardiner to wonder at the gratuity casually handed the two men who brought the cider aboard: Arabian gold coins.

Three days later Kidd sailed back, having apparently decided that Gardiner could be trusted. He asked permission to cache some goods on the 3,300-acre island; in return, Kidd gave the increasingly bemused Gardiner a sash, worsted stockings and a bag of sugar.

Kidd sailed on to Boston, where he was soon clapped into prison by the same Lord Bellomont (now the colonial governor) who had sent him to sea in the first place. Hearing rumors of treasure on Gardiner's Island, Bellomont ordered Gardiner to bring whatever booty was there to Boston at once. Gardiner did this. However, the distrustful Bellomont ordered Kidd to list the hoard from memory. The captain did his best, listing gold, silks, quilts, spices, muslins, calicoes and gems. Kidd did not recall exactly how many gems he had buried—which was just as well for Gardiner. For on his return to the island, a large uncut Golconda diamond rolled unaccountably from his portmanteau.

Boston New England July 25th 1699.

A true Accompt of all such Gold, Silver, Jewels and Merchandize, late in the Possession of Capt. William Kid, which have been Seized and secured by us under written, Pursuant to an Order from his Excellency Richard Earl of Bellomont Captain General and Governour in chief in and over Her Majesties Province of the Massachusetts Bay &c bearing date July 7th 1699.

	Gold Ounces	Silver Ounces	Precious Stones or Jewells	Bags Sugar	Canvis peices	Bailes of Merchandiz
In Capt. Wm. Kids Box vizt. One Bagg of Fifty three Silver Barrs		357				
One Bag of Seventy nine Barrs & pieces of Silver		442½				
One Bag of Seventy four Barrs Silver		421				
One enamele Silver Box guilt in which are						
Found in Mr. Duncan Campbells house No. 1. One Bag of Gold	58½					
2— One Bag of	94					
3— One Handkerchief of	50					
4— One Bag of	103					
5— One bag of	38½					
6— One bag of	19½					
7— One bag of Silver		203				
In Capt. Wm. Kids Chest, Two Silver Bascons, Two silver Candlesticks, one Silver Porringer and some small things of Silver qt.		82				
Rubies small and great Sixty seven green Stones two One Large Load Stone			69			
Recd. of Mr. Duncan Campbell Three Bailes of Merchandize, whereof one he had opened being much damnified by Water qt.						3
Received the 17th Instant of Mr. Jno. Gardner vizt. No. 1. One bag dust Gold qt.	60¾					
2. One bag Coyned Gold qt.	11	124				
3. One bag dust Gold qt.	24¾					
4. One Bag of 3 Silver rings Sundry precious Stones						
5. 1 Bag Silver buttons & lamp qt.		29				
6. One bag broaken Silver qt.		173½				
7. One bag Gold barrs qt.	353½					
8. One bag Gold Barrs qt.	238½					
9. One bag dust Gold qt.	59½					
10. One bag Silver barrs qt.		203				
11. One bag Silver barrs qt.		309				

Also Twenty Dollers, one half and one Quarter piece of Eight, Nine English Crowns, one small barr of Silver, One small lump of Silver, A Small chain, a small bottle a coral necklace, one piece of white, and one piece Checquered Silk.

Recd. of Mr. Duncan Campbell Three Bailes of Merchandize, whereof one he had opened being much damnified by Water qt. Eighty five ps. Silk Romalls Bengalls Sixty peices of Callico & Muslins.

The whole of the Gold above mentioned is Eleven hundred & Eleven Ounces Troy wt.

The Silver is Two Thousand three hundred Fifty three Ounces.

The Jewels or precious Stones weighed are Seventeen Ounces three Eights of an Ounce and Sixty nine Stones by Tale.

The Sugar is contained in fifty seven Bags.

The Merchandize is contained in forty two Bailes.

A true Copy of the first sheet of the Accompt of the Treasure Goods and Merchandizes, imported by Captain William Kidd, and his Company and Accomplices Anno 1699 Seized by Order of the Earl of Bellomont, of which Accompt was presented in two Sheets, under the hands of Samuel Sewall, Nathaniel Byfield, Jeremiah Dummer and Andrew Belcher Esqrs Commissioners appointed to receive and secure the same, and upon their Oaths. And is Lodged in the Secretary's Office at Boston

Exam. W. Isaac Addington Secty.

Lord Bellomont's accounting to the Crown catalogues gold, silver, rubies, diamonds and 57 bags of sugar.

and low for the better part of a day, and eventually found him outside the front door of Bellomont's house. He tried to draw his sword, broke away and rushed into the house. He was caught and his arms pinned in the presence of the chief instigator of the voyage for which he was now being accused—the Captain General and Governor in Chief in and over His Majesty's Provinces of the Massachusetts Bay and Governor of New York, His Excellency, Richard, Earl of Bellomont.

Bellomont had Kidd clapped into the Stone Prison, in solitary confinement, in irons weighing 16 pounds. And from the moment of his confinement he was treated like a wild animal. "Monster" is how Bellomont described the old captain to Lord Somers. For tainting its good name, the English establishment was to exact a terrible revenge.

At the start, a frantic search was made to uncover Kidd's treasure. His lodgings were ransacked and their contents—even his clothes and his wife's things—were bundled away. His gifts to various friends were collected. The sloops that had carried off cargo were tracked down and his treasure on Gardiner's Island was dug up. Three weeks after his arrest an inventory was made of recovered booty: 1,111 ounces of gold, 2,353 ounces of silver, more than one pound of precious stones, 57 bags of sugar, 41 bales of merchandise. The entire proceeds were shipped under close guard to the Treasury in England.

Summer passed, then autumn. With the onset of winter the Council became concerned that Kidd and his fellow prisoners might die of cold in the Stone Prison, and they were allowed warm clothing. In the new year of a new century, H.M.S. *Advice* arrived to take the prisoners back to England for trial. On February 6, 1700, Kidd was escorted on board and locked up in a steerage cabin. The other prisoners were chained in the gun room. On April 11, in the Thames Estuary, Kidd was transferred from the Navy ship onto the royal yacht *Katherine* and rushed to Greenwich. A squad of musketeers on board was ready to march him to the Admiralty headquarters. But when his cabin door was opened early on the morning of Sunday, April 14, he was found unfit to appear. Sick in body and temporarily unhinged in mind, Captain Kidd had begun his descent from purgatory to inferno. He asked for a knife so that he could kill himself. He held out a gold piece to be sent to his wife. And he begged to be shot, not hanged.

Newgate prison was the principal jail of the City of London and already 500 years old. It was, even by the standards of the time, a disgusting place, so overcrowded that prisoners slept two or three to a bed and so verminous that lice crunched underfoot, as one inmate put it, "like shells on a garden path." The stench of ordure and prison damp were so overpowering that visitors often brought bunches of flowers to bury their noses in, and prisoners were washed with vinegar before they appeared in court. Unbelievably, the prison was run as a private business; prisoners were made to pay rent for their cells and jailers exacted extortionate fees for everything.

In this dark, noisome, clamorous, cavernous hole, William Kidd lay in close confinement for more than a year. In May 1700, his jailer reported to the Admiralty Board: "Captain Kidd was troubled with a great Paine in his Head, and shaken in his Limbs, and was in great want of his

Statues of Justice, Mercy and Truth adorn the façade of Newgate, the pestilential London prison where Kidd was held for a year while awaiting trial. Open sewers ran through the cells where drunks, debtors and felons alike were packed in seething masses. One prisoner called the place "an emblem of hell itself."

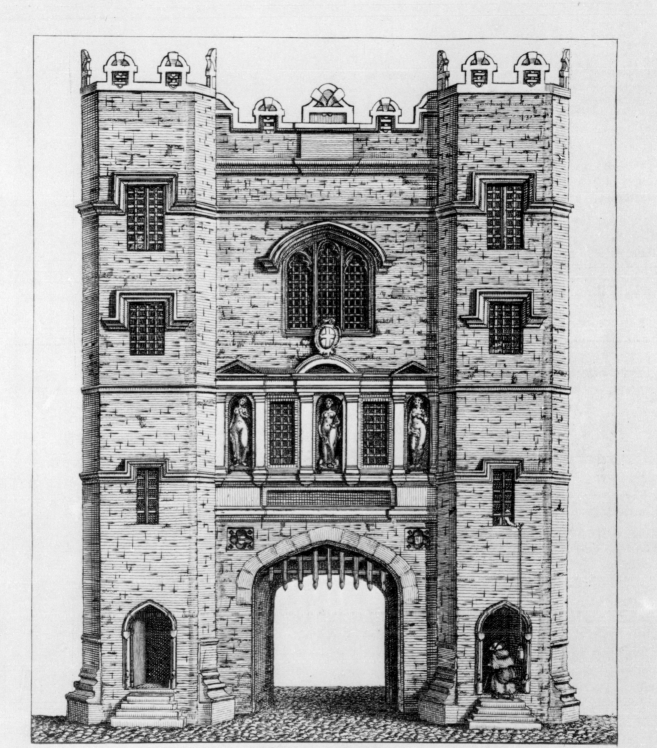

NEWGATE:

Chamberlains Gate, a most miserable Dungeon, was rebuilt by Rich.ᵈ Whittington, in the style here represented and from its newness call'd Newgate, from which Newgate Street was named. Against the west front were four emblematical figures viz. Liberty, Peace, Security, & Plenty, and on the east front were three figures Justice, Fortitude, & Prudence. this Building was destroyed in the Conflagration 1666, & again rebuilt 1672, with great magnificence though nearly on the same plan, as appears by the print given in Maitlands London. At the entire demolition of this Gate, four of the figures were put up on the south wing of the present awfull structure.

see Elstracks print of Whittington, Stow.416. Howells London, Camden.ball Maitland, p.18. Northucks London, p.609. London in Miniature.p212. Ralphs critical Review.p10. & Pennants London.

Cloathes." He was allowed no exercise until the New Year and no visitors except an elderly uncle and aunt. He was not allowed to write letters to his wife or to discuss his case with anyone or prepare his defense. He lay, old and ailing, in a total vacuum.

At the end of March 1701, Kidd was suddenly called before the House of Commons. The abrupt transition from prison to Parliament would have been difficult under the best of circumstances. Kidd did not perform well. Though some members of the House admired his courage, most found him boorish and truculent, and one thought he was drunk. What the House wanted to hear about was not Kidd's personal case but the degree of culpability of the syndicate of Whig lords who had backed him. If he had involved the Whig statesmen who had sponsored his voyage, portrayed them as villains and himself as their victim, he might have yet won a pardon from the Tories. But Kidd had no flair for political intrigue. Instead, he continued to plead his innocence, and by implication, therefore, that of the Whig ministers. "I had thought him only a knave," one member commented, "now I know him to be a fool as well." The next day the House recommended that he should "be proceeded against according to law." The trial was fixed for May 8.

Kidd had spent nearly two years in prison by the time he appeared in

Members of the House of Commons listen expectantly as Kidd (right) testifies on March 27, 1701. The Tories were hoping that he would star in their impeachment proceedings against his Whig backers. But the closest that Kidd ever came to implicating the noblemen was to say later that if he had broken the law, "it was the fault of others who knew better."

De Par le Roy

Vous François Martin Escuier Conseiller Du Roy Directeur
General du Commerce pour la Royalle Compagnie de France dans le Royaume de Bengalle Coste de Coromandelle et autres
Lieux, A TOUS CEUX qui ces presentes lettres verront, Salut Les nommés Coja Ouanesse, et Coja Jacob Armenien, Nacodas
du navire Cara marchand, que le nommé Agapiris Kalender marchand Armenien a frété a Surate du nommé Cohergy
nannabaye Parsy ledit navire du port de trois Cent Cinquante thonneaux ou environ, Sur lequel est Pilotte Rette laudel
ou Bosseman Guuaunalou et Escriuain Gasson, nous ayants remontre qu'ayants pris auant leur depart de Surate vn
passeport de la Compagnie quils nous ont represente en datte du premier Januier mil Six Cent nonante sept Signé
Martin et plus bas de Grangemont, quils aprehendoient destre Inquietez dans le voyage quils doiuent faire de ce port a
Celuy de Surate sous pretexte que ledit passeport est suranne et quasy, Ils nous pri覧ent Instemment de leur en faire
Expedier vn nouueau A CES CAUSES Recommendons et Enseignons a tous ceux qui sont sous l'authorité de la Compag.ie
Prions les Chefs D'escadres et commandans des vaisseaux de sa MAJESTE requerons tous les amis et aliez de la
Couronne de n'aporter aucun Empeschement qui puisse retarder son voyage, ains Luy donner toutes sortes d'ayde
et d'asistance, promettant en Cas pareil faire le semblable, En foy dequoy nous auons signé Ces Presentes fait
Contresigner par le Secretaire de la Compagnie et a Scellé aposer le Sceau de Ses Armes au Comptoir General D'Ougly
Le quatorzieme Januier mil Six Cent nonante huit.

Martin

Par mondit Sieur
Desprez.

Bearing the coat of arms of the French East India Company (lower left), this pass taken from the vessel Quedah Merchant was one of the documents Kidd counted on to uphold his claim that he had seized the ship as a legal privateering prize. But the pass disappeared just as Kidd went to trial. It turned up in the British Public Record Office 219 years later.

the dock at the Old Bailey. This itself was injustice enough. But it was compounded by two further injustices. In the first place, the vital pieces of evidence with which he hoped to defend himself—the French passes that had been turned over to Bellomont—were withheld from him. More dolorous still, Kidd was without any counsel until literally an hour or two before the start of the trial. The Admiralty had appropriated £50 for his defense. But whoever had mislaid the French passes now neglected to deliver the £50 to Kidd's two legal advisers until the night of May 7—and without the money they would not start work. Thus Kidd, after a two-year wait for his trial, had time for one brief consultation with his counsel on the morning before the trial began.

The trial of Captain Kidd was held before no less than six justices and consisted of four separate trials on six indictments on the 8th and 9th of May. The justices were highly talented lawmen; the juries of stalwart Londoners asked fair and pertinent questions. The court gave him, by the standards of his day, a fair trial.

But the standards of his day were grossly unfair to the accused. Kidd could not go into the witness box to testify in his own defense nor could any of his crew testify on his behalf during the piracy trials. Against the biased evidence given by the two King's witnesses, Kidd's former crew members Palmer and Bradinham, who had deserted him at Madagascar, there was therefore no riposte except cross-examination. But court procedure ordained that Kidd's counsel could not cross-examine, only Kidd himself, and the old sailor was obliged to conduct his own defense, in his own fatally clumsy way.

Not that any of this mattered much in the end. The first, shattering indictment was not for piracy at all, but for murder: the death of gunner William Moore on board the *Adventure Galley*. Kidd pleaded provocation. "I had no design to kill him," he protested. "It was not designedly done, but in my passion, for which I am heartily sorry." But he blundered about so badly in his defense that it took the jury barely an hour to return a verdict of guilty.

The outcome of the piracy indictments on the following day was academic. Kidd stood three separate trials on five counts of piracy on May 9, standing in the dock alongside the nine ex-members of his crew who were his codefendants. He was charged with the piracy of the *Quedah Merchant*, the *Maiden*, renamed the *November*, and three unnamed ships, two Moorish and one Portuguese. Kidd, railed the prosecution, "was an arch-pirate, equally cruel, dreaded and hated both on the land and at sea. No one in this age has done more mischief, in this worst kind of mischief, or has occasioned greater confusion and disorder, attended with all the circumstances of cruelty and falsehood." The two King's witnesses—again the prosecution's only witnesses—went through their doctored stories over and over again. Kidd's cross-examination was inept and could not dent the impression that the witnesses had made. He claimed the *Quedah Merchant* and the *Maiden* were lawful prizes because of the French passes and that a mutinous crew had forced him to capture the other vessels. However, he had no material witnesses to call on and no French passes to produce as evidence. In the end Kidd realized the hopelessness of his position.

"This man contradicts himself in a hundred places," Kidd complained as Bradinham gave evidence. "He tells a thousand lies."

"Will you ask him any more questions?" the Solicitor-General asked.

"No, no," Captain Kidd replied, "so long as he swears it, our words or oaths cannot be taken."

"Will you ask him any more questions?" the court clerk repeated.

"No, no. It signifies nothing," Kidd muttered. And as the trial drew to a close, he broke in:

"Mr. Bradinham, are not you promised your life to take away mine?"

The jury was out for scarcely half an hour. They found Kidd and six of his codefendants guilty. Three were acquitted.

"What canst thou say for thyself," the clerk of the court asked Kidd, "why thou shouldst not die according to law?"

"I have nothing to say," replied Kidd, "but that I have been sworn against by perjured and wicked people."

"You have been tried by the laws of the land," the clerk continued. "Nothing now remains but that sentence be passed according to the law. And the sentence of the law is this:

'You shall be taken from the place where you are, and be carried to the place from whence you came, and from thence to the place of execution,

A symbol of the Admiralty court's jurisdiction over crimes on the high seas, an ornate silver oar, such as this embossed 33-inch specimen, lay on a table in front of the judges who tried Kidd.

and there be severally hanged by your necks until you be dead. And the Lord have mercy on your souls.' "

"My Lord," said Kidd. "It is a very hard sentence. I am the innocentest person of all, only I have been sworn against by perjured people."

Bound with chains and encased in an iron framework, Kidd's body hangs as a grisly object lesson at Tilbury Point in the Thames estuary, in this 19th Century illustration. Many a sailor who turned pirate vowed to blow himself to hell rather than "be hang'd up drying, as Kidd."

When Captain Kidd was strung up for a second time at Wapping, the new rope held, and since he was a heavy man, he probably died quickly. When he had stopped twitching, the executioner cut him down and chained his body to a post and left it there until the tidal waters of the Thames had ebbed and flowed over it three times, as Admiralty law prescribed. Then the body was recovered and painted with tar and bound with chains and the head set in a metal harness so that the bones and skull would stay in place when the tissues rotted. It was hung from a gibbet specially constructed at a cost of £10 at Tilbury Point, at a place where it could be seen plainly by everyone sailing in and out of the Thames, so that it would serve, in the words of the Admiralty's final instructions regarding Captain William Kidd, "as a greater Terrour to all Persons from Committing ye like Crimes for the time to come."

No one knows for sure how long Kidd's tarred body swung there. By some accounts it was visible for years. The sun rotted it. the rain lashed at it, the frost prized it apart, the gulls pecked out the eyes. As time passed, the sensation of the Kidd case died away and the dramatis personae went their separate ways.

Only one of the six men convicted with Kidd was hanged. The other five were reprieved. Shortly after the execution, two of them, Nicholas Churchill and James Howe, after paying the Newgate jailers £315 each for their release, sailed past Kidd's gibbet en route to Pennsylvania, where they dug up £2,300 worth of Arabian gold that they had buried when they first arrived in the company of their late captain. The Crown witnesses, Palmer and Bradinham, were duly rewarded with a full pardon three days after Kidd's death. Captain Culliford, the pirate to whose ship Kidd's crew had deserted in Madagascar, was tried and convicted at the Old Bailey on the same day as Kidd but, as he had surrendered under a royal pardon, he was released after a year.

Kidd's family survived the trauma of his imprisonment and death. For two years following his arrest they lived in seclusion in New York, but 18 months after his execution his widow married a prominent politician and lived another 43 years in comfortable circumstances in New Jersey, while his daughters grew up, married and bore children of their own. As for Lord Bellomont, whose wiles had first ensnared the captain, he died nearly three months before Kidd's execution. "He wore out his spirrits," his widow complained in a letter to London, "and put an end to his life by the fatigue he underwent to serve His Majestie." The French passes that Kidd had sent to Bellomont were later discovered in their proper place—the Public Records Office in London. The gold, silver, jewels, silks and muslins from the *Quedah Merchant* were forfeited to the Crown and sold by auction for £6,472. One of the buildings that now houses the National Maritime Museum at Greenwich was bought with part of Kidd's money. Though many have looked for Captain Kidd's buried treasure, no one has ever found it, because none remains.

A brawling lair for a lawless breed

Casting about the Bahama Islands for a base of operations around the turn of the 18th Century, a pirate captain named Henry Jennings happened upon the most felicitous haven that ever met the squinting gaze of an outlaw seaman. The piratical assets of this paradise, the island of New Providence, were immediately apparent. The waters of its snug harbor were a perfect depth—too shallow for large men-of-war, but deep enough for the more nimble shallow-draft craft favored by pirates. The high coral hills that ringed the harbor afforded a hawk's view of an approaching enemy or a potential prize. The reefs abounded with conch, lobster, fish and turtles, while the well-wooded interior of the island contained bubbling fresh-water springs and a bounty of wild pigs, pigeons and fruit.

Jennings happily dropped anchor at New Providence, and others of his persuasion soon followed in his wake. By 1710, a brigand community was thriving on the island. There were perhaps 400 or 500 families living scattered throughout the Bahamas at that time, the remnants of sporadic British attempts to colonize the place. But these settlers posed no threat at all to the pirates and in fact welcomed them for the goods they brought.

When the pirates were not out preying on merchantmen in the coastwise and European trade routes just a short sail away, or converting their prizes into pirate raiders, they debauched themselves in Nassau, the seamy tent town that festered on the white sand beach and coral outcroppings by the harbor. There was no law in Nassau except that of the fist and cutlass. In numerous taverns that were virtually the only permanent buildings, pirates boozed and fought their way into oblivion. They lolled with prostitutes in tents of tattered sail or gambled away fortunes they knew they could replace in yet another foray out to sea.

In that port a pirate felt truly unfettered; he was cut from the moorings of social constraint. Thus originated a saying of those times—that when a pirate slept he did not dream that he had died and gone to heaven, he dreamed that he had once again returned to New Providence.

In the outlaw harbor of New Providence, a pirate raider (center) lowers her sails as she enters an anchorage choked with single-masted sloops, two-masted brigantines and captured three-masted merchant ships. A tender returns to the beach after ferrying out casks of water and crates of food, while beyond, pirate-traders in a small, unarmed, single-masted vessel furl a sail after anchoring. Atop the crumbling limestone fort, a relic of an English settlement, two brigands mount a watch beside a nine-pound cannon now used only to salute comrades or signal danger.

Under a tropical sun that put extra wallop in their rum and heightened the stench of their refuse, New Providence residents —pirates, whores and traders —laze away another day. A mongrel (center) inspects a trio of besotted louts felled by rum, gin and wine from nearby casks, while a pirate cook barbecues a goat on a spit. A lean-to made of driftwood and sail provides a crude shelter, and behind it, two gamblers play dice under the amused gaze of a spectator and his current lady. Across the cove (upper right), a pirate ship is being careened amid the rotting hulks of unwanted vessels used to outfit the raiders' ships.

As a captured square-rigger (rear) glides into New Providence, a pirate crew busily converts a similar three-masted prize into a fighting-man's brigantine. To increase her fighting capacity and speed, the pirates have lopped off her fo'c's'le, pilot's cabin and much of her quarter-deck and railing. Her mizzenmast has been removed and a work gang is straining at the capstan to move her mainmast aft for rerigging with fore-and-aft sails. Other pirates are adding swivel guns and cutting ports for 16 more cannon and holes for oars. Finally, the mermaid figurehead has been replaced by a seahorse to mask the ship's original identity.

Her mainmast toppled by a broadside, a merchant ship wallows in the swells off New Providence as her outnumbered crew fights to repel a pirate boarding party. On the fo'c's'le, a sailor desperately scrambles away from a smoldering keg of gunpowder (upper left) deliberately ignited to explode in the faces of the onrushing pirates. Aboard the pirate sloop, the crewmen are heaving across grappling irons, grenades and sulfurous stink bombs as they continue to blast away with cannon and swivel guns. All the while, pirate bandsmen (right) are adding to the terror of the scene with blaring trumpet and hammering drum.

Richard Schlecht

The terrible Teach and his nemesis

nest of pirates are endeavouring to establish themselves in New Providence," Governor Spotswood of Virginia reported to the British government in July 1716, "and by the additions they expect and will probably receive, may prove dangerous to the British commerce, if not timely suppressed." One of the pirate ringleaders, the Governor added, was a pirate captain by the name of Thomas Barrow. "He is the 'Governor' of Providence and will make it a second Madagascar."

Governor Spotswood's report was well founded—if sorely understated. The pirates had already established themselves on New Providence Island in the Bahamas. The place had attracted the greatest concentration of pirates ever seen in the New World—more than 2,000, distributed among brigantines and sloops in the harbor and in the pirate shantytown on land. The gutted wrecks of some 40 captured ships lay moldering on the beaches. There were no laws. New Providence, in short, was a pirate paradise—as Governor Spotswood had said, a second Madagascar.

From the pirate point of view the new sanctuary had been set up none too soon. Their bases on the original Madagascar had ceased to exist some years before. Even as Captain Kidd was languishing in Newgate prison, a Royal Navy squadron of four warships had arrived off St. Mary's and cruised around Madagascar for the better part of a year: in the face of this force, the pirates had surrendered or fled. Incredibly, for such reputedly fearsome brigands, not a shot was fired during the entire time. The pirates just melted away. Within a year no Red Sea pirates were left—nor any Pirate Round for that matter. After disposing so implacably of Kidd, Lord Bellomont had shut the pirates out of New York and driven them from New England. Virginia's Governor Francis Nicholson had forced them from his colony as well. By 1701, to all intents and purposes, piracy was in collapse. When the War of the Spanish Succession broke out that year—England on one side, France and Spain on the other—the pirates flocked to join the privateers of the British irregular navy.

For almost a decade, piracy was virtually unheard of. Then, in 1713, the war came to an end. Just as the outbreak of hostilities had drained the pirate pool, so the cessation of hostilities flooded it again. Many of the younger seamen on the privateers had known no business other than the legal plundering of enemy shipping. Unemployment forced them one step further, to the illegal plundering of all shipping. But this time, with Madagascar and most North American ports still denied to them, the pirates poured into the safe and immensely profitable Caribbean.

The Bahamas, where they made their base, were not strictly speaking part of the Caribbean at all. A far-flung archipelago of dozens of low-lying islands facing the open Atlantic, the Bahamas were Columbus' first landfall in the New World. But they had remained undeveloped, with only a scattering of English colonists. Their one value, it seemed, was to pirates: their location made them an ideal base from which to prey on the heavy volume of shipping that passed through the Gulf of Florida on the sea-lanes between the Spanish Main, the West Indian colonies and the ports of Europe and North America. Pirate ships based in the Bahamas had no need to emulate the prodigious transoceanic voyages of their pirate roundsmen predecessors. They needed only to lurk in wait for

Garbed entirely in black, the demonic Edward Teach, better known as Blackbeard, flourishes a saber while his men plunder a hapless merchantman in this engraving from Defoe's "History of the most notorious Pyrates." Blackbeard was known even to his crew as "the devil incarnate," and gloried in his image.

their prey among the shoals, bays, reefs and tricky channels, where their small, shallow-draft sloops and brigantines could safely anchor but where no ponderous man-of-war could ever sail, or, alternatively, they could put out from their lairs on short-haul pirate cruises to the Atlantic Coast of America or the Caribbean islands of the West Indies.

In recent years, the Bahamas had fallen on particularly hard times. During the War of Spanish Succession, fierce fighting had erupted in and around the Caribbean. The Spanish and French sacked and burned Nassau with such regularity that the British finally abandoned their useless colony. When the war ended in 1713, they did not move back to rebuild. In their place came the pirates.

By 1715, led by such captains as Thomas Barrow, Charles Vane, Benjamin Hornigold, Thomas Burgess and the fearsome Edward Teach, otherwise known as Blackbeard, the New Providence pirates were ravaging shipping from Florida clear north to Maine. In another year, they were ranging south throughout the West Indies. So desperate was the situation in July 1717 that the Governor of Bermuda complained bitterly, "North and South America are infested with these rogues." Trade in the Caribbean was almost paralyzed; ships could leave Jamaica only in convoy under naval escort. Insurance rates were astronomical. Whatever else one might say about them, Blackbeard and his mates on New Providence were remarkably good at their job. The prizes were not so big as in the Eastern Seas, but there were a lot more of them.

"There is hardly one ship or vessel coming in or going out of this island that is not plundered," complained the Governor of Jamaica. He went on to give a very cogent reason why nothing was done to stop it. "This in great measure I impute to the neglect of the Commanders of His Majesty's ships of war." The Navy was not coping with the pirates in part because its ships were so chronically undermanned through sickness, death and desertion that they often had to remain in port for eight months of the year. But there was another reason: the Navy men in the Caribbean had little interest in suppressing piracy since they themselves had learned to profit handsomely from it.

By Admiralty law, Navy commanders were allowed to charge 12½ per cent of the value of the cargo they were escorting on convoy duty. When a merchant complained about the resulting freight charges, the Navy commanders offered a sub rosa deal: they would transport the goods in their own ships and charge less than cargo vessels. This was illegal, of course, but profitable to most of those concerned. The pirates did not attack the Navy-escorted convoys and the Navy did not attack the pirates, who were thus free to concentrate on unprotected shipping.

Naturally, there were some losers in all of this. First came the cargo ships that lost the business—and were then robbed by the unhindered pirates. Then there were the uncooperative merchants, who paid high rates and received no protection. But perhaps the greatest losers were the governors of the West Indian colonies. They had learned to their sorrow that there was nothing to be gained from the Nassau pirates. The pirates were bringing neither bribes for them nor trade goods for their islands; instead they were plundering the vessels on which the economy of the governors' islands—and ultimately the governors' jobs—depended. The

A small contingent of plunderers, dispatched upriver by privateer Captain Woodes Rogers, politely requires the distraught señoritas of Guayaquil, Ecuador, to surrender their hidden gold chains or submit to a frisking during a raid on the Spanish colonial port in 1709

governors complained bitterly to London. The Admiralty responded with more men-of-war—whose captains were soon at the same game.

Next, the governors asked London to take action against the pirates' nest on New Providence. Nothing was done. Finally, a syndicate of English merchants stepped into the picture, promising to solve the problem. This syndicate leased the Bahamas from the Crown with a view to settling and pacifying the islands, and petitioned the King to appoint as governor the outstanding sea captain of the day, Woodes Rogers.

Woodes Rogers was in his late 30s at the time, and one of the unsung heroes of British Naval history. Born in Dorset about 1679 and apprenticed to the sea as a youth, Rogers had commanded two privateers that had sailed round the world between 1708 and 1711 during the War of the Spanish Succession. Upon his return he was carrying captured Spanish treasure to the value of £800,000—his plunder from the sacking of Guayaquil, in South America, and the capture, off Mexico, of the fabulous Manila galleon, the annual Spanish treasure ship from the Philippines. After paying off his backers, Rogers received only £1,600—a sum considerably less than his debts. But such misfortune did not deter the faithful captain in his pursuit of imperial glory.

Subsequently, Rogers became obsessed with the idea of establishing British settlements to promote trade in the more remote oceans. And it was this grand design that grew into the plan to develop the Bahamas.

The Board of Trade was impressed with Rogers' enterprising proposals. The Secretary of War promised him 100 foot soldiers for the garrison. The Admiralty volunteered an escort of warships. And in the autumn of 1717, the Crown appointed Rogers "Captain-General and Governor-in-Chief in and over our Bahama Islands in America." He was given a commission to wipe out the pirates in any way he chose and permission to establish a plantation colony of some 250 European farmers—Swiss, Huguenots and German Protestant refugees from the Palatinate—in the cutthroats' place. He was supplied with stores, materials and tools, and he received £2.10s. worth of tracts from the Society for Promoting Christian Knowledge (S.P.C.K.) to convert the pirates from their wicked ways. But, alas, he was offered no salary, only a share in any profits that the new plantation colony might make.

All through the winter of 1717 Rogers hastened to get his expedition ready. There were now so many seagoing brigands prowling the Caribbean that the pirates increasingly were forced to sail north, where they lay in wait for cargo boats moving in and out of the North American ports. "The pirates continue to rove on these seas," wrote the Governor of New England, "and if a sufficient force is not sent to drive them off our trade must stop." If Rogers had a plan for dealing with this growing crisis, he kept it to himself. Obviously, he lacked sufficient force to fight the pirates at sea off North American ports. His options were limited to what he could do to them on Nassau, and that would likely depend on what he found when he got there.

At last, on April 11, 1718, Rogers set sail down the River Thames in the 460-ton ex-East Indiaman *Delicia* at the start of his great enterprise. In the Thames estuary he was joined by the convoy squadron of Royal Navy warships—the frigates *Milford* and *Rose*, the sloops *Buck* and *Shark*.

The voyage out took three months, but finally on July 24, the little fleet anchored outside the bar of the pirate harbor at Nassau. Soon after, some of the original English colonists rowed out from nearby Harbour Island. There were about 1,000 pirates presently in Nassau, they told Rogers. And—astonishing news—the majority, having heard that an expedition was making for New Providence, would probably forswear piracy in exchange for a king's pardon. A number of the worst criminals, most notably the hard-core Blackbeard, had decamped to other bases.

Nevertheless, a few other pirates, led by Charles Vane, intended to resist, and they would have to be dealt with. The truth of this soon became evident. The Navy warships *Rose* and *Shark*, with pilots on board, edged into the harbor to reconnoiter. The silence of the Bahamas night was suddenly shattered by a series of explosions, and flames leaped high into the darkness. It was Vane's defiant welcome to Rogers. The pirate captain had loaded a recently captured French prize with explosives, set her ablaze, then cut her loose to drift, fizzing and booming, as a fire ship against the *Rose*. The captain of the *Rose* was forced to run out to sea to avoid this floating inferno. The *Shark* followed.

At dawn Vane ran up the flag of St. George from his main topmast head

When pirates were in the employ of kings

At the turn of the 18th Century, just as the pirates were coming under heavy pressure from the Royal Navy in American and Eastern waters, an event in far-off Spain galvanized the attention of every European maritime power—and for a while gave the pirates assurance of gainful legal employment. The event was the death in November 1700 of King Charles II of Spain, whose disputed will touched off the War of the Spanish Succession. During that conflagration, pirates turned legitimate and became privateers—more or less official Naval auxiliaries whose job was to prey on the enemy's merchant vessels.

Charles had died childless, leaving a vast empire that included territories in Italy and the Netherlands, as well as New World holdings that stretched from the West Indies to the Philippines. In his will, he named as sole heir the grandson of France's Louis XIV, who ascended the Spanish throne as Philip V. But England and the Netherlands backed a rival claimant to the throne, Archduke Charles of Austria. Before long, practically all Europe was at war—England, the Netherlands and Austria, together with Sweden, Denmark, Prussia and the Savoy, in grand alliance against France, Spain and Bavaria.

In May 1702, England's Queen Anne issued a proclamation authorizing private shipowners to seize enemy vessels, and a number of ships were immediately fitted out as privateers. Naturally, given such a license to plunder, many pirates hastened to sign up. For one thing, by doing so they would be exempt from impressment into the exceedingly harsh life of the Royal Navy. For another, they stood a good chance of earning enlistment bonuses.

Between 1704 and 1707, a fleet of 13 privateers operating out of the port of New York captured or destroyed 36 enemy vessels—with a huge profit of £60,000. The price was high, however; by the end of 1707, the colony's privateering fleet had suffered the loss of 260 men in fights with French, Spanish and other enemy ships. Nevertheless, enthusiasm for privateering remained undiminished—especially after 1708, when Parliament renounced its 10 per cent claim to all prizes taken. In the course of the war, British and American colonial privateers captured more than 2,000 prizes, most of them French. There is no record of the value of the total haul, but it was in the millions.

In spite of the heavy inroads made on enemy shipping by privateers, the war itself was decided on land in a series of bloody struggles, commencing with the Battle of Blenheim, in which the Duke of Marlborough dealt France its first military defeat in 40 years. Under the Peace of Utrecht in 1713, Philip V remained on the throne of Spain, but lost his holdings in the Netherlands. France, its economy shattered, yielded to England the dominance of Europe. As for the privateers, the need for these semiofficial commerce raiders vanished as swiftly as it had arisen. Their crews promptly returned to piracy—they performed the identical work, but once again were outside the law.

The Duke of Marlborough accepts the French surrender at the 1704 Battle of Blenheim, where 40,000 Frenchmen were killed or captured.

and the black pirate flag at his mizzen, fired a gun in derisory salute, crowded on sail and, with his vessel loaded with plunder, threaded his way through the eastern narrows to the open sea. The *Rose* and the *Shark* were out of position to intercept him; the sloop *Buck* followed out through the channel in pursuit but was soon left behind as Vane made good his escape. Later he sent word that he would return and burn the *Delicia* in revenge for Rogers' having sent two ships against him. For the next three years he was to remain at large as a constant threat to the security of the embryo colony and to Rogers' peace of mind.

But Vane was the only pirate leader on Nassau to make an open show of defiance. On the morning of July 27, when Governor Rogers finally set foot on Bahamian soil, it was to a flabbergasting reception. There, drawn up in two lines under their leaders—Hornigold, Burgess and others—was a ludicrous honor guard of some 300 dirty, boozy and unkempt pirates firing ragged volleys of musketry over his head and shouting loud huzzas for King George.

Beneath the crumbling ramparts of a small fort, Rogers stopped and turned to address the populace he proposed to rule: the pirates, the pirate traders, the camp followers and adventuresses, the ragged settlers of New Providence. Unrolling his scrolls with a flourish, he shouted out the words of the commission appointing him governor of the Bahamas and the terms of the Royal Proclamation of Pardon. Then, with a dignity befitting His Britannic Majesty's representative in these neglected is-

Frisky dancers caper in front of a blazing bonfire and the spirits flow as fast as the fiddler's tune, while Blackbeard's and Charles Vane's crews revel far into the night on North Carolina's Ocracoke Island in 1718. The saturnalia was one of the largest gatherings of pirates ever held on the mainland of North America.

lands, Rogers was sworn in, while the hairy pirates gawked and their ships rode motionless upon the glassy sea.

Rogers was, in theory, lord of all he surveyed. It did not add up to much. There were virtually no permanent buildings in Nassau. Inside the dilapidated fort there was nothing but a single little hut, and that was inhabited by a mad old eccentric whom the pirates in derision called Governor Sawney. The roads were so overgrown with bushes that an entire invasion force could have hidden in ambush behind them. There was scarcely any agriculture. Rogers' position was most insecure. So long as the four Navy warships remained in the harbor he could use the threat of force to keep the pirates in order. But the warships would not stay there forever. There was no time to lose.

The Governor brought his little band of soldiers ashore and lodged them in crude palm-thatched huts inside the walls of the fort. Outside the fort he housed his settlers in tents rigged up from the spare sails of the *Delicia*. He issued pardons to as many pirates as wanted them—the number eventually totaled 600—while to the waverers he handed out free S.P.C.K. tracts. To persuade reformed pirates to settle down, he offered each man a free plot of land, on condition that he clear the ground and build a house on it within a year, which some of them did. He set up a civil council, and he appointed those who had sailed with him and the most reliable of Nassau's raggle-taggle colonists "who had not been pirates, and were of good repute" to the council and to the posts of Secretary General, Chief Justice, Admiralty judge, provost marshal, justices of the peace, constables and overseers of the ways and roads. From among the citizens and ex-pirates of New Providence he raised three militia companies for defense of the island, while for the defense of Bahamian waters he appointed two pardoned pirate captains—Hornigold and Burgess—as privateer commanders, a shrewd move that nonplused the other pirates. Overlooking the eastern entrance to the harbor Rogers built a small eight-gun redoubt, and he set to work to rebuild the main fort guarding the western entrance. He had now taken the necessary first steps toward the pacification and settlement of the island. All seemed remarkably well. But all was not.

New Providence that summer was particularly hot and unhealthy. Before long an epidemic of fever (attributed by some to the rotting hides of cattle slaughtered for food) had broken out. Scores of the immigrants died, and so did many of the sailors on the warships. The epidemic was a double blow to the Governor. In the first place, the deaths of so many of the immigrants robbed him of his more skilled farmers and artisans and shattered his chances of founding a self-sufficient plantation colony. Worse still, three of the four warships departed. The *Milford* had prior orders to proceed to the Leeward Islands. The crew of the *Shark* was suffering horribly from the mysterious fever, and her captain decided to put to sea before they all succumbed. The sloop *Buck* sailed away with them. Only the *Rose* remained, but her commander was so edgy and insubordinate that Rogers, to enforce his orders, pistol-whipped him on one occasion. Finally (and not surprisingly), even the *Rose* sailed away for more lucrative convoy duties in the Caribbean.

As autumn approached, more and more of the pardoned pirates left

Nassau to resume their old ways, and soon Governor Rogers' position had deteriorated alarmingly. A new war between England and Spain looked increasingly likely, and with it an attack on Nassau by Spanish forces from Cuba. Against these mounting threats, Rogers—himself physically weakened by fever—had only the *Delicia* as guard ship. The militia of ex-pirates was next to useless. "These wretches can't be kept to watch at night," Rogers reported, "and when they do they come very seldom sober, and rarely awake all night, though our officers or soldiers very often surprise their guard and carry off their arms, and I punish, fine, or confine them almost every day." Desperate but undaunted, the Governor of the Bahamas struggled to hold the old pirate base of New Providence in daily expectation of attack, either by the Spanish or by its former pirate inhabitants.

As events in the next months proved, Rogers need not have worried about a mass invasion by the pirates. However fearsome, pirates as a group tended to take the course of least resistance, and few of those who had sailed away, either before or after Rogers' arrival, ever returned to face Nassau's feisty Governor. Charles Vane, one of the men Rogers was most concerned about, came to grief early in 1719, when his vessel was wrecked on an uninhabited island in the Bay of Honduras. Rescued from starvation by a passing ship, he was recognized and later hanged in Jamaica. A second, even more worrisome onetime Nassau pirate was Edward Teach, alias Blackbeard. But he had found a new base and rich pickings along the American coast, where his depredations spawned a legend that made him, along with Captain Kidd, the best-known piratical figure in all history. Indeed as news of Blackbeard filtered back to Nassau he was to cause Rogers trouble in absentia.

Unlike the fumbling, feckless Kidd, Blackbeard was the pirate supreme, perfectly cast for his role and reveling in every bloodcurdling aspect of it. Other pirates—John Taylor, Henry Every, Bartholomew Roberts—may have captured more booty. But no other pirate so closely fitted the public's image of what a real pirate should be. Indeed, Blackbeard, the terror of the American coast, was a master of psychology and consciously tailored his already outsized personality to suit the peculiar requirements of his profession.

Blackbeard's background, like that of most pirates, is obscure. Even his real name is shrouded in mystery. In the official records he is called Teach. But contemporary accounts usually give his name as Thatch, or sometimes Tach, Tatch or Tash. Such names may have been as much an alias as Blackbeard. According to Defoe his real name was Edward Drummond, and he was born in Bristol (others say Virginia or Jamaica). He appears to have learned the skills of his trade on board a British privateer in the West Indies during the War of the Spanish Succession. When that was ended in 1713, Edward Drummond drifted into piracy.

Under the tutelage of Benjamin Hornigold on New Providence, Drummond soon distinguished himself as a natural pirate leader—tall, enormously strong, wild and brave. At some point, he changed his name to Teach and in late 1716 was given command of his own ship, a French vessel captured off St. Vincent in the West Indies. More than a year later,

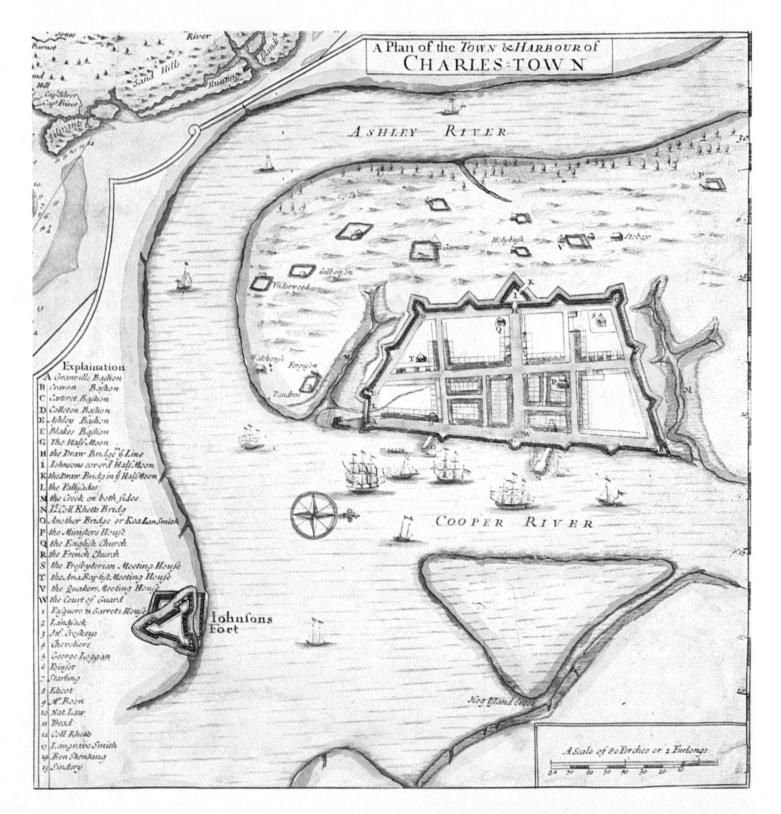

A Plan of the *Town* & *HARBOUR* of
CHARLES=TOWN

A S H L E Y   R I V E R

COOPER RIVER

Explaination
A *Granville Bastion*
B *Craven   Bastion*
C *Carteret Bastion*
D *Colleton Bastion*
E *Ashley Bastion*
F *Blakes Bastion*
G *The Half Moon*
H *the Draw Bridge & Line*
I *Johnsons cover'd Half Moon*
K *the Draw Bridg in y Half Moon*
L *the Pallisades*
M *the Creek on both sides*
N *Lt Coll Rhetts Bridg*
O *Another Bridge or Rea Lan Smith*
P *the Ministers House*
Q *the English Church*
R *the French Church*
S *the Presbyterian Meeting House*
T *the Ana Baptist Meeting House*
V *the Quakers Meeting House*
W *the Court of Guard*
1 *Vasquero & Garrets House*
2 *Lainejack*
3 *Jn. Croskeys*
4 *Chevetiers*
5 *George Loggan*
6 *Pinfet*
7 *Starling*
8 *Elicot*
9 *Mr Boon*
10 *Nat Law*
11 *Tread*
12 *Coll Rhett*
13 *Langrave Smith*
14 *Ben Skenking*
15 *Sindery*

Iohnsons Fort

Hog Island Creek

A Scale of 80 Porches or 2 Furlongs

Pennant-dressed merchant vessels dot the harbor of prosperous
Charleston, South Carolina, which Blackbeard blockaded in
May 1718. Upon the appearance of the pirates the frightened men
of Charleston, expecting a full-scale attack, frantically armed
themselves, observed a contemporary chronicler, while
"the Women and Children run about the Street like made Things."

when word of the Royal Pardon Rogers was bringing reached Nassau, he had already renamed his ship the *Queen Anne's Revenge*, mounted 40 guns on her, and sailed out of Nassau on the cruise that was to turn him into the stuff of folklore.

Teach's beard was the single most important element in the mystique that came to surround him. This beard, wrote Defoe, "like a frightful Meteor, covered his whole Face, and frightened America more than any Comet that has appeared there for a long Time." It was, of course, a black beard, and from it Teach took the name by which he came to be known. It was also—because he never trimmed it—very bushy and very long, reaching down to his chest in one direction and up to his eyes in the other. To emphasize the impact of this horrendous growth, Teach would plait the beard into little tails; some of these tails he festooned with colored ribbons, and others he trained back over his ears.

Before he went into battle he stuck lighted matches under his hat. They were long, slow-burning affairs made of hemp cord dipped in saltpeter and limewater. The effect was terrifying. His face, with its fierce eyes and matted hair, was wreathed in smoke, and he looked to his prey like a fiend from hell. His resemblance to some kind of piratical demon was completed by a bandolier with three braces of pistols, loaded, primed and cocked for firing, and by the additional pistols, daggers and cutlass he carried in a wide belt around his waist.

Blackbeard's temperament was of a piece with his appearance. He was a prodigious drinker, like his crew. A fragment of a journal, said to be his, gives an idea of their dependence on liquor:

"Such a Day—Rum all out:—Our Company somewhat sober: Rogues a plotting;—great Talk of Separation:—So I look'd Sharp for a Prize."

This entry was followed by another, after Blackbeard had successfully captured a merchant ship and replenished his store of spirits:

"Such a Day took one, with a great deal of Liquor on board, so kept the Company hot, damn'd hot, then all Things went well again."

Everything about Blackbeard was larger than life. Contemporary accounts credit him with having bigamously married 14 women, the latest aged 16. She, poor girl, after spending the night with Blackbeard was sometimes forced to spend the day with four or five of his crew; according to Defoe, "he would force her to prostitute her self to them all, one after another, before his Face."

Blackbeard was impetuous, violently competitive and desperately determined to win at everything. One day at sea, related Defoe, Blackbeard suddenly yelled out to his crew that they should make a "Hell of our own and try how long we can bear it." Two or three crewmen accepted the challenge and they all went down into the hold. There they seated themselves on the large stones used as ballast, and Blackbeard ordered several pots of brimstone to be brought down. Then the hatches were closed and the brimstone set on fire. The men sat there in the dark while the hold filled with dense sulfurous fumes. The hatches were opened only when the half-suffocated crewmen cried out for air. Blackbeard, recounted Defoe, was "not a little pleased that he held out the longest." When he came up on deck one of the crew cried out: "Why, Captain, you look as if you were coming straight from the gallows." "My lad," roared Black-

Clutching a farewell nosegay, Stede Bonnet dances the jig of death in the crowded port of Charleston. Bonnet had futilely pleaded for a pardon and in frenzied despair had written the Governor that if reprieved he would make himself incapable of resuming piratical life by "separating all my Limbs from my Body, only reserving the Use of my Tongue, to call continually on, and pray to the Lord."

beard, "the next time we shall play at gallows and see who can swing longest on the string without being throttled."

Blackbeard's unpredictable violence kept his crew in wary subjection. One night, drinking in his cabin with his navigator, Israel Hands, and another crew member, Blackbeard surreptitiously drew two pistols under the table. The other crew member saw this and went up on deck. Hands stayed drinking at the table, however. Suddenly Blackbeard cocked the pistols, blew out the candle and fired. Hands was shot in the knee and crippled for life. When Blackbeard was asked why he had done such a thing, he replied that if he did not now and then kill one of his crew, they would forget who he was.

Such was the man who terrorized shipping along the Atlantic Coast in 1718. And for a time, he had an ally in no less a personage than the Governor of North Carolina. Though most of the colonies had by now turned against piracy in favor of legitimate business, North Carolina was poor and without any appreciable export trade. As Governor Charles Eden and the member of his Council soon made clear, pirates were still welcome there. In January 1718, Eden granted Blackbeard and his crew a pardon under the current Act of Grace in return for a share of his loot, then allowed him to sail off on a foray. Blackbeard openly camped and careened his vessel in the Cape Fear and Pamlico rivers. With the Governor's tacit approval, he boldly sold his merchandise at cut-rate prices direct to the public in the Pamlico River town of Bath.

In the spring of 1718, Blackbeard brazenly blockaded Charleston, capital of the neighboring colony of South Carolina. In the space of a week, he seized eight or nine ships sailing in or out of the harbor. He held Samuel Wragg, a member of the Governor's Council, and his four-year-old son as hostages. He threatened to kill them, send their heads to Governor Robert Johnson and, in the words of the Governor's report, "burn the ships that lay before the town and beat it about our ears" unless the Governor sent Blackbeard urgently needed medical supplies. The Governor complied with a chest containing £300 or £400 worth of medicines—probably mercurial drugs for the treatment of syphilis.

In the 18 months since leaving Nassau, Blackbeard had taken more than 20 prizes in a cruise that had carried him as far north as Virginia and as far south as Honduras. Some of his prizes he kept, and by June 1718 he was in command of a sizable fleet consisting of four ships, several small tenders and some 400 men. Among the ships' captains under his overall command was Major Stede Bonnet, one of the oddest pirate leaders afloat. According to the all-knowing Defoe, the major "fitted out a Sloop with ten Guns and 70 Men, entirely at his own Expence." No other pirate had ever bought his own ship, so it was no wonder that his acquaintances believed that Bonnet's "Humour of going a Pyrating, proceeded from a Disorder of his Mind."

Moreover, Major Bonnet, like Captain Kidd before him, was that rarity in the pirate community, a "gentleman." He came from a good family, was well educated, had served honorably in the recent war, retired from the Army with the rank of major and settled down on his estate on the Caribbean island of Barbados. Why Bonnet should have turned common pirate is a mystery. Defoe says it was because his wife was a shrew and

Blackbeard's nemesis, Virginia Governor Alexander Spotswood, avenged a score of plundered Virginia vessels when he dispatched a naval force to the Carolinas to destroy the pirate and his crew. The feisty Spotswood footed the bill for outfitting the expedition while the antagonistic legislature wasted time bickering over an appropriation.

nagged him—which seems as good a reason as any. Knowing little of nautical matters, the major bumbled about the high seas in amateur fashion until he was taken under the command of Blackbeard, with whom he remained for a number of months.

Eventually, in the summer of 1718, Bonnet went off on his own again. But he did not last long. That autumn he was captured with 30 of his men in the Cape Fear River after a battle with two sloops dispatched by the Governor of South Carolina. He was taken to Charleston and escaped, but then was recaptured, tried and executed in November 1718. Defoe notes that he made an impassioned plea for his life to the Governor and impressed "the People of the Province, particularly the Women," with his "piteous Behaviour under Sentence."

Blackbeard did not outlive him by long. Overconfident, perhaps, because of their connection with North Carolina's Eden, he and his men began to outstay their welcome. Their loutish behavior in the streets upset the respectable burghers of Bath, who only wanted the pirate trade—not the pirates themselves. Before long they commenced plundering any trading sloop that came down the coastal rivers.

Governor Eden still took no action against Blackbeard. But Alexander Spotswood, the strong-minded Governor of the neighboring colony of Virginia, detested pirates in general and Blackbeard in particular. What is more, Governor Spotswood had the use of two men-of-war, H.M.S. *Pearl* and H.M.S. *Lyme*, stationed as guard ships in the James River. In the fall of 1718 Spotswood received word that Blackbeard, now sailing in a sloop called the *Adventure*, had entered North Carolina's Ocracoke Inlet along with a captured vessel. The report continued that the pirate was planning to build a fortress onshore and establish a big base there. Spotswood decided to act, even though it meant usurping the authority of North Carolina's Governor.

Spotswood sent a secret agent into Carolina to acquire details of Blackbeard's personal habits and professional methods and to bring back a couple of coastal pilots who knew the inshore waters. The Governor then conferred with the warship captains on tactics against the pirates in Ocracoke. The men-of-war drew too much water to navigate in the shallow Carolina sounds, so it was agreed that Spotswood was to provide more suitable vessels, and the Navy captains would provide the crews.

As an incentive for the Naval seamen, Spotswood persuaded the Virginia Assembly to post a reward of £100 for the capture of Blackbeard, £40 for any other pirate captains, £20 for pirate lieutenants, masters or quartermasters, boatswains and carpenters, and £10 for ordinary pirate seamen. But he formulated the actual plans to send an expedition after Blackbeard in utmost secret. He did not even let his Council know what was going on "for fear of Blackbeard's having intelligence, there being in this country an unaccountable inclination to favour pirates."

At 3 p.m. on November 17, two shallow-draft sloops procured by Spotswood set sail, one with 35 men under Lieutenant Robert Maynard of H.M.S. *Pearl* and the other with 25 men under Midshipman Baker of H.M.S. *Lyme*. By late afternoon on the 21st, the Navy men had Ocracoke in sight. Some distance up the Inlet they spied two sloops at anchor. One was Blackbeard's *Adventure*, the other the captured merchant prize. The

A brace of hellcats for Calico Jack

Before they were captured in 1720, pirates Anne Bonny (left) and Mary Read cut a bloody swath through the Caribbean.

Howling like banshees, the pirate pair came raging out of the cannon smoke, flashing their cutlasses and singeing the air with shrill oaths and curses. Not one of their mates in Captain Jack Rackam's pirate crew swarming aboard the hapless merchantman off Jamaica that October day in 1720 was putting on a more terrifying show. Yet there was something curious about these two hellions in jackets and long pants. An alert female passenger aboard the merchantman spotted it. "By the largeness of their Breasts," said Dorothy Thomas later, "I believed them to be women."

That they were, and a month later, when Rackam and his crew were captured, Mrs. Thomas testified against the women. In the transcript of the trial, the two murderous Amazons charged with "Piracies, Robberies, and Felonies" were identified as "Mary Read, and Ann Bonny, late of the Island of *Providence* Spinsters." The transcript records their crimes at sea, including an attempt to have Mrs. Thomas killed (she escaped with the aid of some of the men). But the record makes no mention of where these two wildcats came from, or how they turned pirate.

Anne was born in Ireland, the illegitimate child of a prominent lawyer, William Cormac, and Peg Brennan, the family maid. The scandal attending Anne's birth caused her father to leave for Charleston, South Carolina, taking his paramour and daughter. Starting anew as a merchant, he amassed a handsome fortune and Anne had many suitors when she reached marriageable age—13 or 14 in those days—despite tales of her temper, which included one about stabbing a servant girl with a table knife. Though the stories were exaggerated, Anne was fierce enough; when one young buck tried to rape her, she thrashed him soundly.

Eventually, Anne married a penniless ne'er-do-well by the name of James Bonny, who whisked her off to the pirates' lair of New Providence in the Bahamas. Bonny tried to support his new wife by turning informer when Governor Woodes Rogers arrived to clear out the pirates. Naturally, Anne recoiled in disgust. Before long she had transferred her affections to the swaggering Calico Jack Rackam, who had suspended his piratical activities for a royal pardon.

Rackam courted Anne lavishly, buying her flashy baubles in the Bahamas. He even offered to purchase the lady herself—divorce by sale was common then, though not strictly legal. James Bonny not only refused the offer; he ran to the Governor, who threatened to have Anne flogged if she did not return to her husband. But Anne would not crawl back meekly to a man she hated. Instead she and Rackam resolved to run away—and go a-pirating together.

As luck would have it, a merchant sloop renowned as the fastest in the Caribbean lay anchored in Nassau harbor. Anne slipped aboard and determined the number of crewmen on guard and the hour the watch changed. At midnight, Anne, Rackam and a handful of his old cronies quietly boarded the sloop. Dressed as a sailor, with a sword in one hand, a pistol in the other, Anne surprised the two men on watch, and told them she would "blow out your brains" if they offered the slightest resistance. The guards made not a sound, and in no time the sloop was beating out to sea and Anne was free at last of her groveling husband.

Anne and Rackam became, if not the scourge of the Caribbean, at least a major nuisance there—plundering coastal traders and even fishing boats. Like all pirate captains, Rackam pressed skilled sailors from captured vessels to fill out his crew. One such hand was a handsome young sailor from a Dutch ship. Anne Bonny took a liking to the Dutch boy—and then discovered, much to her dismay, that the youth was in truth neither Dutch nor a boy, but a young Englishwoman named Mary Read.

Mary, like Anne, had been born out of wedlock. Her masquerade began when her mother disguised her in the clothing of a recently deceased son in order to deceive her relatives. The ruse worked, and Mary herself perpetuated the fraud. Later she entered the King's service as a cabin boy aboard a man-of-war, and went on to serve first as a foot soldier, then as a dragoon in Flanders during the War of the Spanish Succession. Mary proved courageous, but after a while her zeal for combat began to wane. She had fallen passionately in love with her tent mate, a Flemish youth who returned her ardor and insisted on marrying her.

For the first time in her life, Mary donned women's clothing and the newlyweds set themselves up as tavern keepers in Holland. Alas, their happiness was short-lived. Mary's husband died suddenly of a fever, and Mary, having found it easier to make her way in the world as a man, disguised herself as a sailor and signed aboard a Dutch ship. When the vessel was taken by Rackam, Mary gamely signed the pirate articles, casting her lot with the brigands.

Just as Mary was confiding all this to Anne, Calico Jack came upon the intimately whispering couple. In a fit of jealousy, he would have killed them both had Anne not told him that Mary was a woman.

Rackam agreed to go along with Mary's disguise, and did so until Mary fell in love with a young sailor whom Rackam had forced into the crew. Then, according to one account, "she suffered the discovery of her sex to be made by carelessly showing her breasts, which were very white."

Despite their romantic side, Anne and Mary were lionesses in battle to the very end. In late October, 1720, Rackam dropped anchor off the coast of Jamaica and the pirates were getting riotously drunk when a British Navy sloop surprised them. Rackam and his mates were too besotted to fight and hid in the hold. But the two women flew like furies at the Navy men, firing their pistols and flailing away with cutlasses and axes. When they realized that all was lost, Mary turned raging on her mates, killing one pirate and wounding others, while screaming at the cowards to "come up and fight like men."

At their trial in Jamaica, Mary and Anne were sentenced—like the eight other members of Rackam's crew—to be executed. When the judge asked if they had anything to say, the ladies replied "Milord, we plead our bellies." Both women were pregnant. The judge immediately stayed the order for their execution—no English court had the power to kill an unborn child, no matter how guilty the mother.

As Calico Jack went to his death, the unrepentant Anne told him: "Had you fought like a man, you need not have been hanged like a dog." Mary's lover, being a forced man, was set free. Mary died of fever in prison before the birth of her child. No record of Anne's execution has ever been found, and there is some conjecture that her wealthy father bought her release after the birth of her child.

Ever protective of her lover, Mary Read takes to the sword to slay a fellow pirate who had dared to challenge her man to a duel.

Naval force began to wend its way along the channels. At dusk, among the Inlet's shoals, the Navy men anchored to wait for morning.

Blackbeard was not surprised to see them. Despite all Spotswood's secrecy, Tobias Knight, North Carolina's corrupt collector of customs, had heard that something was afoot and had sent word to Blackbeard. The pirate, though he had only 18 men with him as Spotswood's forces approached, appeared completely unconcerned. Instead of preparing for combat he spent the night drinking and carousing. The stentorian voice of the sozzled pirate must have been clearly audible across the water as Maynard readied his men and weapons. On the next morning, helped on by a little breeze, the lieutenant launched his attack.

Blackbeard's last stand is one of the great battles of pirate history. It was also one of the strangest. Fighting a naval engagement in such shallow waters was something akin to fighting an infantry battle in a bog. At the very start, both Naval sloops ignominiously grounded on sandbars as they tried to close with Blackbeard's *Adventure*. With much huffing and puffing and heaving of ballast over the side, the crews worked the vessels free, and Maynard continued to maneuver awkwardly toward the pirate ship.

According to Defoe's account, Blackbeard, standing on a deck, hailed Maynard across the water separating the combatants. "Damn you for villains, who are you?" he yelled. "And from whence came you?"

At this, Maynard ran up the British ensign and shouted, "You may see by our colors we are no pirates."

Blackbeard roared back that they should come on board so that he could see who they were. To which Maynard replied, "I cannot spare my boat, but I will come aboard of you as soon as I can, with my sloop!"

This verbal shot from the lieutenant seems to have enraged Blackbeard. He took a swig of rum and bellowed, "Damnation seize my soul if I give you quarters, or take any from you." Maynard hollered back that he expected no quarters from him, nor would he give him any.

After this exchange, Blackbeard ran up his black ensign with the death's-head, cut his cables and slid off down the channel. When Baker in the second Navy sloop tried to block his passage, Blackbeard swung his ship round and let go a vicious broadside. Baker was killed along with several of the crew; the sloop's rigging was damaged, so that she drifted helplessly and played little part in the ensuing engagement.

What slight breeze there was now died. The frustrated Maynard ordered out his oars and the crew began to row laboriously toward Blackbeard's ship. When they were within firing range, Blackbeard let go another vicious broadside of swan, partridge and small shot—a blast that devastated the deck of Maynard's sloop and wounded 21 of his crew of 35. In the face of such fire, Maynard was forced to order his men belowdecks, leaving only a mishipman and a North Carolina pilot lying low on deck to keep him informed of developments.

So far the action had been all Blackbeard's. Maynard's crew had been returning the pirates' fire, but for some reason without apparent effect. Blackbeard now launched another attack. He came up alongside the Navy sloop and his men threw across hand grenades made of bottles full of powder, small shot and scrap iron. There were explosions and a lot of

Royal Navy Lieutenant Robert Maynard singlehandedly keeps Blackbeard at bay while the Navy crew sallies from a hiding place. Sailing a shallow-draft sloop, Maynard surprised Blackbeard in the waters of Ocracoke Inlet (below) and later said: "I should never have taken him, if I had not got him in such a Hole."

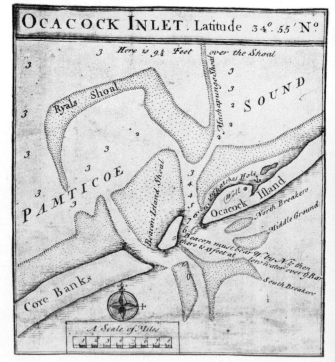

smoke. Blackbeard shouted out to his men that the enemy were "all knock'd on the head, except three or four; and therefore let's jump on board, and cut them to pieces." He himself was the first across, lashing the two vessels together with the rope he carried in his hands.

As the pirates boarded, Maynard ordered all his men who could still fight to dash up on deck. The two crews met head on, amid the shouts and oaths of the men, the clang of cutlasses and the crackle of pistol shots. Suddenly Maynard found himself face to face with his quarry. Both he and Blackbeard fired at almost point-blank range.

It was at this moment, perhaps, that Blackbeard perceived the folly of his ways. The sodden drinking of the night before and the morning jugs of rum had done nothing to steady his hand. Blackbeard's shot missed. Lieutenant Maynard's went straight into the pirate's body.

Incredibly, the heavy ball seemed to have no effect. The howling, raging Blackbeard swung his cutlass, breaking Maynard's in two and leaving him defenseless. But the pirate's *coup de grâce* never came. As he drew back his cutlass to finish off the helpless lieutenant, one of Maynard's seamen slashed Blackbeard across the throat. Still the giant pirate fought on, spouting blood and roaring imprecations. As other Navy men shot and cut at him, Blackbeard grabbed another pistol from his belt and cocked it. Then slowly, like a bull in a bull ring, he toppled

Blackbeard's severed head, its tongue lolling gruesomely from its mouth, swings from the bowsprit of the victorious Maynard's sloop as the lieutenant sets sail back to his base in Virginia. The mutilated body of the pirate was thrown overboard in Ocracoke where he fell. Legend has it that the headless corpse swam around the sloop several times in defiance before it sank from sight.

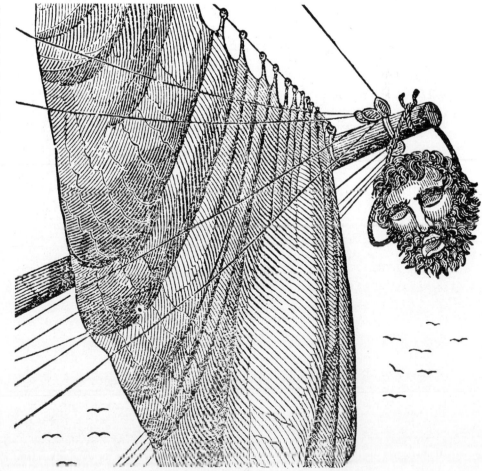

over and fell to the deck. That was the end of it. With their leader dead, the rest of the pirates cast down their weapons and surrendered.

Ten of the pirates had been killed; all nine survivors were wounded. Maynard had 10 dead and 24 wounded. Examining Blackbeard's corpse, he found no fewer than 25 wounds, five from pistol shots. He ordered Blackbeard's head to be cut from his body. With that grisly trophy swinging from his bowsprit, he sailed back in triumph to Virginia.

The death of Blackbeard marked the virtual end of piracy in American coastal waters. No pirates ever again attempted to make their base in North Carolina; as they had on other occasions, they faded away in the face of determined resistance. The scandal involving North Carolina's Governor Eden and Tobias Knight was never satisfactorily resolved. Though Maynard found an incriminating letter from Knight among Blackbeard's belongings, and Spotswood reported the whole affair to the Council for Trade in London, Knight successfully defended himself before the Governor's Council, which found the evidence against him to be "false and malitious." Governor Eden likewise remained in office; he succumbed to yellow fever three years after the battle of Ocracoke Inlet. The wrangling over the reward money went on for four years. The captains of the two men-of-war, H.M.S. *Pearl* and H.M.S. *Lyme*, maintained that it should be shared out equally among all their crewmen. Lieutenant Maynard argued that only those who had fought deserved a reward. It was eventually decided not to allow any reward at all for Blackbeard or the other pirates killed since they had not been taken alive. The amount finally allocated came to £334, 13s 6d: those who had fought got £1, 13s 6d; those who remained behind got 9s 6d. Lieutenant Maynard was allowed two combat shares in recognition of his leadership.

Though Blackbeard's demise put paid to piracy along the immediate American coast, it was a while before Woodes Rogers could feel secure on New Providence. All during Blackbeard's coastal rampage, news of his successes had acted as a tonic among his onetime pirate cohorts on Nassau. Rogers' position deteriorated until late in 1718, when several lapsed pirates were brought in. They were the remnants of the crews of three ships Rogers had sent off some months earlier to Hispaniola for provisions; only two days out from Nassau, the men had reverted to piracy. When this news reached Rogers, he dispatched his now-loyal ex-privateer commander, Benjamin Hornigold, to capture the mutineers. Hornigold brought back 13 men, three of whom died of their wounds.

Strictly speaking, Woodes Rogers had no powers to try the 10 prisoners for piracy. But he decided that nothing would suffice save to make a terrible example of the miscreants. On December 9 and 10, 1718, in the guardroom at Nassau, a vice-admiralty court was assembled composed of eight judges including the Governor and two pardoned pirate captains, Thomas Burgess and Peter Courant. The pirates had been caught by ex-pirates. Now they were to be tried and sentenced by ex-pirates. The evidence was overwhelming against nine of the defendants. They were found guilty and condemned to death. One was spared on the grounds that he had been forced to join the pirates.

Rogers' justice was swift. Barely two days later, at 10 o'clock on the

A 1798 London playbill announcing the opening of J. C. Cross's spectacle "Black Beard; Or, The Captive Princess" testifies to the popularity of the brigand as a folk legend. Cross embellished Blackbeard's story by having him kidnap a beautiful Mogul princess who is saved by her handsome fiancé in the play's finale.

morning of Friday, December 12, the provost marshal took the condemned men out of their irons, pinioned their hands in front of them and ordered the guards to escort them to the beach at the foot of the fortress wall where the gallows had been erected.

The condemned pirates' attitudes varied widely. Dennis Macarty, 28, dressed like a prizefighter, with long blue ribbons festooning his neck, wrists, knees and hat, cheerfully kicked his shoes over the parapet, saying he had promised not to die with his shoes on. Thomas Morris, 22, decked out in red ribbons, grinned and shouted from the scaffold that he might have been a greater plague and now wished he had been. John Augur, 40, was remorseful; he wore old clothes and had neither washed nor shaved; on the scaffold he drank a small glass of wine and toasted the success of the Bahamas and their governor. William Dowling, 24, who had murdered his own mother in his native Ireland, was churlish and unrepentant. George Bendall, 18, was sullen and denied being a pirate. William Cunningham, 45, a onetime gunner of Blackbeard's, was contrite. William Lewis, 34, an ex-boxer, was determined to die drunk and loudly demanded wine. William Ling, 30, a true penitent, thought water more appropriate. At the very last moment, Rogers reprieved the ninth prisoner, George Rounsivil, 18, having heard that he had "loyal and good" parents in Rogers' own home county of Dorset, England. Then the marshal pulled the butts away with a rope, the stage fell and the variously beribboned, unshod, unshaven, drunk, matricidal and contrite pirates suffered Woodes Rogers' ultimate revenge for their betrayal of his trust.

Rogers had no way of knowing the impact of his Draconian measures against piracy. He had executed eight convicted pirates, but there were still hundreds of onetime pirates in his colony and hundreds of practicing pirates on the loose among the islands. But the hanging of the eight backsliders marked the beginning of the end for the pirates of the Golden Age. There would be a last spasm of piracy in the Eastern Seas around Africa and India in the next few years. But in the New World the incidents grew fewer and fewer. As time passed in Nassau, Rogers began to fear a Spanish invasion more than the increasingly remote possibility of an internal pirate rebellion or a concerted pirate attack from the sea.

And indeed, he was never bothered by pirates again. All of his troubles thereafter were with his own country and her enemy, Spain. Another of the interminable wars between the two nations broke out soon after the hangings in Nassau. Rogers wrote to London asking for troops and warships. But no reinforcements arrived. Left to his own devices, he labored feverishly to finish the fort, stirring the populace to fitful effort by playing on their fears of the Spanish. Once, by bribing them with lavish handouts of food and liquor, he managed to extract a fortnight of more or less continuous labor. By January 1720, the fort was finished and mounted with 50 guns. In February the Spanish attacked.

The Spanish force of four warships and 1,300 troops under the command of Don Francisco Cornejo had sailed from Cuba through the Florida Channel, approaching New Providence from the north. At noon on February 24, 1720, the Spaniards anchored off the eastern entrance to Nassau harbor. To oppose them Rogers had only one infantry company and his local militia of 500 drunken ex-pirates. Even so, Cornejo would not risk a direct frontal attack. He sent a squadron of ships to cruise off Hog Island and block the eastern entrance to the harbor, and on the night of the 25th this force launched the long-awaited Spanish invasion.

It was a farcical failure. Two sentries on shore, blazing away with their muskets at the raw Spanish troops in the approaching boats, were sufficient to repel this eastern thrust. The Spanish withdrew in confusion, mutinous and ashamed. Though they remained in Bahamian waters for some time after, they never dared set foot on Bahamian soil again.

Rogers had thus held New Providence for the British Crown against two powerful enemies—the pirates and the Spanish. Probably no single individual had done so much on his own to bring piracy to an end in the New World. But for all this he received as much congratulation from the British Government as he had for his round-the-world cruise—that is to say, nothing. By early 1721, he was at the end of his tether. For two years he had received no support in money, men or supplies. On the contrary, he had paid the garrison and the settlement's food bill with £11,000 of his own money, in the process wiping out his share of the treasure taken during his great privateering days. "It is Impossible I can subsist here any longer," he said in a dispatch to London, "on the foot I have been left ever since my Arrivall." Finally, in March 1721, weary at heart and sick in body, he gave up and sailed away. Back in England, Woodes Rogers was dismissed from his post. He was then declared bankrupt and thrown into debtors' prison.

But it would not have been like him to give up. Having been treated with disdain by the Admiralty, Rogers put his case to the Army. A board of eight generals considered his plight. They decided that he merited being placed on the infantry rolls on half-pay as a captain of foot and declared that he fully deserved the royal favor and bounty.

In 1728, restored to honor and rescued from poverty, Rogers was reappointed Governor of the Bahamas with proper powers and a proper salary of £400 a year. He spent his day struggling to establish a viable economy based on sugar and cotton. But the idleness of the islanders and the infertility of the coral soil soon wore him out. He died in 1732, at the age of 54, still grappling with his old ambition of turning a pirate land into a prosperous British colony of honest Englishmen.

Rogers' proud son, William, shows the 50-year-old Governor a map of growing New Providence as the family waits for afternoon tea at Fort Nassau. This tranquil scene is by William Hogarth, who also painted the family in London.

At the beginning of Woodes Rogers' second term as governor of the Bahamas in 1729, the colony's great seal featured a merchant vessel sailing triumphantly into Nassau harbor as pirate ships flee over the horizon. The motto translates, "The pirates having been expelled, trade is restored."

Chapter 6

The last and most lethal of the captains

he Fanti fishing village and English trading station of Anamaboe on the Guinea Coast of Africa was the sort of place white men ventured to visit only out of greed. There could be no other reason. The furnace days under a blinding equatorial sun, the humid, windless nights, the poor food, resentful natives and myriad tropical diseases made it an earthly hell for Europeans. Yet in 1719, Anamaboe was one of the richest and most important of the chain of permanent European posts along the West African littoral. The slave trade was then entering its most prosperous period, and Anamaboe, at the seaward end of an easy route from the interior, was among the busiest of the slaving entrepôts dotting the African bulge from the Senegal River to Whydah.

At Anamaboe the Royal African Company had built a triangular stockade called Fort Charles, with sharp, sheer corners like the bows of a ship, surmounted by guard turrets. Here, within the protective walls of their castle, the English traders lived and—with appalling frequency—died. The toll was so great that it was said three governors were appointed for every post—the incumbent, his replacement traveling out by sea, and one in England about to board ship to replace the replacement. Only alcohol and the African girls in the village—or the arrival of a ship in the roadstead beyond the pounding surf—relieved the oppressive isolation and boredom. There was no harbor at Anamaboe, nor at most of the European posts along the coast. African bum boats—canoes hollowed out of the great trees of the rain forest—ferried slaves, gold and ivory between shore and ship across a shark-infested sea.

Between 12 and 1 o'clock on the afternoon of June 5, the *Princess*, a merchant galley from London, was taking on slaves from the compound at Fort Charles, and the captains of two other English merchantmen, the *Hind* and the *Morrice*, were bartering with Africa Company traders when two strange sails approached the roadstead and bore down swiftly on the ships anchored there. From their appearance, the slavers knew them to be pirates. The first of the visitors to come up was a rakish, black-hulled vessel with a black flag flying from the masthead and the deck crowded with well-armed, belligerent-looking men. This was the *King James*. Close on her stern came her sister ship, the *Royal Rover*, a Dutch trading ship recently captured off Capo Three Points by the Welsh pirate captain Howell Davis, and mounting 32 cannon and 27 swivel guns.

The two pirate ships looked so businesslike that the ill-prepared slavers struck their colors at once in token of surrender. Unaccountably, possibly because of illness, the traders manning the company fort offered hardly any resistance. A few sporadic cannon shots from them were soon stifled by a broadside from Davis' *Rover*. Then all was quiet.

This chance meeting of the slaver *Princess* with the pirates on a drowsy afternoon off Anamaboe was to prove most fateful for the history of the remaining years of piracy's Golden Age. For among the merchant seamen taken aboard the pirate ships as forced hands was Bartholomew Roberts, third mate on the *Princess*. He was soon to turn pirate and to become the most lethal captain of his time.

The return of the brigands to the Eastern Hemisphere was the direct result of Woodes Rogers' success in breaking up the pirates' nest in New

Howell Davis, who invaded African waters after Bahamian Governor Woodes Rogers made the Caribbean unhealthy for pirates in 1718, cuts a dramatic figure as he leads an attack on a Portuguese settlement in this 1846 engraving. Davis was mentor of the greatest pirate of the Golden Age, Bartholomew Roberts.

Providence and the rising resistance to pirates of Blackbeard's stripe in the American and West Indian colonies. By 1719 the New World as a whole had begun to be an untenable place for pirates, and the more dynamic leaders, men like Howell Davis, John Taylor, Edward England and Christopher Condent—most of them old New Providence hands— turned their gaze once more to the East.

Condent had led the assault, reestablishing Madagascar and the surrounding islands as pirate havens after a lapse of nearly 20 years. Following the old routes to the Red Sea and the Malabar Coast, Condent took an Arab ship near Bombay with a cargo of about £150,000 in gold and silver, a yield of close to £2,000 per man—shares of a size that pirates had not seen for many a year. When Condent's company broke up at St. Mary's after the share-out, the beach was littered with unwanted luxuries —silks, gold-embroidered muslins, spices of all kinds.

Having such success, Condent and about 40 of his men decided not to risk their luck again, and gave up piracy. They received a French pardon from the Governor of Bourbon (later called Réunion) and settled down. According to Defoe, Condent married the Governor's sister-in-law, emigrated to Saint-Malo in France and became a wealthy shipowner.

Following Condent across the Atlantic came a stream of dispossessed New World pirates who now operated not only in the Red Sea and Indian Ocean but also all around the east and west coasts of Africa, wherever there was booty to be had. The Royal African Company and the East India Company reacted to this surge of piracy with predictable concern— and this time their entreaties had the desired effect on the Royal Navy. The Admiralty put Commodore Thomas Matthews in command of a squadron of four men-of-war and dispatched him around Africa to the Indian Ocean. Arriving at Madagascar ahead of the other ships in his squadron and not wishing to dally, Matthews left a letter instructing his captains and sallied forth on patrol. The pirates intercepted this letter. And as so often in the past, most of them declined to confront the Royal Navy. Though Matthews never fought or captured any pirates in the Indian Ocean, his mere presence there was enough to convince them that the game was not worth the candle. They drifted away—some into retirement, a number around the Cape of Good Hope to the west coast of Africa, where for a time they continued their activities. And this was where Captain Bartholomew Roberts came on the scene.

This greatest of the pirate captains was born around 1682 and probably, like virtually all his fellows, saw active service on board a Naval ship or privateer during the prolonged War of the Spanish Succession. It is known that at the time of Blackbeard's exploits he was the mate of a Barbados trading sloop. By his mid-thirties he was clearly an outstanding master mariner. In the pirate's parlance of the time, he was "pistol-proof," meaning a man expert in ship handling, crew control and the tactics of naval warfare.

Roberts' very expertise was in all probability an important reason for his turning pirate after 20 years as an honest seaman. As a ship's officer of working-class origins he could not have expected a command of his own in legitimate service at sea. Only as a pirate could he attain the supreme rank to which his training, experience and ability fitted him.

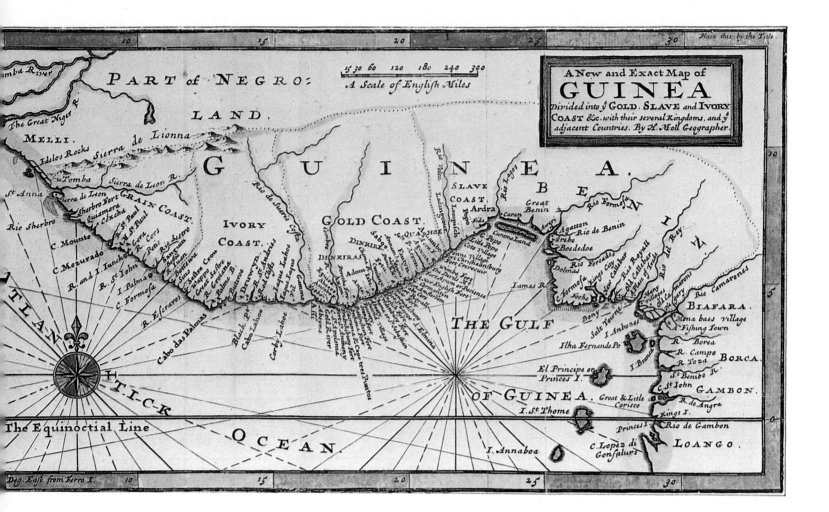

The 3,000-mile-long Guinea Coast in the early 1720s drew treasure-hungry pirates like a lodestone—and for good reason, as shown in this contemporary English map. The coastline was dotted with European trading posts from which the fabulous wealth of Africa—gold, ivory and slaves—was shipped abroad.

Nevertheless, he was averse at first to taking up pirate life on Davis' ship. But then events led him to change his stance. Six weeks after the engagement at Anamaboe, Davis was slain, pistols blazing, in a Portuguese ambush on Princes Island, where he had put into to reprovision. The pirates retreated out to sea in the *Royal Rover* to nurse their wounds. And there, on the rolling ocean, the crew elected Roberts captain; clearly he had already proved himself to be their superior.

Roberts accepted the position. If he was reluctant to become an ordinary pirate crewman, he apparently found that he could reconcile himself to piracy when he was chosen as captain. "It is better to be a commander than a common man, since I have dipped my hands in muddy water and must be a pirate," was how Roberts himself put it.

What sort of man was this towering captain of pirate history? Defoe calls him "black," implying that he was a swarthy, Celtic kind of Welshman. Though he was probably short in stature, like most Welsh hill people, he was blessed with a powerful personality and a natural flair for leadership. And he brought to his new rank as captain—or acquired as a result of it—some of the mannerisms and affectations of the gentleman officers of the regular Navy quarter-decks. His style of dress served to emphasize his distinction from his men: rich crimson damask waistcoat and breeches, red feather in his tricorn hat, gold chain around his neck with a diamond cross suspended from it, two pairs of pistols on the end of a silk sling over his shoulders and a sword at his side. He drank great quantities of tea, which was the gentlemanly thing to do, and he had a corresponding dislike for the sort of alcoholic excesses that pirate crews habitually indulged in—not because he was a puritan but because he believed drink impaired the efficiency of his ship. "Being almost always mad or drunk," wrote Defoe of such men, "their Behaviour produced infinite Disorders, every Man being in his own Imagination a Captain, a Prince, or a King."

According to Defoe: "When Roberts saw there was no managing of such a Company of wild ungovernable brutes by gentle Means, nor to keep them from drinking to Excess, the Cause of all their Disturbances, he put on a rougher Deportment and a more majesterial Carriage towards them." He made every member of the crew swear to obey his articles and was swift to enforce these rules. "And if any seemed to resent his Usage," wrote Defoe, "he told them they might go ashore and take Satisfaction of him, if they thought fit, at sword and pistol, for he neither valued or feared any of them."

Flying the cross of St. George, symbol of British rule, Fort Charles looks out on the Guinea Gulf at Anamaboe, an important gold- and slave-trading station. Such forts generally mounted 25 to 30 guns and were virtually impregnable against local uprisings — or pirates.

On one occasion during a cruise, a drunken crewman insulted the captain to his face. Roberts, beside himself with fury, killed the man on the spot—an act that was resented by many of the drunk's equally besotted shipmates, most notably one Thomas Jones. Jones was onshore at the time of the killing, but when he came back on board and was told what had happened, he cursed Roberts and said he ought to be done away with himself. At this the enraged captain drew his sword and stabbed Jones in the body. Whereupon Jones, sorely wounded though he was, picked Roberts up, threw him over a cannon and beat him up—"handsomely," says Defoe.

This riotous incident, not surprisingly, threw the whole ship into an uproar. Some of the crew sided with Roberts, others with Jones. It took the full authority of the quartermaster, who was responsible after Roberts for the ship's discipline, to calm the tumult. In the inquiry that followed, the majority of the crew gave their view that the dignity of the captain ought to be upheld on board, and since it was a post of honor, no crew member was entitled to violate it. So poor Jones was sentenced to be severely punished. As soon as his stab wound had healed, he was tied up and given two lashes by every member of the crew—and the crew

African canoes paddle out to European vessels anchored beyond the bar on the Gold Coast, where bartering took place. One early English traveler found the Africans reluctant to come aboard until the captain splashed three drops of sea water in his eye as a sign of friendship.

a to Mowri, *from* Barbot & Smith.

Fort Royal at Manfrow

Mowri

numbered 180 men. This terrible punishment did not, however, convince Jones that he was in the wrong; and at the earliest suitable moment, he and some cronies left Roberts to go off on their own account.

The *Royal Rover's* crew could not have imagined the full depth of Roberts' personality, or the adventures in store for them when they first set sail with their new captain in July of 1719. But Roberts, or "Black Bart" as he has come to be known, lost no time in making his name as a pirate captain. In a whirlwind act of revenge he returned to Princes Island and devastated the Portuguese settlement where Davis had been ambushed and slain. The account squared, Roberts set out south along the sweeping bend in the African coast called the Bight of Biafra, where he quickly seized and plundered two prizes, a Dutch trading vessel and a Royal African Company slaver. He then put in at the small island of Annobon to decide where to head next. Tiring of the oppressive latitudes of the Guinea Coast, Roberts and his crew decided by a majority vote to sail for the rich Portuguese colony of Brazil. Roberts shaped a course from tiny Annobon for the scarcely larger island of Fernando de Noronha, 2,300 miles away, off the coast of South America. Twenty-eight days later, in a virtuoso feat of navigation, Roberts brought the *Royal Rover* into a cove on this uninhabited pinprick of volcanic rock in the South Atlantic. And here the pirates watered, made some repairs to their ship and prepared for their Brazilian foray.

For several weeks, Roberts and his crew patrolled the Brazilian coast without finding suitable prey. At last, in September 1719, they came upon a fleet of 42 Portuguese merchant ships off Bahia preparing to form up with two men-of-war that would escort them across the Atlantic to Lisbon with their cargoes of Brazilian gold, tobacco, sugar and hides. Sailing boldly into the middle of the fleet, the pirates boarded the richest, most heavily laden ship and plundered her of her cargo, including 40,000 gold moidores, worth £50,000 in English currency. The other merchantmen could only cluck and cackle in dismay, firing their cannon and raising their topgallant sails as distress signals to the convoy's two men-of-war escorts. But the warships' commanders either could not or would not make sail quickly enough to intercept Roberts; they remained at anchor until the pirate had sailed away with his prize.

From Brazil the pirates headed north. On Devil's Island, a sleazy Spanish colony off Guiana (later notorious as a French penal colony), they traded their loot for money and women, and spent several weeks roistering and gambling in an orgy of self-indulgence. From Devil's Island they sailed into the Caribbean, but the Royal Navy and the islands' privateer naval auxiliaries chased them out. So they carried on northward, aiming for Newfoundland, where pirates in the past had found quarry among the merchantmen preparing for the North Atlantic crossing.

In June 1720, with colors flying, ship's band braying and drumming and the Jolly Roger fluttering from the mast top, Roberts sailed brazenly into the port of Trepassi, where 22 merchant ships lay anchored with 1,200 men and 40 cannon on board. Not a shot was fired in self-defense and ships' crews fled to the shore. Roberts and his crew plundered those vessels at their leisure, along with another four that had the misfortune

Portuguese settlers drive Howell Davis' pirate crew off Princes Island, a Portuguese colony in the Guinea Gulf. Davis attempted to persuade the colony's Governor that he was captain of an English man-of-war hunting pirates. The Governor, unconvinced, laid an ambush in which Davis was killed.

to come on the scene. The fishing fleet of 150 ships in Trepassi was at his mercy as well, and to enforce his will, he sank a number of them. By now, the *Royal Rover* was showing her hard usage. Roberts converted the best of the prizes, a Bristol galley, for his own use, aptly renaming her the *Royal Fortune*. Wrote the Governor of New England in his report of Roberts' descent on Trepassi: "One cannot withhold admiration for his bravery and daring."

Roberts had now entered the most prolific spell of his incredible career. Off the Newfoundland Banks he captured another half dozen prizes, all French. Since he was always searching for a better ship, he exchanged his recently acquired Bristol galley for the best of the new vessels, mounted 28 guns in her and gave her the same name as her predecessor, the *Royal Fortune*.

Sailing south now, Roberts took a succession of English prizes off the New England coast, the richest being the sloop *Samuel*, bound from London to Boston. The *Boston News Letter*, in its issue of August 22, 1720, reported the eyewitness accounts of several passengers who were robbed of all their money and finery and were threatened with death if they did not disclose where their valuables were. The pirates tore up the hatches and entered the hold "like a parcel of furies." They broke open every bale, case and box they could find. Everything they did not want they threw overboard, cursing and swearing as they did so.

They stole sails, guns, powder, rigging and nearly £10,000 worth of goods. They hauled the chief mate, Harry Glasby, out of his hiding place and forced him on board the *Royal Fortune*. Though Roberts rarely impressed captured sailors, he did on occasion press such high-ranking artists. The raiders told the *Samuel*'s captain: "We shall accept no Act of Grace, may the King and Parliament be damned with their Act of Grace for us, neither will we go to Hope Point"—that is, Execution Dock—"to be hanged a-sun-drying." They let it be known that they would look for a pardon only when they had made enough money.

What Roberts' crew considered money enough was, according to one of them, "seven or eight hundred pounds each." Some of the steadier pirates seemed to have reached this goal already; they left the crew to retire a short time thereafter. But they were the rare ones. The majority heartily agreed with the one who made it plain to the *Samuel*'s captain, "If we are captured, we will set fire to the powder with a pistol, and all go merrily to hell together."

By September 1720, Roberts was back in the Caribbean. From his previous experience, he knew the West Indies was no longer the healthiest of places for a pirate. But the vagaries of wind and weather had left him no choice in the matter. Sailing south from New England, he had arrived at Deseada Island in the Lesser Antilles, where he took on provisions and water and set off again with the aim of sailing back across the Atlantic to Africa. He meant to make his first stop at Brava, the southernmost of the Cape Verde Islands. But the winds pushed him too far to the north and he found it impossible to beat southward down to Brava against the prevailing southerly breeze. Instead he was forced to return across the ocean, and beat back down to the Caribbean on the northeast trades in the Western Atlantic. He had already been at sea for some time when he made the turn to go back across the Atlantic. And now another long voyage stared him in the face.

For this venture Roberts had only one hogshead of water remaining from the stores taken on at Deseada. It contained 63 gallons for a crew of 124 men. Eventually, as the days dragged into weeks, the pirates were down to one mouthful every 24 hours, and some were driven so mad with thirst that they drank sea water or their own urine. A number of the crew died of "fluxes" and "apyrexies"—dysentery and fever. The ones who did best were those who drank nothing save their meager ration.

The day came when the men ran out of water altogether, and it seemed miraculous the next day when their soundings registered a shelving of the seabed, indicating the proximity of land. They anchored on their last waterless night in only seven fathoms. Soon after they set sail the next morning, the lookout at the masthead sighted land. They launched their boat and it returned that evening with water from the Maroni River in Surinam on the northern coast of South America.

Thereupon, Roberts embarked on a campaign of heroic proportions in the Caribbean—and the Royal Navy be damned. He took dozens of prizes, and impudently landed onshore even under fire in fortified harbors. He sailed boldly into the harbor of St. Christopher (now St. Kitts) in the British Leeward Islands; there he looted the shipping and landed a boat to rustle a few sheep while under the fire of fortress guns.

A month later, the Governor of the French Leeward Islands complained that "between the 28th and 31st October these pirates seized, burned or sunk fifteen French and English vessels and one Dutch interloper of 42 guns at Dominica." Basing himself off St. Lucia, Roberts inflicted such a toll on French shipping from Martinique that the Governor there was forced to send a message to the Governor of British Barbados pleading for help. The Governor of Bermuda wrote home that the Martinique prisoners the pirates took in their encounters with the French were "barbarously abused, some were almost whipped to death, others had their ears cut off, others they fixed to the yardarm and fired at them as a mark and all their actions looked like practising of cruelty."

A few months later the Martinique Governor sent another call for help to the Governor of the British Leeward Islands. That worthy responded by ordering the Royal Navy guardship H.M.S. *Rose*—one of the four ships that had escorted Woodes Rogers to New Providence—to set off in pursuit of Roberts. The Navy captain replied tartly: "You know, sir, you have no power to give me orders, but I will concert any affairs that shall be for my King's service, and I am sorry I am forced to say I wish you'd do the same." He then sailed in the opposite direction.

Roberts displayed his contempt for these efforts by designing a new pirate jack, showing a figure of himself with a sword in his right hand and each foot standing on a skull. One skull had written beneath it the initials ABH, for A Barbadian's Head; the other had AMH, for A Martinican's Head. The plate on his cabin door bore the same design.

By the spring of 1721 Roberts had nearly brought Caribbean shipping to a halt. Without prey, there was no longer anything to keep him in the Caribbean. He had retained two of the captured ships to carry his loot, and to serve as back-up fighting vessels. The holds of these ships were

A View of a Stage & also of ỹ manner of Fishing for, Curing & Drying Cod at NEW FOUND LAND.
A. The Habit of ỹ Fishermen. B. The Line. C. The manner of Fishing. D. The Dreſſers of ỹ Fiſh. E. The Trough into which they throw ỹ Cod when Dreſſed. F. Salt Boxes. G. The manner of Carrying ỹ Cod. H. The Cleanſing ỹ Cod. I. A Preſs to extract ỹ Oyl from ỹ Cods Livers. K. Casks to receive ỹ Water & Blood that comes from ỹ Livers. L. Another Cask to receive the Oyl. M. The manner of Drying ỹ Cod.

Fishermen dry codfish on Newfoundland— a fertile northern port of call for pirates— in this 1715 engraving. The brigands found easy pickings among the cargo-laden merchant ships that put in here for reprovisioning before setting out on the long journey across the Atlantic. They also found eager recruits among the local fishermen who were tired of their hard life.

full of plunder. He needed to exchange this merchandise for gold, for only in this concentrated, indestructible form could his crew realize the real wealth of their piracy. But the American ports were too dangerous for Roberts, and he knew that eventually, despite all the shilly-shallying, a powerful expedition would be sent against him. He held a conference with his crew, and they voted to attempt another passage back to Africa, where they could dispose of their loot.

At the beginning of April Roberts and his crew set out on their eastward voyage. This time Roberts found favorable winds, and the *Royal Fortune* made its landfall at Senegal. From Senegal, Roberts sailed to Sierra Leone. For six weeks, while they careened and refitted their ships, the pirates enjoyed the hospitality of the freelance English traders of Sierra Leone. Though the Royal Africa Company had an official monopoly on all English trade along the coast, about 30 of these illicit entrepreneurs had set up their own posts on the coast and up the major rivers. These merchants of fortune proved good friends of the pirates, much as the Madagascar traders had sustained the pirates of a generation before. The most prosperous among them was ex-buccaneer John Leadstone, called Old Crackers, who kept the most hospitable house on the coast and had several guns mounted by his door with which he saluted the pirates whenever they arrived at his port. Another was Benjamin Gun, who ran a port on the Rio Pungo and served as Robert Louis Stevenson's model for the Ben Gunn of *Treasure Island*.

Yet there was no question of Sierra Leone's becoming a vast pirate hangout like Madagascar. The country was too unhealthy, the pirates and pirate-traders too few, the Royal African Company too well established in its fortified posts along the coast. Still, the traders managed a modest business, sending their employees upriver in boats to swap brass pots, pewter pans, old guns and English gin for slaves, ivory and dyewoods, which they sold to English merchantmen who had the courage to defy the Royal African Company by trading with them.

It was from these traders that Roberts and his crew learned for the first time of the presence of two British men-of-war on the coast—the *Swallow* under Captain Chaloner Ogle, and the *Weymouth* under Captain Mungo Herdman—both formidable ships of 60 guns each, sent by the Admiralty at the insistence of the Royal African Company as a protection against Roberts and the other pirates still operating in the region. The Navy ships had left Sierra Leone on patrol a month before the pirates arrived and planned to return before Christmas. Their presence did not dismay the pirates. But—as events were to show—it should have.

At the end of August 1721, Roberts set sail from Sierra Leone, heading east. Off Sestos, in Liberia, he captured the Royal African Company frigate *Onslow*, increased her guns from 26 to 40, and converted her into his last *Royal Fortune*. Continuing east, plundering endlessly as he went, he put into the disease-ridden, rain-forested creeks of the Calabar River in the Bight of Biafra, where he careened his ships—and, when rebuffed in his attempts to trade, fought with the local tribes so fiercely that 200 years later Bartholomew Roberts' visit was still remembered in the oral history of the natives of Old Calabar. At Cape Lopez, 400 miles south, Roberts turned around and headed west again.

It was now Christmas. Roberts evidently believed that sufficient time had elapsed for him to be safe in reversing course. If the warships followed their schedule, they should by now have returned to Sierra Leone. Thus, Roberts could count on sailing safely in waters already vacated by the Navy. What he did not know was that the Navy ships had been delayed at Princes Island, where their crews had been swept by malaria and venereal disease, and 100 men had died. With his crews so badly depleted, Captain Ogle, commander of the patrol, was unable to continue to Sierra Leone as planned. Instead he had put in short of his goal at Cape Coast Castle to press-gang a few merchantmen for crew replacements. This meant that when Roberts, after sailing westward, made his landfall at what is now the Ivory Coast, the Navy ships were still nearby. At this point Roberts turned east once again to resume his piratical cruise; he was now sailing directly toward the men-of-war.

On the reedy bank of the Guinea Coast's Old Calabar River, Bartholomew Roberts' rum-swilling crew celebrates a successful raid. Pirates often cleaned and refitted their ships in the Calabar's shallow waters, which the larger men-of-war were unable to navigate.

The maneuvers that led to the final encounter between the flotilla of Captain Roberts and that of Captain Ogle were haphazard but curiously predestined. On Thursday, January 11, 1722, Roberts sailed into Whydah, the greatest slaving port on the coast. To do so, he had to sail right past Cape Coast Castle, where the Navy ships were anchored. There is no indication that Roberts knew of their presence at the time—he was very likely out of sight of land, prudently steering clear of the heavily fortified Royal African Company post—but there is every indication that the Navy suddenly became aware of his passing, and set out in pursuit.

Unaware of his danger, Roberts set about plundering Whydah. Anchored in the roadstead were 11 slave ships, and they surrendered to him without firing a shot. All the captured ships were ransomed for eight pounds of gold dust (about £500) apiece except for one, whose captain refused to pay, and whose ship was then set on fire (against Roberts' orders) with 80 slaves still fettered two by two together on board. They had either to jump over the side to be torn to pieces by the sharks, or remain on the ship and die screaming in the flames.

On Saturday, January 13, the pirates got their first inkling of trouble. They intercepted a message from Cape Coast Castle to the Royal African Company's agent in Whydah. It warned him that the pirates were heading in his direction—with H.M.S. *Swallow* hot on their tail. Roberts immediately put to sea.

Beyond Whydah to the south, the African coast consisted of a labyrinth of lagoons and swamps devoid of a single permanent European settlement. The pirates set course for the remote little island of Annobon. But the winds were contrary and they missed Annobon and arrived again at Cape Lopez. It was a fateful landfall.

The two Navy ships, H.M.S. *Swallow* and H.M.S. *Weymouth*, had spent the last six months in frustrating patrol up and down the West African coast. At every turn they had received reports of Roberts' ravages. But now Captain Ogle in the *Swallow* was at last catching up with him. Ogle came into Whydah only two days after Roberts left. Ogle followed after him, guessing that he had gone south. At daybreak on February 5, 1722, searching the inlets toward Cape Lopez, Ogle was surprised to hear, in all that vastness of swamp and lagoon, the firing of a gun. Casting about for the source of the noise he at last spotted Roberts' little fleet—the *Royal Fortune*, the *Great Ranger* and the *Little Ranger*—anchored beneath the Cape.

Aboard the *Royal Fortune*, Roberts saw the approaching vessel and committed the first of a series of errors that would, in the end, prove fatal. He mistook the *Swallow* for a large merchant ship—not a difficult thing to do in those days, particularly at a distance. He ordered the *Great Ranger*, commanded by Captain James Skyrme, to pursue the presumed victim; it was, Roberts believed, a routine capture of a routine prize.

At this point, Ogle pulled a cunning trick. He turned the *Swallow* away, and the *Great Ranger* pressed after him. Ogle kept out to sea, running before the wind, but allowed the pirate to gain on him slowly.

At 10:30 a.m., when Cape Lopez has fallen out of sight and Ogle reckoned the sound of gunfire could not be heard by the ships there, he allowed the *Great Ranger*, flying a bewildering array of flags, including

most noticeably a Jolly Roger, to come up within range. Captain Skyrme let fire his bow chase guns to force the *Swallow* to come to, and ordered his men to battle stations, whacking sluggards with the flat of his cutlass.

By **11** a.m. the *Great Ranger* was within musket shot of the *Swallow*. Incredible as it may seem, it was not until this point that Skyrme, to his horror, realized that both he and his commander had made a terrible mistake. Suddenly, with speed and precision, the Navy ship turned to starboard, ran out her lower guns and let fly a devastating broadside.

This turn of events seems to have befuddled the pirates. For a moment they dithered. They hauled their pirate flag down. Then they hauled it back up again. Rather than flee they decided to fight. They fired a return broadside at the *Swallow*. They stood on the poop wildly swinging their cutlasses in an optimistic gesture of aggression. They shot ahead of the *Swallow*'s bow, and then slowed in readiness to board her.

Ogle's men, meanwhile, spurred on by rumors of vast treasures in the pirates' ship, had kept up a withering fire. One of Skyrme's legs was shot

A dandified Bartholomew Roberts brandishes his sword at the slave station at Whydah, "that port" according to Defoe "where commonly is the best booty." In this 18th Century engraving, the 11 slave ships that Roberts seized in one swoop in 1722 lie at anchor under the menacing care of Roberts' two ships, the Great Ranger (left) and the Royal Fortune.

off. The main-topmast was shattered and came crashing down to the deck. For an hour the two ships, rolling in the Atlantic swell under the boiling sun of the West African noon, slugged it out. Skyrme, sword still in hand but bleeding badly and half mad with pain, continued to direct his men, and repeatedly urged them to board the warship. But they could not bring themselves to take this drastic and dangerous step and by 3 o'clock it was too late.

Ten of the pirates lay dead. Twenty were wounded, 16 severely. A number had deserted their posts. The *Great Ranger* had been so badly shot up that she was no longer capable of either fighting or fleeing. Bitterly, Skyrme was forced to call for quarter. As he struck, he threw his pirate colors into the sea, so that they could not be used in evidence against him. Not all his crew was ready to be taken prisoner however. Half a dozen ran down into the magazine in the steerage, and one of them, John Morris, took a pistol and fired it into a barrel of gunpowder, hoping to blow the ship and everyone in it to kingdom come. But there was not enough powder in the barrel. There was a small explosion. Morris was burned to death and the rest of the men suffered terrible flash burns that scorched the clothes off their backs and the skin off their faces.

The Naval boarding party found 100 morose men on the *Great Ranger*, many of them wounded; 59 were English, 18 French and 23 were African slaves. There was no gold on board, but there was blood everywhere, the injured thrashing around in it in their agony. John Atkins, the Naval surgeon from H.M.S. *Swallow*, who later provided Defoe with most of his material about the capture and trial of Roberts' men, tended the wounded as best he could.

Among the pirates disfigured by the powder blast were the boatswain, William Main, and a seaman named Roger Ball. Surgeon Atkins, seeing the badge of office, a silver whistle, hanging at Main's waist, said to him: "I presume you are boatswain of this ship."

"Then you presume wrong," replied Main, "for I am boatswain of the *Royal Fortune*, Captain Roberts, commander."

"Then Mr. Boatswain you will be hanged, I believe," Atkins told him.

"That," said the pirate, "is as your honor pleases."

Atkins asked him how the powder had come to catch fire.

"By God, they are all mad and bewitch'd, for I was blown out of the cabin gallery into the sea and I have lost a good hat of it."

"But what signifies a hat, friend?"

Main at this moment was being stripped of his shoes and his stockings by the Navy crew. "Not much," he acknowledged. He commented that he wished he was back on the *Royal Fortune*, and when the surgeon gravely said, "No doubt of it," Main, looking down and seeing himself quite stripped, said wryly, "By God, it is the naked truth!"

As soon as the *Great Ranger* had been patched up, Captain Ogle sent her off with the wounded prisoners under guard to Princes Island. With the remaining prisoners shackled and pinioned on board the *Swallow*, he then returned to Cape Lopez to deal with the other two ships of Roberts' fleet. Amazingly, Ogle had suffered not a single casualty in his first encounter with the pirates and the morale of his men was high.

On the morning of February 10, Bartholomew Roberts was in his great

cabin on board the *Royal Fortune* breakfasting on his favorite dish, salmagundi, when word was brought down to him that a strange sail was
approaching. This was a commonplace event and Roberts did not pay
much attention to it; nor, apparently, was he concerned that five days
had passed since Skyrme had gone off in pursuit of another strange sail.
Roberts continued his breakfast. His crewmen were badly hung over
after a night's hard drinking and they dozed or nursed their heads on
deck. The sail drew nearer. Some of the pirates blearily debated what she
might be. Soon they could see that she was flying a French ensign. The
debate continued. She drew nearer still, headed straight for them. Roberts in his great cabin wiped his mouth. Suddenly a Navy deserter on
board the *Royal Fortune*—a deserter, as it happened, from the *Swallow*—recognized his old ship. It was the *Swallow*, he cried, and she was
coming to get them!

Roberts was up on deck at once. His crew, with their bad heads, were
not very lively. He ordered the men from the *Little Ranger*, anchored
nearby, to board the *Royal Fortune* at once. At 10:30 a.m. he slipped his
cable and calmly ordered his men to arms and to their stations. He sent a
pirate to find out from the deserter how the *Swallow* sailed and the man
came back and told him: she sailed best upon a wind—that is, with the
wind striking her abeam; to get away from her it would be wisest to run
before the wind. Roberts ordered full sail set. His men were unfit for
combat and he was determined to get away. If he was outsailed he would

*After months of seeking her quarry
along the tortuous African coast,
H.M.S. Swallow (left) finally bears down on
the Royal Fortune, the flagship of
Bartholomew Roberts' fleet. Roberts' crew,
reveling over a recent haul, failed
to recognize the Swallow as a man-of-war;
their ship was taken and Roberts slain.*

Chaloner Ogle, as the captain of H.M.S. Swallow, was the person who finally brought down Bartholomew Roberts, in February 1722. The British government attached such importance to this coup that it knighted the doughty Ogle.

run his ship aground so they could scramble ashore. Failing that, he would try to board the warship and then blow up both ships. He ducked below and changed into his crimson waistcoat and breeches and a hat with a big red feather in it. He took his sword and his silk sling with its two pairs of pistols and put his gold chain around his neck. He went back onto the poop deck. Then, in a totally unexpected maneuver, as impudent as it was pointless, he set course not away from but toward the *Swallow*. It has been said that his purpose was to gauge the warship's firepower. If so, he fatally succeeded.

Sharply at 11 a.m., the two ships came within range of each other. To be in a better position to direct his own fire, Roberts leaped onto a gun carriage. With an immense roar, the Navy guns delivered their broadside. It sent the pirates' mizzen topmast crashing down. Almost immediately the pirates delivered their reply. As the noise subsided and the smoke cleared, Roberts was seen slumping on the rope tackles of one of the guns. The helmsman ran to help him. He could see no marks of injury on the captain's body—until he looked at Roberts' throat. Grapeshot had struck him there and torn it open. The helmsman, hardened killer though he was, saw that his captain was dead and burst into tears.

So, not yet in his 40th year, died Bartholomew Roberts. He had had an incredible career; for sheer daring, bravado and stunning success, no pirate in the decades of the Golden Age could match him. In less than four years, he had captured a staggering total of more than 400 ships. Though he had started out off the West African coast, he had made the entire Atlantic his hunting ground. Crossing and recrossing the vast ocean, Roberts had dared the increasingly heavy odds by preying on shipping all along the North and South American seaboards and the Caribbean as well. On this zigzag course of lunatic virtuosity, like a piratical bird of passage, following the winds and his own volition till time ran out, Roberts had played a long end game before the forces of retribution finally checkmated him in the Gulf of Guinea.

His death unnerved the crew of the *Royal Fortune*. Roberts had been no mere nominal captain in a shipboard pirate commune. His charisma, his brains, his nerve and courage had alone inspired his crews and held them together in times of tribulation. Without him they were confused and lost. With the battle still going on, his body, in all his finery and wearing his arms and ornaments, was thrown overboard, as he had always requested. There was no second in command on board, so Harry Glasby, the sailing master, took command. A forced man, he was no lover of piracy and he tried to persuade the crew to surrender. But a number of diehard veterans from Howell Davis' command, who had been pirating continuously for nearly four years now, could not face up to the prospect of the noose. They refused.

The *Royal Fortune*, sailing badly, was relentlessly overhauled by the *Swallow*. The pirates had made no attempt to run her aground, nor to stand and fight. They kept up a haphazard fire but the crew no longer had any heart for the fray. One was seen to slide down into a drunken heap by his gun. Many of the crew of 152 were in this besotted condition. At 1:30 p.m. the damaged mainmast toppled to the deck. At 2 p.m. the pirates struck their colors and asked the Navy for quarter. They threw incriminating documents—the signing-on papers that showed which men were volunteers—overboard, but they were unable to retrieve their pirate flag, which portrayed Roberts as an avenging skeleton, from the tangled wreckage. It was found later by the Navy boarding party, which also found a quantity of gold dust and trade goods belowdecks. Even the pirates were embarrassed after the surrender when one of their number, who had remained in a drunken coma throughout the battle, suddenly woke up, saw H.M.S. *Swallow* close by, leaped to his feet, shouted: "A prize! A prize!" and urged his companions to board her.

At about 7 p.m. the prisoners were all on board the *Swallow*, shackled together with their old comrades from the *Great Ranger*. Altogether there were 254 of them, including 70 Africans. In mid-March, when the *Swallow* reached Cape Coast Castle, they were transported through the surf in canoes and thrown into a vast dark cavern carved out of the solid rock—the underground slave hole beneath the castle ramparts. From there, on March 28, they were taken in irons, pale and blinking, to the Great Hall of the castle and put on trial for their lives.

A trial in a Vice-Admiralty court especially convened within the stout walls of a British castle was a very different affair from the pirates' own mock trials, and it had a sobering effect on them all. From being mutinous and blasphemous they became quiet and serious. Few, however, were actually contrite. The hardest cases among them were the members of Roberts' original crew. These men had taken to calling themselves "The House of Lords"; they were the elite, they felt, and mocked the aristocracy by prefixing their names with the word "Lord." Thus there was a pirate known as Lord Sutton, and he complained bitterly when the man with whom he shared the same irons said his prayers.

"What," he asked, "do you propose by so much noise and devotion?"

"Heaven I hope," the other man replied.

"Heaven, you fool?" said Sutton. "Did you ever hear of any pirate going thither? Give me hell, it's a merrier place. I'll give Roberts a salute of 13 guns at entrance."

Sutton then asked the prison officer to move the man or take his prayer book away because he was disturbing the peace.

Altogether 169 men were charged when the trial began. Of the 254 men captured, 15 had died in the *Swallow* en route to Cape Coast, and four more died in the slave hole there during the trial. The 18 Frenchmen from the *Great Ranger* were acquitted on the grounds that they were forced men and foreigners. The remainder received an extraordinarily fair trial. The court sat far from the legal corruption and chicanery of the London law courts. The court officers—Captain Mungo Herdman of H.M.S. *Weymouth*, James Phipps, the director-general of the Royal African Company and three other members of that company—lived nearer the scene of the action and understood better the circumstances that forced men into piracy. To some extent, considering the hard life they lived on the Coast, they were subject to the same pressures themselves.

All the prisoners pleaded not guilty, claiming they had been forced. If they could substantiate that claim the court was ready to acquit them, even if they had served a long time under Roberts. Glasby, Roberts'

Peter Delime; John King; Willm Phillips; Saml Fletch.
Phillip Bill; Willm Maine; Willm Mackintosh;
Willm Williams

Ye and each of you are adjudged and
Sentenced to be Carried back to the Place from
whence yo came; from thence to the Place of
Execution without the Gates of this Castle, and
there within the Flood Marks to be Hanged by
the Neck 'till yo are Dead, Dead, Dead.

And the Lord have Mercy on y.^r souls.

Dated at Cape Cors Castle
this 5.th of April 1722

Herdman
James Phipps
Henry Dodson
Boyes
Edmund Hyde
Chas Fanshaw
Jno Barnsley

A parchment sheet spells doom for eight
of Bartholomew Roberts' comrades,
condemned to death for piracy on April 5,
1722. The document is from the court
proceedings at Cape Coast Castle, on the
Guinea Coast, where the British
Admiralty tried 169 pirates in the largest
such prosecution ever mounted.

sailing master, and chief prosecution witness in the trial, was one of those acquitted as a forced man. So were the musicians and other reluctant artists. In all, 74 men were acquitted, 54 sentenced to death (two of whom were later reprieved), 17 were committed to the Marshalsea Prison in London (all but four died on the voyage home) and 20 were sentenced to seven years' hard labor in the Royal African Company mines in the Gold Coast (a living death that none of them survived).

Fifty-two men, including Captain Skyrme, who had miraculously survived his injury, made the final journey from the slave hole to the scaffold outside the castle ramparts. They were hanged in batches from day to day, the first to go being the old House of Lords, as cocky as ever, except for Lord Sutton, who had dysentery. Surgeon Atkins acted as chaplain, but he could extract no repentance from them. "We are poor rogues," one told him, "and so must be hanged, while others, no less guilty in another way, escaped."

They walked with an escort of the Company's soldiers through a crowd of company employees, visiting sailors and local Africans. A pirate known as Lord Sympson spotted a woman he knew in that expectant throng, a passenger on one of the ships Roberts captured, named Elizabeth Trengrove. "I have lain with that bitch three times," he exclaimed when he saw her, "and now she has come to see me hanged." The condemned asked for water and complained about the way they were manacled, with their hands tied behind them. They were well up in the details of execution. "I have seen many a man hanged," said the pirate known as Lord Hardy, "but this way of having our hands tied behind us I am a stranger to, and I never saw it before in my life."

Surgeon Atkins asked each condemned man his age and birthplace before he was strung up. The answers produced a few interesting statistics. The oldest pirate to be executed was 45, the youngest 19 (he had been 16 or 17 when he first signed on with Roberts). The average age was rather high for a pirate crew—not quite 28. The House of Lords, for all their seniority, averaged 30 years. Only four men were 20 or under. Only four were over 40. More than a third came from the west of England, the rest from Wales, London and the north. Atkins' data were not, however, quite complete. Against the name of William Williams, for example, he could only record the poignant remark: "Speechless at execution."

For more than a fortnight the hangings went on. The last batch of 14 were hanged together on April 20, 1722. The bodies of 18 of the worst offenders were dipped in tar, bound with metal straps and hung in chains from gibbets on three prominent hills overlooking the roadstead—as Kidd had been in England 21 years before. They rotted rapidly in that sweaty climate, then dried in the sun and lightly swayed in the noonday onshore breeze—macabre shapes looking out across the sea to where the sails crept over the horizon and the storm clouds of the approaching rainy season towered into the sky.

After the mass hangings at Cape Coast, profound relief was expressed in mercantile centers as far apart as New York, Jamaica and Bombay. Captain Ogle was knighted for his triumph, the only Naval officer to be honored expressly for his actions against pirates. He rose steadily thereafter to the rank of Admiral of the Navy; his personal fortune he had secured by illicitly purloining the hoard of plundered gold dust he found in Roberts' cabin on the *Royal Fortune*.

Roberts' rampage along the Gulf of Guinea was the last great act of this extraordinary saga. His defeat marked the end of the Golden Age of piracy. And yet, awesome though the mass hangings at Cape Coast had been, they represented the loss of only a small proportion of the total pirate population at large. The rest just vanished.

Where did they go, and why?

No one knows the answers for sure. The end of Roberts' men was a salutary shock, certainly. Yet for the remainder of the century conditions at sea in merchant and Navy ships remained as bad as ever, and the pressures to go pirating were as cogent. Occasionally, the records reveal an instance of pirate activity—in 1769, for example, a gang of seagoing thugs from Hastings, Sussex, were sentenced to death at the Old Bailey for boarding a Dutch coaster off Beachy Head and robbing it of 60 men's hats. But by comparison with the big pirate flings of the Golden Age such acts were petty and meaningless local outbreaks.

The end of the Golden Age was not due to any diminution in the amount of treasure traversing the world's sea-lanes. East Indiamen were

Cape Coast Castle, the principal English fort in Africa during slaving days, overlooked the Gold Coast and gave entry to the rich slave land beyond. It was the treasure collected at posts such as this that brought the pirates into the area to lie in wait for departing merchantmen.

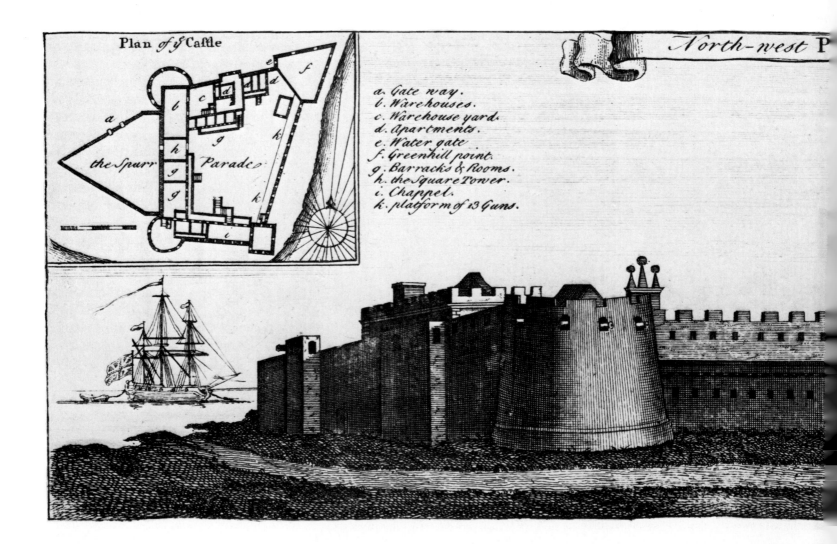

Plan of ỷ Castle

a. Gate way.
b. Warehouses.
c. Warehouse yard.
d. Apartments.
e. Water gate.
f. Greenhill point.
g. Barracks & Rooms.
h. the Square Tower.
i. Chappel.
k. platform of 13 Guns.

North-west P

still carrying large amounts of specie with which to trade in India and China, and were returning with jewels and riches of all sorts. Consignments of silver from Mexico to Spain were increasing; and large amounts of gold were being shipped from Brazil to Lisbon.

But now these cargoes were better guarded than ever before. As trade increased, the Western nations could support larger and more efficient navies. Colonial administrators were tougher and more honest. Overall, there was a greater sense of international responsibility toward the maintenance of civilized standards by the leading seafaring nations. In the face of this, the pirate ethos vanished like a will-o'-the-wisp.

The Golden Age had lasted barely 30 years, a fraction of a man's lifetime: a young pirate who had sailed out in 1691 could theoretically have sailed back again in 1723 and still not have reached his fiftieth year.

Yet this brief flowering of talented villainy on the high seas, its style, its bravura, left an indelible mark on the psyche of the Western world. For all their loutishness, the pirates appealed to something deep in the oppressed soul of common man: the lure of the far horizon, the promise of a different tomorrow, the fantasy of breaking out of the trap of human existence, of breaking the rules and of becoming rich in the bargain.

of the same.

The scavenging sharks
of an inglorious later day

Piracy could never be eradicated completely. After the Golden Age had passed, isolated incidents of piracy were reported, and from time to time a seagoing brigand was put to death for his crimes. But there was no real epidemic of piracy for almost 100 years—and then suddenly at the beginning of the 19th Century there occurred one final savage explosion that for a decade rivaled the Golden Age in its white-hot intensity.

The circumstances that triggered this rebirth of piracy were two. The ending of a plague of wars—the War of 1812, the Napoleonic Wars, the Latin American wars of liberation—left thousands of privateers out of work and primed for that short step into piracy. At the same time, the burgeoning Industrial Revolution swelled the Atlantic and American coastal sea-lanes with ever-increasing fleets of cargo-carrying vessels.

The pirates who came to ravage this trade were a far cry from the great seafaring figures of the preceding century. Striking from bases among the coves and cays of Cuba and Puerto Rico, they acted like nothing so much as scavenging sharks—mindlessly brutal, and as willing to steal a sack of coal as a bag of gold. A Captain Lander of the brig *Washington* recounted in 1822 that the pirates who boarded his ship in the Caribbean took $16 from his trunk, ordered the cook to hand over the potatoes, and then stole the cooking utensils, most of the crew's clothing, the ship's compass, a hailing trumpet and a quantity of twine before departing.

This 19th Century parody of piracy would have been ludicrous—except that Lander was lucky to live to tell the tale. In this last spasm of piracy, many a captain—along with his crew—was cold-bloodedly murdered for less.

Armed to the teeth, a pack of scoundrels crouch on deck while their disguised mates attempt to lure a prize into their clutches in this rendition of a 19th Century painting by French artist Auguste-François Biard. The fanciful scene reflected the popular romance still attached to piracy; in reality the later pirates were cutthroats, lacking the imagination to stage such a charade.

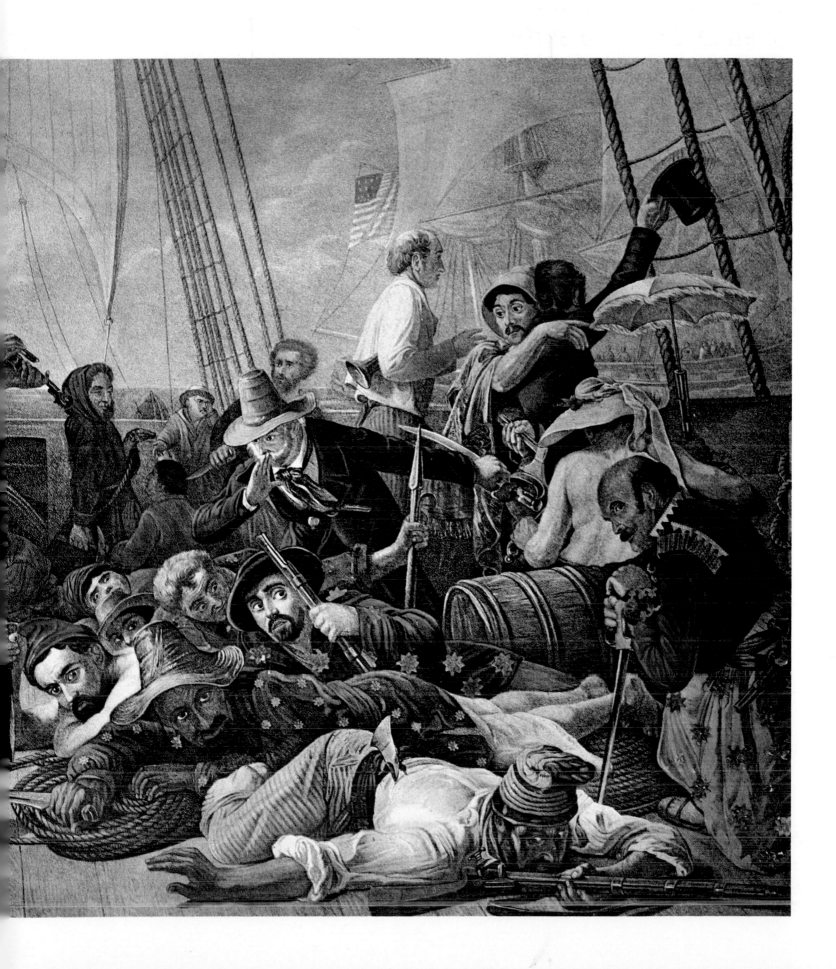

A first victory over the marauders

Though many nations suffered at the hands of the new pirates, the young United States was hardest hit—and the quickest to respond. In 1820 alone, 27 American vessels were plundered in the Atlantic and West Indies, with heavy losses of both life and cargo. Maritime insurance rates doubled, and Congress, in response to the clamor, not only prescribed the death penalty for piracy but also granted President James Monroe wide powers to chase down the pirates.

By the summer of 1821 the U.S. Navy had sent six warships and three gunboats to cruise the Gulf of Mexico and the Caribbean. On October 16, one of them, the U.S. brig *Enterprise*, under Lieutenant Commander Lawrence Kearney, made a spectacular catch of four pirate schooners commanded by Charles Gibbs, an ex-privateer and as vicious a rogue as ever sailed. On one occasion, Gibbs had chopped off a captured captain's arms and legs; on another he had burned an entire merchant crew to death.

Kearney found Gibbs and his villainous crew of 100 in the act of plundering three merchantmen off Cape Antonio, Cuba. In a fierce fight the pirates were put to rout. Forty were captured, and the rest fled into the jungles—including Gibbs, who was finally caught and hanged in 1831.

American mariners were heartened by Kearney's success. "It is probable that this fortunate and well-managed affair," reported one newspaper, "will check, if it does not break up, piracy in this quarter." Even that qualified judgment, however, was premature.

Lieutenant Commander Lawrence Kearney's brig Enterprise *(far left) rides off the Cuban coast in 1821 after launching five boats (center) to attack Charles Gibbs's pirate fleet as it was plundering several prizes. In this contemporary watercolor, the pirate schooners are in the background, and two of them are on fire.*

A special squadron of pirate killers

In the years 1822 and 1823, pirate attacks against shipping in the West Indies continued unabated despite the best efforts of Kearney and his fellow captains. For one thing, there were simply too many pirates to cope with; by one estimate, more than 2,000 were operating in the area. For another, the U.S. frigates and sloops of war were too big and heavy to operate effectively among the shallow reefs and banks of the area. At last, Congress commissioned a special West India Squadron under the command of Commodore David Porter (inset), an officer noted for both his brilliance and his temper.

Armed with a $500,000 appropriation, huge for the time, Porter proceeded to organize the perfect pirate-catching fleet. For the backbone of his force, he purchased eight fast-sailing schooners of light draft. Next, he secured a Connecticut steamer, the first steam-propelled ship engaged in naval warfare. Needing landing craft to attack pirates ashore, he added to his fleet five flat-bottomed barges with 20 oars each. The last element was a decoy ship that resembled a merchantman but mounted six cannon.

With 1,150 sailors and Marines, Porter sailed from Norfolk, Virginia, and headed south to join the six U.S. warships already cruising the Caribbean. In April 1823, his force put an end to the ferocious Cuban pirate Diabolito (Little Devil) after a bloody battle in which 70 pirates were killed. During the next two years Porter's West India Squadron bagged hundreds more, and most of the remaining evaporated in the face of this determined campaign.

Flying the Stars and Stripes, West India Squadron barges (right) row up in a surprise attack on the pirate Diabolito's two-masted schooner in 1823. Within two years, the Squadron, under Commodore David Porter (inset), had crushed the pirates. It was disbanded soon after.

The murdering master of the "Black Joke"

Only a few pirates remained to annoy shipping in the Atlantic as the 1820s ended. But if these diehards were mere irritants in the overall picture, they loomed large enough to their victims on the vessels they accosted.

The very name of Benito de Soto, a Portuguese who sailed a sleek brigantine aptly named the *Black Joke*, was a synonym for psychopathic savagery among merchant sailors of the day. Thus the crew of the British barque *Morning Star*, homeward bound in the South Atlantic from Ceylon, was filled with dread at dawn, on February 21, 1828, when de Soto's *Black Joke* appeared alongside. The pirates blasted the unarmed *Morning Star* with cannonshot, wounding many aboard and cutting up her rigging. The vessel's captain was then summoned to the pirate ship, but he was slow in arriving. As he stood before de Soto, the pirate raised his cutlass and roared out, "Thus does Benito de Soto reward those who disobey him!" and with one blow cleft the captain's head to the chinbone. The pirates next brutally raped the women passengers, threw them and all the men on board into the hold, riddled the ship's hull with holes and left, certain she would sink.

By a miracle, the crew managed to force open the hatch, man the pumps and plug the leaks. De Soto made his way to Gibraltar, where he was recognized by some of the crew of the *Morning Star*. There he was tried, convicted and hanged.

In a desperate scene, often used to illustrate Benito de Soto's vicious action against the Morning Star in the South Atlantic in 1828, a pirate vessel sails away leaving its prey down by the head and apparently sinking. The rendition by marine artist Clarkson Stanfield is flawed, however: de Soto's Black Joke is thought to have been a brig or a brigantine whereas the vessel in this picture is a topsail schooner.

Ordeal by fire aboard the "Mexican"

One of the last recorded instances of piracy in the Atlantic took place on September 20, 1832, when the American brig *Mexican*, bound from Salem to Rio de Janeiro with $20,000 in silver, was taken by the pirate schooner *Panda*. When the pirates asked their captain, Pedro Gibert, what to do with the captives, he said, "Dead cats don't mew. You know what to do."

The pirates locked the *Mexican*'s crew in the fo'c's'le while they looted the vessel. They then slashed the rigging and sails, filled the galley with combustibles, set it afire and sailed away from what was now a smoldering funeral pyre. But after an hour, the crew broke out of their prison and gradually doused the fire—letting enough smoke billow to fool the pirates until they were over the horizon.

The *Mexican*'s crew made it safely back to Salem, after six harrowing weeks at sea. As for Gibert, he was caught in Africa by the British in 1834, and extradited to Boston where he was tried and hanged.

Pirates from the schooner Panda (left) row toward the brig Mexican in 1832. The Mexican's 19-year-old mate, Thomas Fuller (shown below in old age), gave key testimony at the pirates' trial — and grew so angry in court that he rushed up and struck a pirate who had beaten him.

Bibliography

Allen, Gardner W., *Our Navy and the West Indian Pirates*. The Essex Institute, 1929.

Barlow, Edward, *Barlow's Journal*, Vol. I and II. Transcribed by Basil Lubbock. Hurst and Blackett, 1934.

Biddulph, Colonel John, *The Pirates of Malabar*. Smith, Elder and Co., 1907.

Bosman, William, *A New and Accurate Description of the Coast of Guinea*. 1704; reprinted, Barnes and Noble, Inc., 1967.

Bradlee, Francis B. C., *Piracy in the West Indies and Its Suppression*. The Essex Institute, 1923.

Brooke, Henry K., *Book of Pirates*. J. B. Perry, 1847.

Brooks, Graham, editor, *Trial of Captain Kidd*. William Hodge and Company, Ltd., 1930.

Cochran, Hamilton, *Freebooters of the Red Sea*. Bobbs-Merrill, 1965.

Course, Captain A. G., *Pirates of the Eastern Seas*. Frederick Muller, 1966.

Craton, Michael, *A History of the Bahamas*. Collins, 1962.

Defoe, Daniel, *A General History of the Pyrates*. Edited by Manuel Schonhorn. University of South Carolina Press, 1972.

Dow, George Francis and John Henry Edmonds, *The Pirates of the New England Coast 1630–1730*. Argosy-Antiquarian Limited, 1968.

Drury, Robert, *Madagascar; Or, Robert Drury's Journal*. 1890; reprinted, Negro Universities Press, 1969.

Ellms, Charles, *The Pirates Own Book*. 1837; reprinted, Marine Research Society, 1924.

Fuller, Basil, and Ronald Leslie-Melville, *Pirate Harbours and Their Secrets*. Stanley Paul, 1935.

Gascoigne, Bamber, *The Great Moghuls*. Harper and Row, 1971.

Gosse, Philip: *The History of Piracy*. Burt Franklin, 1968.

The Pirates' Who's Who. Burt Franklin, 1968.

Grey, Charles, *Pirates of the Eastern Seas (1618–1723)*. 1933; reprinted, Kennikat Press, 1971.

Innes, Brian, *The Book of Pirates*. Bancroft and Company, Ltd., 1966.

Jameson, John Franklin, *Privateering and Piracy in the Colonial Period: Illustrative Documents*. The Macmillan Company, 1923.

Jobé, Joseph, editor, *The Great Age of Sail*. New York Graphic Society, 1967.

Johnson, Captain Charles (Daniel Defoe), *A General History of the Robberies and Murders of the Most Notorious Pirates*. 1724; reprinted, Routledge and Kegan Paul, Ltd., 1926.

Karraker, Cyrus H., *Piracy Was a Business*. Richard R. Smith, 1953.

Lee, Robert E., *Blackbeard the Pirate*. John F. Blair, 1974.

Little, Bryan, *Crusoe's Captain*. Odhams Press, 1960.

Mitchell, David, *Pirates*. Thames and Hudson, 1976.

Paine, Ralph D., *The Book of Buried Treasure*. Macmillan, 1926.

Parry, J. H., *Trade and Dominion: The European Oversea Empires in the Eighteenth Century*. Sphere Books Ltd., 1974.

Pringle, Patrick, *Jolly Roger*. Museum Press Limited, 1953.

Rankin, Hugh F., *The Golden Age of Piracy*. Holt, Rinehart and Winston, Inc., 1969.

Richards, Stanley, *Black Bart*. Christopher Davies Ltd., 1966.

Seitz, Don C., *Under the Black Flag*. 1925; reprinted Gryphon Books, 1971.

Snelgrave, Captain William, *A New Account of Some Parts of Guinea, And the Slave-Trade*. James, John and Paul Knapton, 1734.

The Tryals of Captain John Rackam, and Other Pirates. Robert Baldwin, 1721.

Wilkins, Harold T., *Captain Kidd and His Skeleton Island*. Cassell and Company, Ltd., 1935.

Williams, Neville, *Captains Outrageous: Seven Centuries of Piracy*. Barrie and Rockliff, 1961.

Winston, Alexander, *No Man Knows My Grave*. Houghton Mifflin, 1969.

Woodbury, George, *The Great Days of Piracy in the West Indies*. W. W. Norton & Company, Inc., 1951.

Wright, Arnold, *Annesley of Surat and His Times*. Andrew Melrose, Limited, 1918.

Acknowledgments

The index for this book was prepared by Peter del Valle.

The editors wish to thank the following artists: John Batchelor *(pages 32-41 and 112-113)*, Richard Schlecht *(pages 128-135)* and Jerry Dadds *(end-paper maps)*.

The editors also give special thanks to Hugh F. Rankin, Professor of History, Tulane University, New Orleans, La. They also wish to thank the following: In London, England: Mildred Archer, India Office Library and Records; E. H. H. Archibald, R. B. Knight, David Lyon, Joan Moore, J. Munday, Roger Quarm, Elizabeth Wiggans, National Maritime Museum; B. W. Bathe, Science Museum; H. L. Blackmore, Tower of London; E. J. Freeman, Wellcome Institute for the History of Medicine; Madeleine Ginsburg, Anthony Latham, Betty Tyers, Victoria and Albert Museum; R. N. Hyde, Guildhall Library; Brian Innes; Peter Jackson; C. J. Kitching, Public Record Office; Victoria Moger, Museum of London; R. B. Pugh, Professor of English History, University of London; R. Williams, British Museum. Also in England: Ian V. Hogg, Upton-upon-Severn; Quentin Hughes, Department of Architecture, Liverpool University; Richard Vaughan, Professor of History, University of Hull; Terence Wise, Doncaster. In Paris, France: Claire Bertinetti, Denise Chaussegroux, Hervé Cras, Ghislaine Larmoyer, Marjolaine Mathikine, Marcel Redouté, Musée de la Marine; Hubert Deschamps; Françoise Jestaz, Monique de la Roncière, Bibliothèque Nationale; Marie-Antoinette Menier, Section Outre-Mer, Yves Metman, Archives Nationales. Also in France: Jean Bruneau, Nantes; Dan Lailler, Musées de Saint Malo, Saint Malo. In the Netherlands: L. M. Akveld, E. A. De Vries, B. C. W. Lap, Maritiem Museum Prins Hendrik, Rotterdam; A. J. Hilgersom, Scheepvaartmuseum, Amsterdam; Nederlandsch Historisch Scheepvaartmuseum, Amsterdam. The editors also wish to thank Paul Albury, Bahamas Historical Society, Nassau; Esin Atil, Freer Gallery of Art, Washington, D.C.; Milo C. Beach, Professor of Art History, Williams College, Williamstown, Mass.; Catherine Bennington, Jerry Cotten, University of North Carolina, Chapel Hill; Ann Blum, Marte Shaw, Harvard University, Cambridge, Mass.; Howard Brokaw, Wilmington, Del.; Georgia B. Bumgardner, American Antiquarian Society, Worcester, Mass.; B. R. Burg, Professor of History, Arizona State University, Tempe; James W. Cheevers, Bob Sumrall, U.S. Naval Academy Museum, Annapolis, Md.; Maud D. Cole, New York Public Library, New York City; William P. Cumming, Davidson, N.C.; Thomas Declaire, Library of Congress, Washington, D.C.; Richard Doty, American Numismatic Society, New York City; William C. Ellington Jr., Richard J. Rademacher, Wichita Public Library, Wichita, Kan.; Rowland Elzea, Phyllis Nixon, Delaware Art Museum, Wilmington; Robert David Lion Gardiner, Gardiner's Island, N.Y.; Larry D. Gilmore, Linda Kelsey, Mariners Museum, Newport News, Va.; Marguerite

B. Hubbard, Franklin D. Roosevelt Library, Hyde Park, N.Y.; Jacob Judd, Sleepy Hollow Restorations, Tarrytown, N.Y.; Lucinda Keister, Dr. Peter Olch, National Library of Medicine, Bethesda, Md.; John G. Leland, Charleston, S.C.; Ann Mayer, Brandywine River Museum, Chadds Ford, Pa.; Nancy Merz, Linda Roe, Colonial Williamsburg Foundation, Williamsburg, Va.; Barbara Miller, Bahamas News Bureau, Coral Gables, Fla.; Harold L. Peterson, Arlington, Va.; Eleanor M. Richardson, University of South Carolina, Columbia; Ford Rockwell, Wichita, Kan.; Helen Sevagian, Boston Public Library, Boston, Mass.; Wendy Shadwell, New-York Historical Society, New York City; Philip C. F. Smith, Peabody Museum, Salem, Mass.; Gerald Somes, The Title Guarantee Company, New York City; Dorothy Swerdlove, New York Public Library at Lincoln Center, New York City; Bryant F. Tolles, Essex Institute, Salem, Mass.; Rev. Gerald P. Van der Hart, Tarrytown, N.Y.; Dr. H. J. Warthen, Richmond Academy of Medicine, Richmond, Va.; Stuart C. Welch, Fogg Art Museum, Cambridge, Mass.

Picture Credits

Index

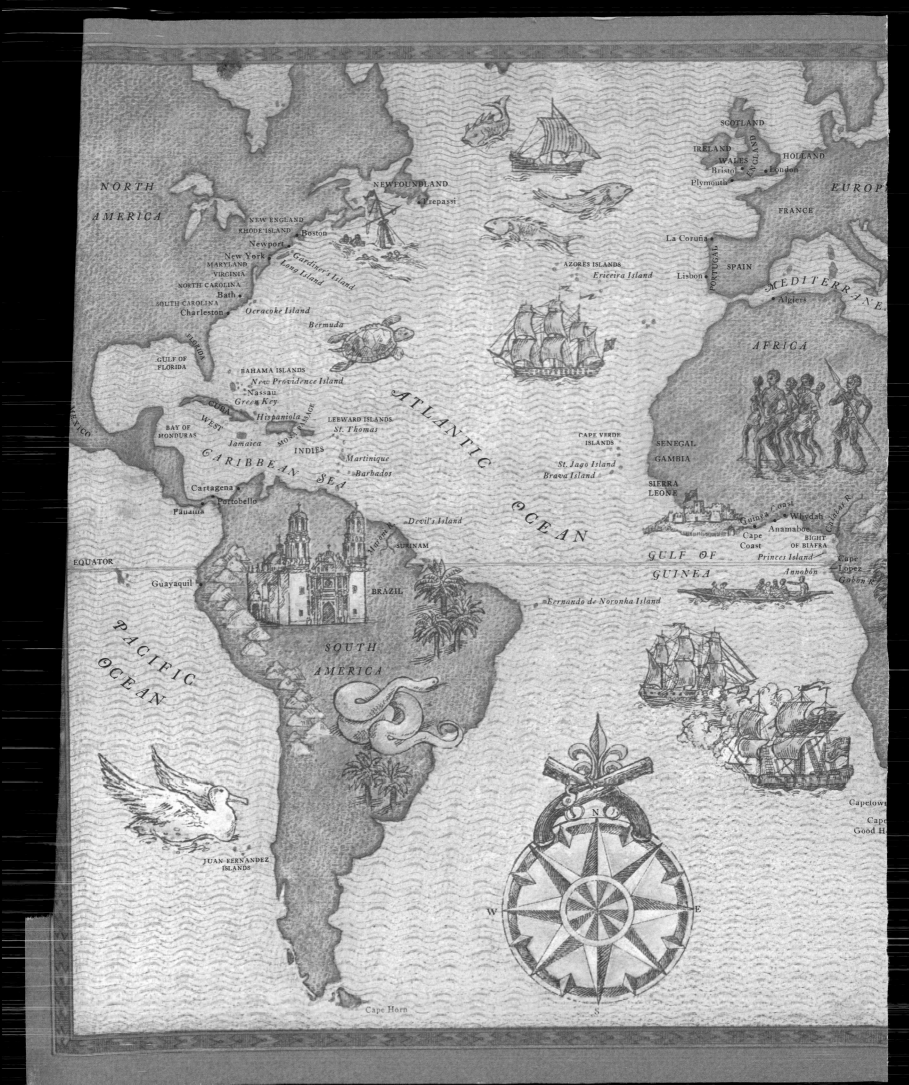